RIPLEY'S
Believe It or Not!®

Vice President, Licensing/Publishing and Online Marketing Amanda Joiner
Senior Creative Content Manager Sabrina Sieck

Editor Jordie R. Orlando
Text Geoff Tibballs
Feature Contributors Emily Harriss, Jordan Neese, Sabrina Sieck, Meghan Yani
Proofreader Rachel Paul
Fact-checker James Proud
Indexer Jordie R. Orlando

Designers Rose Audette, Luis Fuentes, Julia Moellmann
Reprographics Bob Prohaska
Cover Designers Luis Fuentes, Michael Jurado

Creative Solutions Steve Campbell, Kieran Castaño, Yaneisy Contreras, Jeff Goldman, Emily Harriss, Allyson Iovino, Michael Jurado, Colton Kruse, Matt Mamula, Julia Moellmann, Jordan Neese, Shania Osburn, Andrew Petersen, Ekechi Pitt, Suzanne Smagala-Potts
Special Thanks Tacita Barrera, John Corcoran, Barbara Faurot

Dedicated to Norm Deska.

ISBN 978-1-60991-514-8
ISBN 978-1-60991-519-3 (Walmart U.S.)
ISBN 978-1-60991-517-9 (Costco Canada)

For more information regarding permission, contact:
Vice President, Licensing/Publishing and Online Marketing
Ripley Entertainment Inc.
7576 Kingspointe Parkway, Suite 188
Orlando, Florida 32819
publishing@ripleys.com
www.ripleys.com/books

Manufactured in China in May 2023 by Leo Paper
First Printing

Library of Congress Control Number: 2023932933

PUBLISHER'S NOTE
While every effort has been made to verify the accuracy of the entries in this book, the Publisher cannot be held responsible for any errors contained in the work. They would be glad to receive any information from readers.

WARNING
Some of the stunts and activities are undertaken by experts and should not be attempted by anyone without adequate training and supervision.

RIPLEY'S Believe It or Not!®

LEVEL UP

RIPLEY®
PUBLISHING
a Jim Pattison Company

Level 20 UNLOCKED

You have reached Level 20 in the Ripley's Believe It or Not! annual series. That's right, this is the twentieth edition of Ripley's beloved book. So, where did it all begin, what's it all about, and who's responsible for leveling it up?

Leveling Up Ripley's Books

Ripley's has been publishing books since 1929, but the annual didn't hit the shelves until 2004 thanks to the company's EVP of Intellectual Property, Norm Deska. Before then, Ripley's books were mostly paperbacks focused on the company's cartoons, history, and archives.

Norm took things to the next level with the annual, introducing the world to a magazine-style hardback full of new and current unbelievable features and photos.

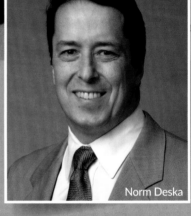

Norm Deska

THE FIRST RIPLEY'S ANNUAL!

The book's first edition sold well over 500,000 copies and quickly became a *New York Times* bestseller. Its popularity led to the creation of a legacy series (hint: the epic book in your hands right now) and translations into dozens of languages around the world!

2

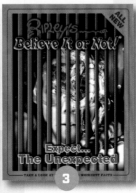

3

4

5

6

High Score: Norm Deska

With the success of the annual series, Norm expanded Ripley's publishing program, championing in-house production for full creative control and that extra layer of fact-checking. Now retired, he is who we have to thank for where we are today, leveling up your reading experience with games, extra content, and fun new features! For this, Ripley's is proud to dedicate *Level Up* to Norm Deska!

> "
> *The internet didn't exist [when I started my career at Ripley's]. Ripley's researchers were still combing the public library. We've evolved to being an aggregator of unbelievable content for people. It makes our jobs easier in some respects and more difficult in others.*
>
> – Norm Deska

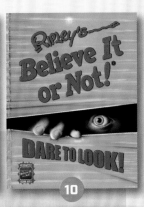

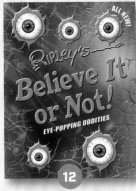

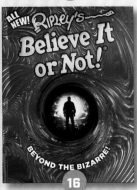

THE 20TH ANNUAL!

LEVEL UP

Explore the pages of this book and scan the QR codes to unlock interactive bonus content that will level up your reading experience with mini games, quizzes, videos, and more!

At the end of each side quest, part of a secret password will be revealed. Successfully enter the password at **RipleysLevelUp.com** to complete the challenge!

Help Robin clean up
Page 14

Take a quiz to unlock a masterpiece
Page 186

Match strange stars
Page 204

Ripley's hopes that this book—with the help of the amazing creators, creatures, and curiosities inside it—inspires you to push the limit, progress, and pride yourself on what makes you stand out.

It's time to Level Up—Ripley's way!

How to Play

1. SCAN TO PLAY!

Scan the QR codes throughout this book to play and collect secret letters.

2. CRACK THE CODE!

Reveal the password created by the letters you unlock in each challenge.

3. LEVEL UP!

Visit RipleysLevelUp.com and enter the password to complete the challenge.

Use this area to keep track of secret letters and reveal the password!

___ ___ ___ ___ ___ ___ ___
1   2   3   4   5   6   7

___ ___ ___ ___ ___ ___ ___ ___
8   9 10 11 12 13 14 15

LEVEL UP
SOLVE HERE

SCAN AND PLAY!

WHAT'S NEW?

Ripley's has been busy finding all-new stories to tell, introducing fresh faces, and opening numerous new experiences around the world for you to level up your next adventure!

Strike a Pose

Ripley's Selfie Studios in Niagara Falls, Ontario, invites visitors to express themselves in more than 20 scroll-stopping themed installations, while new and trending wax figures greet guests at Louis Tussaud's Waxworks—ready for their close-up. Don't put your phones away yet! Ripley's Mirror Maze in Orlando, Florida, takes things to the next dimension with illuminated infinity rooms and bottomless floors.

Amazing Animals

Ripley's Aquariums introduced many new species this past year, including axolotls, internet-viral orange lobsters, lemon sharks, and even two-toed sloths at Ripley's Aquarium of Myrtle Beach's all-new Sloth Valley habitat.

Meet Ripley's Cartoonist

Ripley's Believe It or Not! has been presenting the incredible and the unusual in illustrated form since Robert Ripley's first "Champs and Chumps" comic was published in the *New York Globe* on December 19, 1918.

Today, artist Kieran Castaño is the eighth cartoonist to take up the pen of this legacy panel. Kieran resides in Central Florida with his bird Rosie and pup Trini—who can often be spotted in his work!

What's INSIDE?

219
NEW ADDITIONS
TO RIPLEY'S
EXHIBIT
COLLECTION!

RIPLEY'S
UP CLOSE &
PECULIAR

80
OUT-OF-THIS-WORLD LISTS

100
INTERACTIVE
GAMES

46
YOU'VE GOT
QUESTIONS.
WE'VE GOT
ANSWERS!

RIPLEY'S EXCLUSIVE

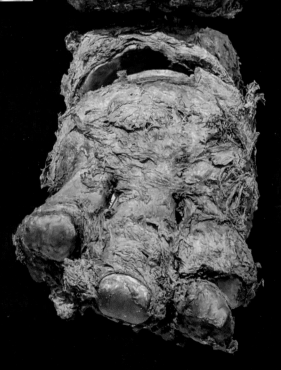

HUMAN PINBALL

Latvian freerunner Pavel "Pasha" Petkuns teamed up with Red Bull to create a five-story-tall pinball table where Pasha could jump, flip, and swing his way around miniature versions of global icons like the Statue of Liberty and the Eiffel Tower.

Creating "The Human Pinball" was a dream come true for Pasha, who came up with the idea years before pulling it off, having developed an affinity for the nostalgia of pinball machines after moving to the U.S. to work as a stunt double on Hollywood films. The scaled-up pinball table weighed around 50,700 pounds (23,000 kg) and featured a 75.5-foot-long (23-m) wall tilted at a 45-degree slant. It was inspired by a bridge in Latvia where Pasha perfected his craft. Believe it or not, the flippers actually moved and were operated by two strong men each!

It took seven weeks to build the elaborate set!

JUMP, FLIP, AND SWING!

ONE MAN'S TRASH

Environmental activist Robin Greenfield added every piece of trash he generated to a plastic suit he wore for 30 days!

From April 20 to May 20, 2022, Robin donned his trash suit and took to the streets of Los Angeles, sparking conversations and demonstrating just how much of an impact one person can have on the environment. But just because he looked like trash doesn't mean he wanted to smell like it. In an effort to avoid scaring people away with his stench, he replaced raw food waste with the equivalent weight of dry rice.

Robin ended up carrying around 72 pounds (32.7 kg) of trash on his body by the end of the month, having added about 2.5 pounds (1.3 kg) each day. And if you think that is a lot of garbage, consider the fact that, as a highly eco-conscious person, he only produced half the amount of waste as an average human!

LEVEL UP
SEE PAGE 7!

SCAN AND PLAY!

ANOTHER MAN'S TREASURE

A November 2022 art festival featured two trash towers of epic proportions, measuring 30 feet (9.1 m) tall each! Created by Pasadena-based artist Brent Spears, a.k.a. Shrine, the seven-sided towers featured 1,200 10-inch (25.4-cm) steel food can tassels, 4,800 steel can lids, 400 plastic bottles, and a garland of 1,100 aluminum cans! The trash-tastic piece debuted at Art With Me Miami, an international arts, music, and cultural festival. The garbage-fueled installation was created to raise funds for Highway Sanctuary, a nonprofit that allows local people to take part in workshops with artists at no cost.

RED HOT
A lightning bolt is only the width of a human thumb, but its temperature can reach 54,032°F (30,000°C)—five times hotter than the surface of the Sun.

FRIES PERFUME
The Idaho Potato Commission created a limited-edition perfume, Frites by Idaho, which smells of french fries.

TALKING MUSHROOMS
Mushrooms communicate with each other through electrical impulses which spike when the fungi come into contact with food sources or potential dangers. They have a vocabulary of over 50 "words."

BLUE SNOW
In December 2021, scientists discovered blue snow in the Russian Arctic that glowed like Christmas lights. It was believed to have been caused by tiny aquatic crustaceans called copepods which had been swept ashore by powerful currents and emit a faint blue glow when touched. So the scientists' footprints left a blue glowing trail.

FLOODED FLOOR

Customers at the Sweet Fishs Café in Khanom, Thailand, walk to their tables through ankle-deep water that covers the entire floor and contains dozens of koi fish. Before entering the café, people must remove their shoes and disinfect their feet. They are not allowed to touch the fish.

MAIL BOAT
Since 1993, Jill and Jim Koch have been making weekly mail deliveries by boat to the residents of Hells Canyon, a remote stretch of the Snake River on the border of Oregon and Idaho. They deliver to 52 mail stops and the 200-mile (320-km) round trip takes 10 hours.

PASSWORD DAY
World Password Day, celebrated annually on the first Thursday in May, was devised to remind computer users to keep their passwords updated and secure.

CARPET CAR
Georgy Makarov, a Russian automobile enthusiast, covered the metal bodywork of an old Soviet-produced Zhiguli VAZ car in a layer of colorful, patterned Persian-style rugs. He wanted a car that would stand out, but not something too expensive.

BIKE SEATS
Two McDonald's restaurants in Guangdong and Shanghai, China, replaced their seats with stationary exercise bikes so that customers could work out while eating.

2022 CHAMP: GUITARANTULA!

ROCKIN' WITHOUT

Since 1996, the Air Guitar World Championships have promoted world peace through musical mimicry! According to the event's organizers, "all bad things will vanish when all the people in the world play the air guitar." At the 2022 Championships in Oulu, Finland, contestant Kirill "Guitarantula" Blumenkrants from France shredded some sweet power chords in front of 3,500 people, impressing the judges enough to beat 17 other finalists and become World Champ. In addition to world peace, the Air Guitar World Championships also promotes inclusivity—there is no right or wrong way to shred, and air guitar can be played by anyone regardless of gender, age, ethnicity, sexual orientation, or social status. So, what are you waiting for? Grab your invisible Strat and rock out!

MEGAVALANCHE

The Megavalanche is a bike race of epic proportions! The track is snowy, steep, and covered in rocks, but the most dangerous part is the very beginning. All at once, hundreds of riders take off from the top of Pic Blanc, a 10,925-foot-tall (3,330-m) mountain in the French Alps, resembling an avalanche as they approach the first turn—a nearly 90-degree corner resulting in mass crashes and pile-ups. Believe it or not, riders who make it past that first challenge can reach speeds of 70 mph (113 kmph) as they plummet down the mountain!

To keep them intact, the black puddings are wrapped in tights!

THE OFFICIAL WORLD BLACKPUDDIN THROWING CHAMPIONSHIP

SAUSAGE TOSS

At the World Black Pudding Throwing Championships in Ramsbottom, England, contestants attempt to knock pastries off a 20-foot-tall (6-m) tower by hurling sausages at them!

Hitting the stacks of savory bread-like dishes known as Yorkshire puddings is a lot easier said than done. Each participant receives three black puddings—a type of blood sausage—as their ammunition, which must be thrown underhand while standing on a special brick called the "golden grid." The competitor who knocks the most Yorkshire puddings off the platform wins! Local legend states the event's origins date back to 1455 during the War of the Roses, when soldiers on both sides ran out of ammunition and resorted to launching puddings at one another.

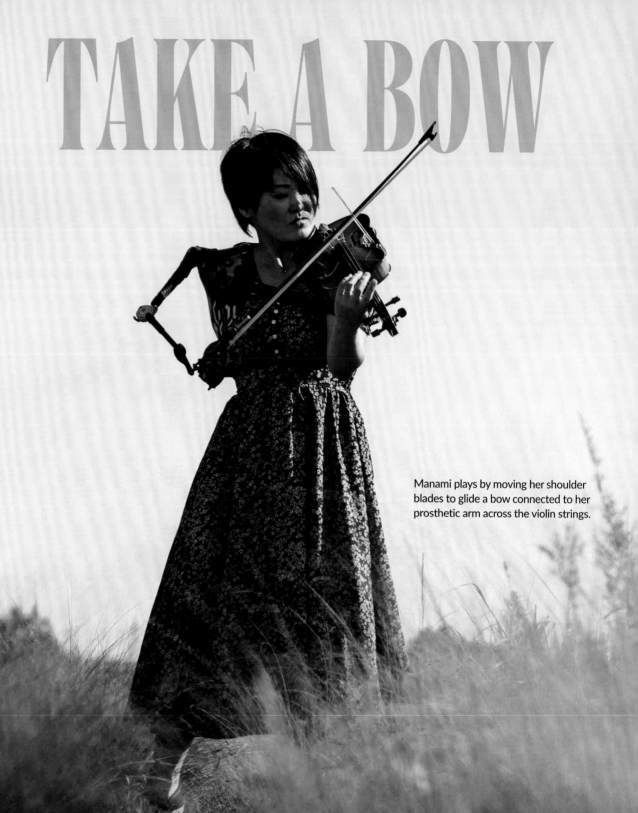

TAKE A BOW

Manami plays by moving her shoulder blades to glide a bow connected to her prosthetic arm across the violin strings.

Japanese violinist Manami Ito defies expectations, making beautiful music with the help of a prosthetic arm customized just for her!

Manami started playing the violin at seven years old and was just 20 when a motorcycle accident led to her right arm being amputated. After a period of thinking she would never leave the house again, Manami dusted herself off and set out to show the world nothing is impossible. Now in her thirties, she has since become Japan's first nurse with a prosthetic arm, swum in two Paralympic Games, and relearned how to play the violin, even performing at the Opening Ceremony of the Tokyo 2020

Composing Change

Gaelynn Lea of Duluth, Minnesota, makes beautiful music from her wheelchair by playing her violin like a cello! Since beating out more than 6,000 artists to win NPR's Tiny Desk Contest in 2016, Gaelynn has opened for major acts like Wilco, The Decemberists, and LOW, and even composed the entire score for *Macbeth* on Broadway! Born with brittle bone disease, Gaelynn is a passionate advocate for disability rights. She uses her music and voice to promote positive social change and accessibility in the arts. She is also a cofounder of the Recording Artists and Music Professionals with Disabilities (RAMPD) group.

Foot Notes

Born without arms, professional musician Felix Klieser instead plays the French horn with his toes! The German performer had his first horn lessons at age five, undeterred by what others might consider a disadvantage. As he already used his feet for everything from eating and dressing to writing, playing a musical instrument with his tootsies was not unusual for Felix. He performs by keeping his horn on a stand while using his left foot to press the instrument's valves. According to him, the majority of playing the French horn comes down to lip position and air control. Felix has played in symphony orchestras worldwide, toured with Sting, and released multiple albums of his own!

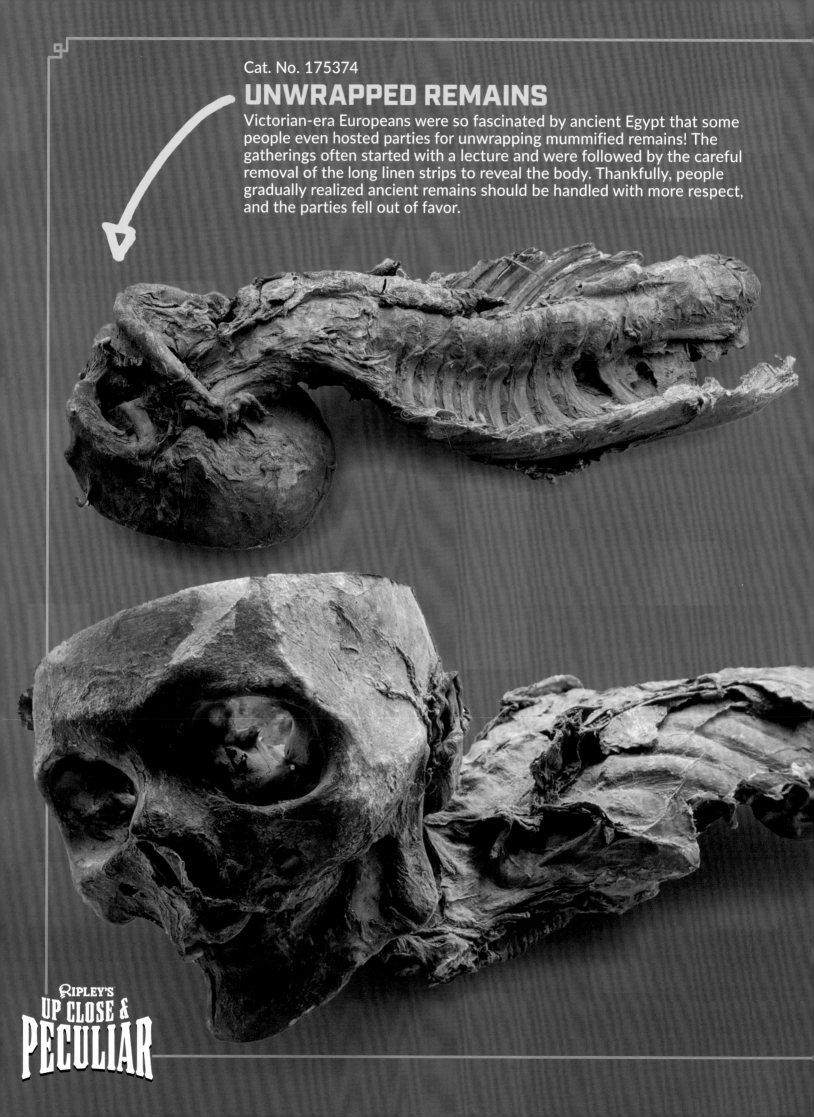

Cat. No. 175374

UNWRAPPED REMAINS

Victorian-era Europeans were so fascinated by ancient Egypt that some people even hosted parties for unwrapping mummified remains! The gatherings often started with a lecture and were followed by the careful removal of the long linen strips to reveal the body. Thankfully, people gradually realized ancient remains should be handled with more respect, and the parties fell out of favor.

Cat. No. 174347
PAPYRUS SCROLLS

These three scrolls were created more than 2,000 years ago during Egypt's Ptolemaic dynasty. The exact contents of these ancient scrolls is unknown. The writing is in Demotic script, which during that time period was used for a variety of reasons, including administrative, religious, and literary texts.

Cat. No. 11597
MUMMIFIED FALCON

In addition to humans, ancient Egyptians also mummified animals such as cats, birds, dogs, snakes, and crocodiles. This falcon is one of hundreds of thousands that were mummified and buried in sacred sites throughout the country. The bird was often associated with power and kings, as it was the form taken by Horus, one of the most important gods in ancient Egypt.

COLOSSAL UNDERTAKING

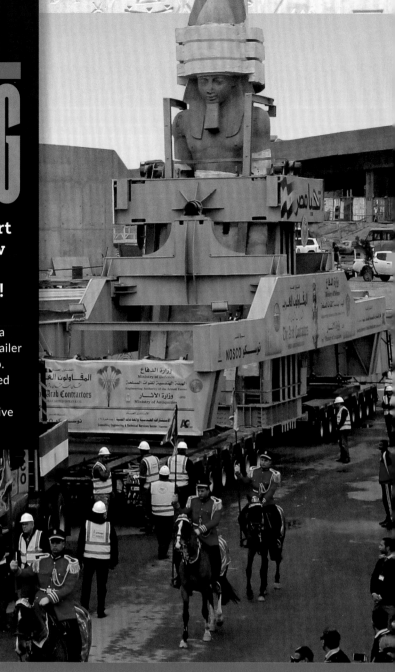

Extreme measures were taken to transport a giant statue of King Ramses II to its new home at the Grand Egyptian Museum, resulting in a procession fit for a pharaoh!

On only its fourth voyage in 3,200 years, the 30-foot-tall (9.1-m) sculpture of Egypt's most powerful pharaoh was accompanied by a marching band and military guard as it was towed along on two trailer beds. Safely transporting 83 tons of granite wasn't easy—or cheap. The ancient statue was strapped into a custom cage and suspended from a steel beam to ensure it wouldn't be damaged during the 10-hour move, while road surfaces were treated to bear the massive weight. All in all, the 1,200-foot (366-m) journey cost $770,000.

E · G · Y · P · T · O

Although not native to Egypt, **baboons were considered sacred** to ancient Egyptians and were even **kept as pets**.

Pharaohs wore **false beards to look more like their gods.** Even female pharaohs like **Hatshepsut**, seen here, wore one!

When ancient Egyptians' pet cats passed, every member of the family would **shave off their eyebrows** in mourning.

83 TONS OF GRANITE!

M · A · N · I · A

More than **4,000 square feet (372 sq m)** of linen could be used during the **mummification process!**

Ancient Egyptians used **moldy bread as an antibiotic** to treat wounds.

Ancient Egyptians loved a **board game called Senet.** Some pharaohs were even buried with **sets to play in the afterlife!**

NIGHT LIGHT

Believe it or not, scorpions glow under ultraviolet light! The desert arachnid's blue-green radiance comes from its exoskeleton and is less vibrant right after it molts. Scientists aren't fully sure why scorpions glow, but some theorize that these nocturnal creepy-crawlies use their fluorescent glow to gauge the Moon's brightness and avoid revealing themselves to predators when it is too bright out!

UNSCHEDULED STOP

Finnish skier Kalle Jalkanen helped his team to win gold at the 1936 Winter Olympics despite stopping to pick up his dentures on the last leg of the cross-country skiing relay after he accidentally spat them out onto the snow.

FLOATING HOUSE

When Daniele Penney and her partner Kirk Lovell learned that a two-story house they had long admired on the shore of the Bay of Islands inlet in Newfoundland, Canada, was due to be demolished, they moved the building to their own coastal property in McIvers. It was too difficult to move the house by land, so instead they used six small boats to push and tow it 0.6 miles (1 km) across the ocean—a journey that took eight hours. Barrels were placed under the house, which was strapped to a metal frame packed with old tires to keep it afloat.

HAIRY EAGLE

The Onondaga Historical Association in Syracuse, New York, is home to a decorative eagle made entirely out of hair donated by 37 leading U.S. politicians and their spouses. First displayed in 1864, the eagle's head was made from President Abraham Lincoln's hair, its back from Vice President Hannibal Hamlin's hair, its beak from Secretary of the Treasury Salmon Chase's hair, and its wings from the hair of various senators.

PRINTED BRIDGE

A 3D-printed steel bridge was opened to pedestrians and cyclists in Amsterdam, the Netherlands, in 2021. It took a team of four giant robots six months to print the bridge, which is 39 feet (12 m) long and weighs 4.9 tons.

CLEVER PET

Coco, a guinea pig owned by Gwen Ford, of High Point, North Carolina, has mastered 70 different tricks, including jumping over Ford's arm, pushing a soccer ball, jumping through a hoop, and ringing a bell.

PRECIOUS WOOD

A single gram of kynam, a very rare type of agarwood with a strong fragrance, can fetch over $10,000, making it nearly 200 times more expensive than gold. It is found in aquilaria trees, which, if infected by a particular mold, produces a dark resin that forms the precious agarwood used in the perfume industry. It is expected that a 200-year-old aquilaria tree at the Wat Bang Kradan Temple in Cambodia will one day produce kynam, prompting Japanese buyers to offer the monks $23 million for the tree. The monks declined and the tree was placed under military guard.

SHELL SHOCK

In May 2022, Switzerland's Tropiquarium zoo welcomed the world's first known albino Galápagos tortoise! Animal enthusiasts and scientists alike were stunned when the red-eyed, pigmentless creature came crawling out of its shell. With only about 15,000 members of the species in existence, the birth of these giant reptiles is rare on its own, but the chances of one being born with albinism is estimated to be 1 in 100,000! Despite the hatchling weighing just 1.8 ounces (50 g) at birth, Galápagos tortoises are the world's largest living tortoise species and can grow to more than 500 pounds (227 kg)!

POWERFUL EYES!

EYE SEE YOU

When it comes to scallops, these seemingly simple creatures are more than meets the eye—or, if you're a scallop, up to 200 eyes!

Close examination of a scallop's peepers reveals complex biological engineering. Rather than using a lens to focus light onto the retina like a human eye does, scallops have a curved mirror at the back of their eyes that functions like a high-tech telescope! Incredibly, each mirror consists of more than 20 layers of tiled crystal plates and is calibrated for varying wavelengths to ensure a clear picture. On top of all that, the light gets reflected onto a double-layer retina, allowing scallops to see both peripheral and frontal views—at the same time!

Cartoon CAKES

Australian baker Tegan "Tigga Mac" MacCormack creates unbelievable cakes that look like 2D cartoon drawings!

For Tigga, who co-owns a Melbourne-based bake shop called Cake for Days, removing dimension from a cake's appearance is a matter of artistry. She first covers the cake in a smooth ganache before wrapping it in colorful fondant and outlining all of the features in black icing. When she posted her first cartoon cake online, Tigga's Instagram and TikTok followers were in total disbelief. And even after she uploaded a video of the entire baking process, her comment sections were still filled with people who thought it was fake—mission accomplished in the eyes of the baker! It took posting a video of herself cutting the cake to get followers to believe their own eyes.

YOU HAVE TO CUT IT TO BELIEVE IT!

FROZEN FOOD

Checking out a menu is only a scan away these days, but 100 years ago, it was rare to find any kind of menu at all in Japanese restaurants! Rather than write down what they had to offer, restaurants displayed meal options in window displays. To avoid waste—and because leaving food sitting in a window all day would get kind of gross—they'd create realistic replicas out of wax and plastic called "shokuhin sampuru." The practice remains common today, and artists have only gotten more elaborate with their designs. Some tourists even collect the frozen-in-time food as souvenirs!

UNDERWATER PIZZA

Thane Milhoan works as a scuba diving pizza deliverer, bringing meals to guests at Jules' Undersea Lodge, an underwater hotel in Key Largo, Florida. He uses a dry box and extra bags to keep the pizzas from getting wet and adds weights to ensure the box remains level in the water so the toppings don't fall off.

SNOWBALL LAW

Throwing snowballs was illegal in Severance, Colorado, until 2018. The law was only changed because nine-year-old Dane Best petitioned his hometown to overturn a 100-year-old ban on snowball fights.

CANDY TOWER

Brendan Kelbie from Queensland, Australia, successfully arranged six M&M candies into a vertical stack that did not topple. He can also flip a drumstick 98 times in one minute and stack 13 dice on the back of his hand in 30 seconds while blindfolded.

SAUSAGE ROLLS

Nearing 30 years old, Megan Topping of Manchester, England, has already eaten more than 10,000 sausage rolls in her lifetime. Her latest quest is to visit all 2,078 Greggs bakery stores in the UK and eat a sausage roll at each.

ACROBATIC BACKFLIP

Ashley Watson, a gymnast from Leeds, England, successfully performed a spectacular backflip between two horizontal bars placed 19.66 feet (6 m) apart.

LUCKY CLOVER

Betina Reich, of Eau Claire, Wisconsin, collected a four-leaf clover every day for 258 days straight—from March 22, 2021, to December 4, 2022, when heavy snow fell for the first time that winter.

BIG MACS

Don Gorske, from Fond du Lac, Wisconsin, has eaten a Big Mac nearly every day for half a century, missing out on only eight days in five decades. He ate his first on May 17, 1972, and has been averaging almost two a day ever since, estimating that he has eaten more than 33,000 Big Macs in total. He celebrated the fiftieth anniversary in 2022 by visiting his local McDonald's, where a sign was erected in his honor.

High Roller

French inline skater Florian Petitcollin can jump over a 5.6-foot-tall (1.71-m) bar while rollerblading—without using a ramp! While Florian won his first free jump competition with a 4.8-foot (146-cm) jump in 2015, he took rollerblading to new heights at 2022's Paris Slalom World Cup, where he not only won the free jump category but set a world record for good measure!

BLUE BEER

French company Hoppy Urban Brew adds spirulina, an algae with a natural blue pigment, to its beer during the brewing process to create a blue beer called Line.

BALL WALL

When Melissa Brodt began removing the dark green roof shingles covering the wall of a bedroom in her family's recently purchased home in Boise, Idaho, she discovered about 1,600 baseball cards that had been glued to the plaster as decorative wallpaper. The cards, which dated back to the 1970s and 1980s, had been arranged there by the house's previous occupant, Chris Nelson.

FEEDING SPIRITS

Before dawn for 15 days in September and October, families in Cambodia visit graveyards and temples and throw small sticky rice balls into the air to feed the spirits of deceased relatives. This Buddhist ritual is called "bos bai ben" and is part of Pchum Ben, the Khmer people's annual ancestors festival.

SKYSURFER SPINS

Daredevil Keith "KĒBĒ" Snyder, from Eloy, Arizona, completed 160 helicopter spins in freefall while skysurfing over Egypt. He strapped his skysurfing board to his feet and jumped out of an airplane at an altitude of 13,500 feet (4,116 m), performing the spins while plummeting toward the ground headfirst before flipping over and releasing his parachute.

Remote Control

Swedish freight technology company Einride's new all-electric truck, the Pod, has plenty of space for cargo, but none for a driver! That's because the vehicles are autonomous, meaning they are self-driving. Not to worry, there will still be human eyes on the road—kind of. Remote Pod Operators will monitor the trucks from a live video stream provided by on-board cameras at all times.

REMOTE POD DRIVER

YOUR CHARIOT AWAITS

Though chariot racing was largely forgotten after the ancient Olympic Games, the daredevil event made a comeback in the 1920s—only this time with motorcycles!

The success of the 1925 movie *Ben-Hur: A Tale of the Christ*, which included a chariot race sequence, sparked the sport's resurgence and prompted thrill seekers to add a modern twist by replacing horses with motorcycles. Riders would dress in their finest Roman-like costumes before strapping bikes to a chariot, with some amping up the action by welding multiple motorcycles together before taking off around a dirt track. The new-again pastime was so popular it was often accompanied by parades and stunt shows, with interest lasting well into the late 1930s, only to dwindle again by the time World War II came around.

The sport has resurfaced a few times since its heyday, like at this 1970s stunt show in Australia.

OH MY GOURD!

LEVEL UP SEE PAGE 7!

SCAN AND PLAY!

The Ludwigsburg Pumpkin Festival in Germany is considered the world's largest pumpkin exhibition, featuring over 400,000 gourds!

Spooky jack-o'-lanterns and pumpkin spice lattes are synonymous with autumn in the U.S., but pumpkin patches are harder to come by in Europe, making the festival an even bigger deal. Some of its most unique attractions are the massive pumpkin figures, all of which correspond to a different theme each year, such as underwater, rainforest, and music. Believe it or not, more than 600 squash varieties are used in the sculpture gardens every year, showcasing the incredible creativity of the artists behind the pumpkins.

LONG LEMON

Filippo Manzoli of Rivoli, Italy, reached out to Ripley's to share this bizarre fruit that grew from his lemon tree. Looking nothing like the citrus found in your typical grocery store, this sour oddity is closer in appearance to a banana than it is to a lemon!

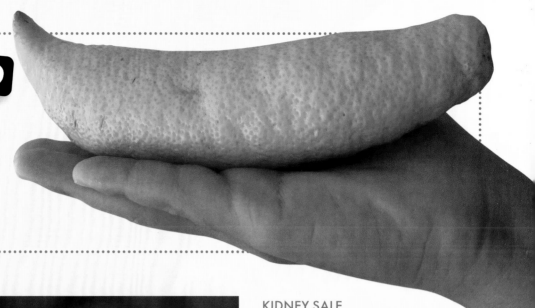

Swirly Succulent

The twisted cactus is sure to prickle your fancy with its strikingly unique appearance! The cultivar—a type of plant bred for a specific trait—is appropriately named "Spiralis" and occurs in South American cacti in the *Cereus* genus. Also called a spiral cactus or contorted cereus, it is trunkless and forms tall, column-like stems that corkscrew upwards. Strangely, the origins of the twisted cactus are not fully known. It was originally believed to have been man-made, but evidence of the plant appearing naturally in the wild has been recently discovered.

KIDNEY SALE

Many villagers in impoverished Shenshayba Bazaar, Afghanistan, have raised money by selling one of their kidneys. A healthy kidney can sell for about $3,000 and so many residents have undergone the procedure that their home is known locally as "one kidney village."

GOOSE PATROL

In October 2021, a team of 500 geese was employed to monitor a portion of China's border with Vietnam. The ever-alert birds are very sensitive to sound and are used to help detect and detain people crossing the border illegally.

BROOMSTICK BAN

In Swaziland, witches on broomsticks are not legally permitted to fly above an altitude of 500 feet (150 m). Any witch breaking the law is liable to a fine of $35,000.

EARLY CELEBRATION

The small village of Villar de Corneja in Spain celebrates New Year at noon instead of midnight because many of the residents are elderly and want to go to bed early.

TREE VENUE

Redwoods Treehouse is a pod-shaped structure located 33 feet (10 m) above ground in a redwood tree in Warkworth, New Zealand. The venue has a capacity of 30 guests who reach it via an elevated treetop walkway.

LARGE LEMON

Tammy Warren purchased a 9-inch-long (22.9-cm) lemon from a farm fruit stall in Wiltshire, England, and when she took it home she found that it was bigger than her baby Sebastian's head. The 4-pound (1.8-kg) fruit was 17 times the size of an average lemon.

NEW FLAVOR

Van Leeuwen Ice Cream of Brooklyn, New York, teamed up with Kraft Heinz to release a limited-edition macaroni and cheese flavor ice cream.

BAT CAVE
Icelandic musician Björk recorded her vocals for her song "Cover Me" in a bat-infested cave in Nassau, the Bahamas.

INSCRUTABLE JUDGES
Judges in China used to wear eyeglasses with smoke-colored quartz lenses so that nobody in court would be able to see their reactions to evidence until the conclusion of the trial.

HUGE HAILSTONES
Hailstones measuring 6.4 inches (16 cm)—the size of a human hand—fell in Yalboroo, Queensland, Australia, in October 2021, shattering car windshields.

NFL TOUR
Football fan Ryan Bailey, from Charlotte, North Carolina, attended home games for all 32 NFL teams in only 74 days.

STICK BALANCE
Raj Gopal Bhoi, from Odisha, India, balanced a field hockey stick on his right index finger for 3 hours 35 minutes.

LIP BALMS
Six-year-old Scarlett Ashley Cheng and her eight-year-old sister Kaylyn, both from Hong Kong, have collected more than 3,380 different lip balms from around the world.

THREE WHALE ROCK

Situated in Thailand's Kala rainforest, Hin Sam Wan is a 75-million-year-old rock formation that looks like a family of whales swimming through the trees!

Also known as Three Whale Rock, the massive stone creatures are open to the public and can be reached by a number of trails. Hikers can spend the day enjoying waterfalls and spotting local wildlife on their way to the "whales." After climbing to the top of the rocks, travelers are treated to incredible views of the Mekong River, Phu Wua Wildlife Sanctuary, and Pakkading mountains of the Lao People's Democratic Republic.

CHIN-UPS
Jonathan Young, of Gulf Shores, Alabama, completed 15 chin-ups in one minute while wearing a 100-pound (45.4-kg) pack strapped to his back.

MOST TOILETS
Wembley soccer stadium in London, England, has 2,618 toilets—more than any other venue in the world.

PERFECT BALANCE
If a bald eagle loses a wing feather while molting, it will drop a matching feather from the other side to remain balanced in flight.

SURPRISE WINNER
The winner of the 2021 New Zealand Bird of the Year competition was a bat! The critically endangered long-tailed bat beat 75 bird species to win by 3,000 votes.

GOLD RUSH
If all the gold was extracted from the world's seafloors, there would be about 9 pounds (4 kg) of gold for every person on Earth. However, it's almost impossible to mine it all.

WINE GIFT
The Swiss canton of Fribourg offers 100 bottles of wine to any of its residents who reach the age of 100.

BUGGIN' OUT

Spain's fiery Fil Loxera Festival celebrates the time the municipality of Sant Sadurní d'Anoia defeated a plague of insects that destroyed their vineyards!

In the mid-nineteeth century, the invasive phylloxera hitched a ride on a cargo ship from their native North America to France, devastating the countryside as they traveled. Despite their giant name, the pesky insects are actually very tiny, so it took a long time to identify what was destroying the vineyards the region heavily relied on for wine production. Once they were found out, winemakers were able to keep the bugs at bay by grafting North American and French vines together.

More than a century later, revelers commemorate the triumph over the phylloxera with the Fil Loxera Festival, a big shebang that kicks off with fireworks and live music every September 7, followed by a parade of people dressed as the pest, with even more fireworks shooting out of their antennas!

CAR CRASH

Right after purchasing a brand-new $300,000 red luxury Ferrari sportscar, a man in Derby, England, crashed it, causing major damage to the vehicle. He had driven it for less than 2 miles (3.2 km).

SLOW GAME

All four Chinese badminton players taking part in a quarter-final game at the Fuzhou Open tournament were given a three-month ban from all badminton-related activities for not trying hard enough.

TEENS' PLEA

In 1966, 15-year-old friends Jennifer Coleman and Janet Blankley wrote a message in a bottle asking for any boys between 16 and 18 to write back to them. They threw the bottle into England's River Humber but didn't receive a reply until 56 years later when the bottle was found in nearby Lincolnshire.

SERIAL DIVORCERS

A young couple in Hachioji, Japan, divorce and remarry every three years just so that they can take turns using their family surnames. Under Japanese law couples must agree on a single last name to use after marriage, but this couple could not decide which one to choose.

PET SOUNDS

In the 1993 movie *Jurassic Park*, some of the sounds of the fearsome *Tyrannosaurus rex* were actually made by sound designer Gary Rydstrom's tiny Jack Russell terrier, Buster. The growling noise when the *Tyrannosaurus* shakes a smaller dinosaur, *Gallimimus*, to death is that of Buster playing tug-of-war with a rope.

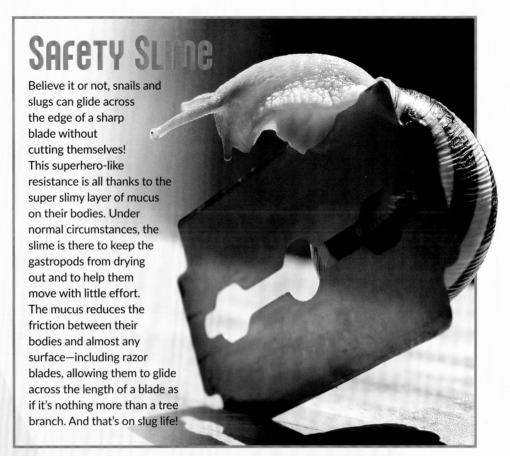

Safety Slime

Believe it or not, snails and slugs can glide across the edge of a sharp blade without cutting themselves! This superhero-like resistance is all thanks to the super slimy layer of mucus on their bodies. Under normal circumstances, the slime is there to keep the gastropods from drying out and to help them move with little effort. The mucus reduces the friction between their bodies and almost any surface—including razor blades, allowing them to glide across the length of a blade as if it's nothing more than a tree branch. And that's on slug life!

36-HOUR SWIM

In February 2022, long-distance swimmer Pablo Fernández Álvarez of Spain swam nonstop in an endless pool for 36 hours.

POT LUCK

When torrential rain hit Kerala state in southern India in October 2021, a young couple rode to their wedding venue in a giant metal cooking pot, which was steered through the flooded streets by friends.

SENIOR SOFTBALLERS

Maggie McCloskey plays for the Colorado Peaches women's softball team, even though she is over 90 years old. All of the players in the team are at least 50, and several are aged over 70.

MAP EXPERT

Eight-year-old Rehaan Khan, from Kent, England, can identify 72 different countries in one minute just by looking at their outline.

Love is Blind

Looking for love at the bottom of a bottle—at least, that's what it seems like male Australian jewel beetles are trying to do! Across Western Australia, the insects have been caught trying to mate with glass beer bottles that have been littered in their natural habitat. The beetles mistakenly confuse the trash for female jewel beetles, and upon closer inspection, it's hard to blame them. The females are much bigger than the males, a golden-brown color, and covered in dimple-like bumps—characteristics that are shared with some brands of beer bottles.

Early Start

Emmie Bay of Pembrokeshire, Wales, started skateboarding when she was just two years old! She was inspired to borrow her father's board after watching videos of Sky Brown, who was just 13 when she skated in the Tokyo Olympics. Now seven, Emmie practices nearly every day with her sights set on becoming a professional skateboarder and competing in the 2028 Olympic Games. At this rate, it seems she is right on track to achieve her goals!

WALKING TALL
Brother and sister Jordan Wolf and Ashley McCauley walked on 54.1-foot-tall (16.5-m) stilts—three times the height of an adult giraffe—at the 2022 Dairyfest in Marshfield, Wisconsin.

SKATEBOARD TRICKS
Although he has suffered from arthritis in both of his hips since 2015, 34-year-old skateboarder David Tavernor, from Norwich, England, performed 323 consecutive ollies—a trick where skateboarders perform a jump without their feet leaving the board.

CHAMPAGNE GLASSES
To herald the start of 2022, Atlantis, The Palm hotel in Dubai, United Arab Emirates, displayed a 27-foot-tall (8.2-m) pyramid constructed from 54,740 champagne glasses. It took 55 days to build the pyramid.

DOUBLE SKIPS
In 12 hours, Ryan Ong Alonzo (a.k.a. "Skipman"), of the Philippines, performed 40,980 double-under rope skips. A double-under requires the athlete to jump higher than usual because the rope has to pass beneath twice for each skip.

QUICK COOK
SN Lakshmi Sai Sri, a young Tamil Nadu girl, cooked 46 dishes in 58 minutes in Chennai, India, averaging 1.2 minutes per dish.

FISHY RULING
In 2022, a court ruled that under the California Endangered Species Act, bees in the state are legally classified as fish.

WALKS UPRIGHT
After losing one of his front legs in a road accident, Dexter, a Brittany spaniel dog owned by Kentee Pasek of Ouray, Colorado, taught himself to walk upright on his two hind legs—like a human.

HOG HAVEN
There are more than twice as many pigs in Denmark as people. There are 13.2 million pigs compared to 5.8 million humans.

OYSTER PEARLS
While dining at a restaurant in New Orleans, Louisiana, in December 2021, Keely Hill discovered 12 pearls inside an oyster that she was eating. There is a 10,000-to-one chance of even finding one pearl in an oyster.

ISLAND MONARCH
Whoever is landlord of the 300-year-old Ship Inn, the only inhabited building on the tiny island of Piel off the coast of Cumbria, England, also gets the title of King or Queen of Piel. At their coronation, new landlords sit on the pub's oak throne, wearing an old helmet and wielding an ancient sword while being showered with buckets of beer.

Ruff Rider

Henny the bulldog was 10 weeks old and walking with her owner, Ryan Lynch, when a passing skateboarder changed her life forever. The California cool girl got so excited the skater hopped off to let her sniff the board. It was love at first whiff—almost instinctively, she put her front paws onto the deck, started pushing, and then hopped on with all four feet! Ryan swiftly got Henny her own board, and she was cruising down the streets of Long Beach in no time. In the decade since, she's taken her skills to the next level, becoming a pro at pushing herself along, turning, and maneuvering better than some humans (including Ryan)!

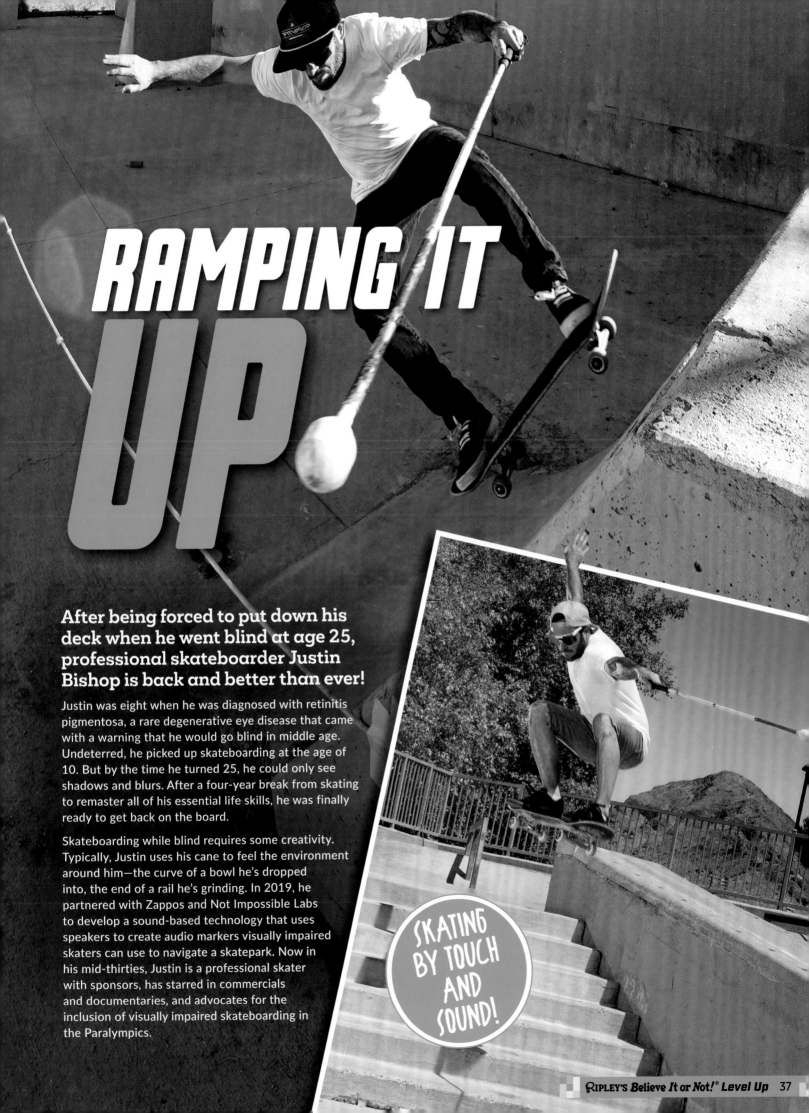

RAMPING IT UP

After being forced to put down his deck when he went blind at age 25, professional skateboarder Justin Bishop is back and better than ever!

Justin was eight when he was diagnosed with retinitis pigmentosa, a rare degenerative eye disease that came with a warning that he would go blind in middle age. Undeterred, he picked up skateboarding at the age of 10. But by the time he turned 25, he could only see shadows and blurs. After a four-year break from skating to remaster all of his essential life skills, he was finally ready to get back on the board.

Skateboarding while blind requires some creativity. Typically, Justin uses his cane to feel the environment around him—the curve of a bowl he's dropped into, the end of a rail he's grinding. In 2019, he partnered with Zappos and Not Impossible Labs to develop a sound-based technology that uses speakers to create audio markers visually impaired skaters can use to navigate a skatepark. Now in his mid-thirties, Justin is a professional skater with sponsors, has starred in commercials and documentaries, and advocates for the inclusion of visually impaired skateboarding in the Paralympics.

SKATING BY TOUCH AND SOUND!

OBJECTIVE

Approach

For the entire month of January 2022, fashion writer Taryn de Vere created outfits inspired by everyday household items.

Taryn decided to take on the challenge as a way to remain creative while staying at home on a break from work. They had just one rule as they embarked on their fashion journey: They could not buy anything new to create the outfits, something that was important to them from a sustainability perspective.

Luckily for Taryn, often described as "the most colorful person in Ireland," they had plenty of clothes in their closet to choose from! Some of the outfit inspirations included a milk carton, toilet cleaner, curry powder, hairspray, cheese puffs, trash bags, and even cat food!

JANUARY 18: CURRY POWDER

JANUARY 28: CUSTARD

JANUARY 7: TOILET CLEANER

JANUARY 2: CHOCOLATE TIN

JANUARY 31: SPARKLING DRINK

JANUARY 23: CHEESE PUFFS

JANUARY 3: CANNED BEANS

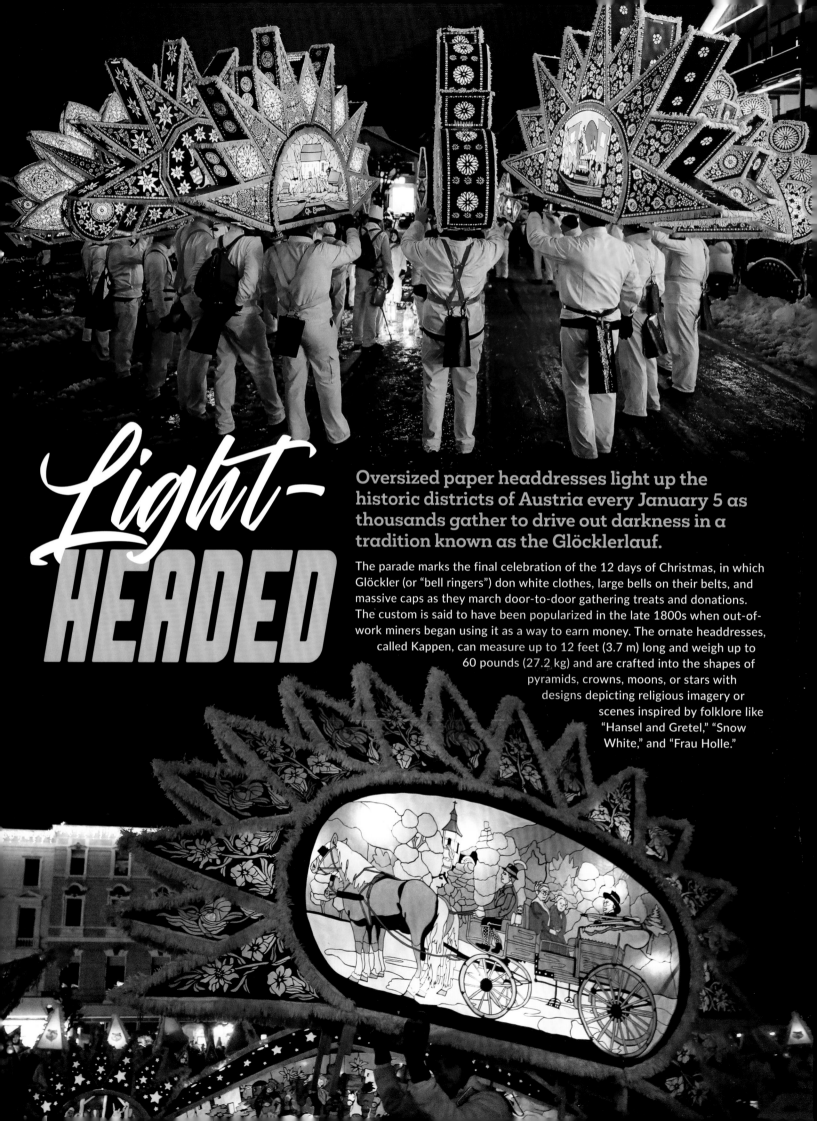

Light-HEADED

Oversized paper headdresses light up the historic districts of Austria every January 5 as thousands gather to drive out darkness in a tradition known as the Glöcklerlauf.

The parade marks the final celebration of the 12 days of Christmas, in which Glöckler (or "bell ringers") don white clothes, large bells on their belts, and massive caps as they march door-to-door gathering treats and donations. The custom is said to have been popularized in the late 1800s when out-of-work miners began using it as a way to earn money. The ornate headdresses, called Kappen, can measure up to 12 feet (3.7 m) long and weigh up to 60 pounds (27.2 kg) and are crafted into the shapes of pyramids, crowns, moons, or stars with designs depicting religious imagery or scenes inspired by folklore like "Hansel and Gretel," "Snow White," and "Frau Holle."

AUTOMOBILE ACCOMMODATIONS

Blink as you cruise through the Jordanian desert village of Al Jaya, and you might just miss the "world's smallest hotel," a converted Volkswagen Beetle parked on the side of the road! Created by Mohammed Al Malaheem, the unique guest experience begins in a small cave-turned-hotel lobby. From there, the budding hotelier shows you to the cozy accommodation—his old car from which he removed the engine and interior, painted white, and adorned with a mattress, colorful pillows, and tapestries. The car more than makes up for its lack of space with charm and originality. The hotel has hosted more than 200 guests, who also get to enjoy home-cooked food made by Mohammed's wife and daughter.

TEA COZY

A group of knitters based in Frankston, Victoria, Australia, knitted a tea cozy that measured 16.7 feet (5.1 m) tall and had a circumference of 63.3 feet (19.2 m). It was made from 186 miles (298 km) of yarn.

KIND GESTURE

At the 1928 Olympic Games in Amsterdam, the Netherlands, Australian rower Henry Pearce stopped mid-race during the quarter-finals to let a family of ducks cross his lane safely. He still won that race and went on to win the gold medal.

TOUGH BUBBLE

A team of French physicists at the University of Lille blew a bubble that lasted for 465 days before popping. They used glycerol and water to create a tough "gas marble" bubble that lasted 200,000 times longer than a standard soap bubble.

STRONG CENTENARIAN

Competitive powerlifter Edith Murway-Traina, from Tampa, Florida, could still lift weights of up to 150 pounds (68.1 kg) three days a week at age 100. A former dance teacher, she only took up weightlifting when she was 91.

FIGHTING FESTIVAL

People in Chumbivilcas province, Peru, are encouraged to settle disputes by fighting each other in public on Christmas Day as part of a festival called Takanakuy. Each fight lasts for about a minute and combatants range from young children to the elderly.

TIME ZONES

A journey along the full 5,772 miles (9,289 km) of the Trans-Siberian Railway from Moscow to Vladivostok takes seven days, crosses 3,901 bridges, and passes through eight different time zones.

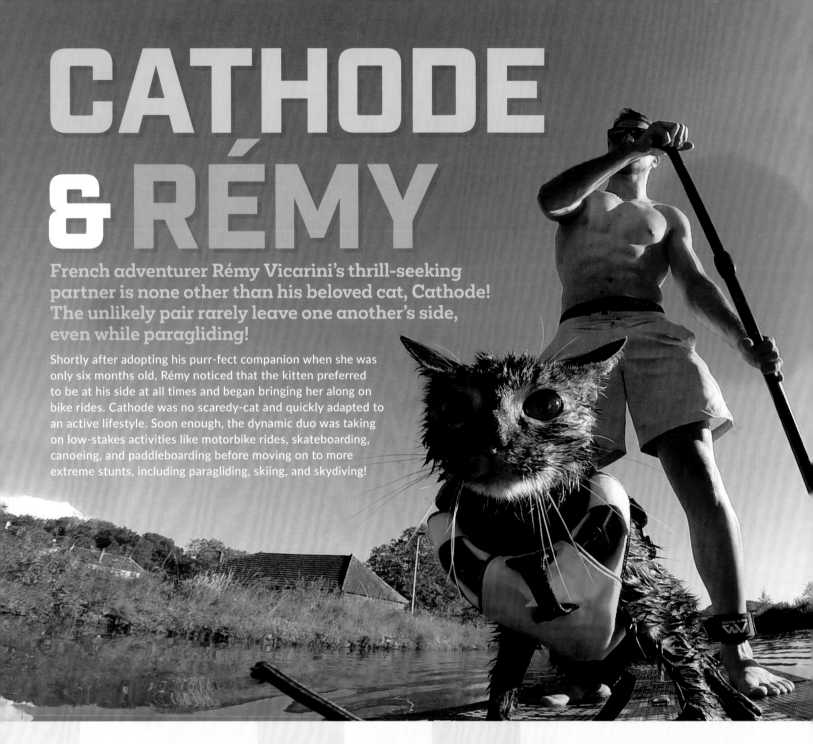

CATHODE & RÉMY

French adventurer Rémy Vicarini's thrill-seeking partner is none other than his beloved cat, Cathode! The unlikely pair rarely leave one another's side, even while paragliding!

Shortly after adopting his purr-fect companion when she was only six months old, Rémy noticed that the kitten preferred to be at his side at all times and began bringing her along on bike rides. Cathode was no scaredy-cat and quickly adapted to an active lifestyle. Soon enough, the dynamic duo was taking on low-stakes activities like motorbike rides, skateboarding, canoeing, and paddleboarding before moving on to more extreme stunts, including paragliding, skiing, and skydiving!

BRIDEZILLA

Victor Hugo Sosa, mayor of San Pedro Huamelula, Mexico, married an alligator! The "wedding" is actually a centuries-old tradition in the small fishing community and is meant to bring good luck and prosperity. The ceremony involved clothing the seven-year-old alligator in a white wedding dress and plenty of dancing for the reptile bride and her human groom, who frequently kissed the alligator's head as a symbolic connection between people and nature. The toothy newlywed was then carried through the village streets for the locals to see.

Safety is always first for Rémy, who uses a 3D printer to create custom helmets and goggles that protect Cathode during their adventures.

FLYING CAT!

GRAPE TRADITION
A New Year tradition in Spain is to eat 12 grapes—one at each of the 12 chimes of midnight. But the choking risks have prompted doctors to ask the government to extend the time between chimes.

BASE RUNNER
Macho, a five-year-old Jack Russell terrier owned and trained by Lori Signs, ran the bases at Dodger Stadium, Los Angeles, in only 21.06 seconds. Signs placed balloons at each base and encouraged Macho to pop them.

FRUIT CYCLE
The kākāpō—a critically endangered, flightless parrot from New Zealand—only mates every five years to coincide with the ripening of the rimu fruit. The birds only breed in years when rimu trees carry enough fruit to feed their chicks.

REPTILE STASH
A man who was stopped at the San Ysidro, California, port of entry border crossing with Mexico in February 2022 was found to have nine live snakes and 43 live horned lizards hidden in his clothing.

BREAKING NEWS
On January 19, 2022, Tori Yorgey, a reporter for WSAZ-TV in West Virginia, was hit by a car during a live broadcast in Dunbar, but quickly climbed back to her feet to finish her report.

MAEHEM MAYHEM
Maehem, a three-year-old Kai Ken dog owned by Autumn Arsenault, of Gladwin, Michigan, escaped from her temporary home in Bay City and, while on the loose for four days, walked 7 miles (11.2 km) across ice on frozen Saginaw Bay before being rescued.

RUSSIAN RAPUNZEL

Anzhelika Baranova of Irkutsk, Russia, hasn't had her hair cut for over 23 years—since she was five—and now it reaches all the way down to her ankles, almost touching the ground.

T-REXCELLENT

Minnesotan Paul Larcom uses the state's harsh winters as a creative outlet by constructing elaborate snow sculptures, like this 12-foot-tall (3.7-m) *T. rex!*

Paul has been delighting his neighbors with fantastical frozen figures for about a decade, and at 23 feet (7 m) long, his 2022 creation was the largest to date. The prehistoric project took him three weeks of on-and-off work to build, and he shaped everything by hand! For stability, Paul constructed a frame out of large sticks and branches. The wood was then encased in tightly packed snow, which he sculpted into shape with a loop tool. To truly bring his creation to life, Paul used spray paint to add skin, eyes, and other dino details. Frosty beware, this snow sculpture is terrifyingly realistic!

Paul hand-carved the teeth out of ice!

Spitting Fire

Inside the Kudykina Gora theme park near the Russian village of Kamenka stands a three-headed, fire-breathing dragon! Made of iron and concrete, the 49-foot-tall (15-m) statue represents the villainous dragon of Russian and Ukrainian folklore, Zmei Gorynich—or "Dragon, the Son of the Mountain." It took two years for Ukrainian artist Vladimir Kolesnikov to complete the sculpture, which features intricate details like scales, claws, and teeth, and on weekends and holidays, even emits perfectly-timed roars before spouting real flames and smoke out of its three mouths!

SAUSAGE BAIT

Millie, a Jack Russell terrier pup owned by Emma Oakes, was trapped on mudflats in Hampshire, England, for four days before rescuers eventually lured her away from the dangerous incoming tides by attaching a tasty sausage to a drone.

TIDY CROWS

A Swedish company, Corvid Cleaning, trains crows to pick up trash from streets in exchange for food. More than one billion cigarette butts are discarded on Sweden's streets each year and the crows are rewarded with a treat for each one they collect.

KITTEN CHAOS

A six-week-old kitten survived a four-hour, 230-mile (368-km) journey from South Wales to Leeds, England, in the engine compartment of a car. The driver only discovered the cat when he opened the hood to investigate a strange noise.

CLEVER CATERPILLAR

A Japanese butterfly, *Niphanda fusca*, lays its eggs in the nest of a carpenter ant. The caterpillars that hatch then trick the ants into feeding them instead of the ants' own young by chemically mimicking the odor of a male ant.

BURIED TREASURE

During World War II, the British monarch's Crown Jewels, which are usually kept in the Tower of London, were instead stored for safe keeping in a cookie tin buried in the grounds of Windsor Castle.

Cube Cloud

Megan Coombs was hiking in the Devil's Punch Bowl, a popular nature site in Surrey, England, when she spotted a strange cloud that looked like something straight out of *Minecraft*! She shared the unusual sight on social media, where it quickly went viral as people tried to guess what caused the seemingly unnatural shape. Some suggested the cloud was being used to hide alien spaceships, while others claimed it was proof that we are living in a simulation!

POLICE BOARD

Applicants for a post with the Gulf Shore Police Department in Alabama in 2021 were surprised to find that one of the seven interviewers was Oscar-winning actor Morgan Freeman who lives locally.

GARDEN ORNAMENTS

A couple in Suffolk, England, unknowingly used two stone statues from ancient Egypt to decorate their garden for 15 years. When the sphinxes' true value was discovered, they sold for $265,510.

NUGGET SPILL

Route 309 in Bucks County, Pennsylvania, was closed for several hours on April 27, 2022, when an overturned tractor-trailer spilled its load of 40,000 pounds (18,160 kg) of chicken nuggets onto the highway.

WHISKY BOTTLE

In 2021, a team of treasure hunters led by Dieter Mueller, of Barrie, Ontario, Canada, searched Otter Lake and found a bottle of whisky that sank there in 1964. Even after all those years underwater, the bottle was still sealed and intact and therefore drinkable. The cargo of spirits ended up in the lake when a boat crashed into the dock.

PERMANENTLY HUNGRY

David Soo, a 10-year-old boy from Singapore, has been diagnosed with the rare genetic disorder Prader-Willi Syndrome, which leaves him feeling permanently hungry no matter how much he eats. His family has to lock the kitchen door to keep him from overeating.

LEVEL UP
SEE PAGE 7!
SCAN AND PLAY!

RIPLEY'S EXCLUSIVE

TICKLED *Pink*

Known as the Pinkest Person in the World, Kitten Kay Sera is a Barbie girl living in a Barbie world. Everything in Kitten's life is pink—even her dog!

Kitten's enthusiasm for pink began on her twentieth birthday when she dressed head to toe in the color. In what she describes as a "spiritual awakening," she found herself and has never looked back. She immediately gave all of her clothes to her four sisters and set out to buy herself a wardrobe with a rosier outlook. After more than 40 years of wearing only pink, she married it in a symbolic ceremony! The monochromatic maven brings her pink power to the masses through her Instagram page and as the lead singer of "Barbie-core" band Pinktastic Plastixx.

Eager to know more about her rose-tinted life, we reached out to Kitten for an interview. Here's what she had to tell us.

Q: After 40 years of "dating," what made you decide to take the leap and marry the color pink?
A: I really did it out of fun. The true story is that a kid on a skateboard abruptly stopped when he saw me all dolled up in pink and said, "If you love the color pink so much, then why don't you marry it?" He was being a brat, but I thought it wasn't a bad idea!

It took me two years to plan the wedding. It took place on New Year's Day 2022 in Las Vegas and in the actual pink Cadillac owned by Elvis Presley!

Q: How do you feel your relationship with the color changed after marrying it?
A: It's been a wild ride. My story has been shared all over the world, and I find a lot of people are now emulating my all-pink style. I love that I am a source of "pinkspiration" for so many. And as the longest living monochromatic person, I do believe that pink is for everyone!

Pinktastic Plastixx
Clockwise from top-left: Rocky Rose (keytar and backing vocals), Aurora Celena (bass guitar), Alexa Rae (drums), Kitten Kay Sera (lead vocals), and Celinda Chang (guitar).

Q: Besides your clothes and home, what else in your life is pink?
A: I *love* pink foods and make all-pink meals. And I always, always dream in pink. Oh! I also use beet juice to color my pup pink; it is totally safe and vet-approved! Her name is Pinkaboo! She is a little Pomeranian and so sweet.

Q: What are some pros and cons to dedicating your life to a single color?
A: Oh, it's SO easy to do the laundry! All pinks!

But seriously, I have made a paycheck out of my passion for the color pink, which is unheard of. I have done commercials for major makeup brands, appeared on the cover of an international edition of *Vogue* magazine, and been featured on an interior design show for my home, the Pink Palace.

I'm creating a dream life which I am grateful for every single day. There are absolutely no cons, whatsoever.

> 66
> *I just wanted to prove my commitment to the color pink in an over-the-top way.*

Pretty in Pink

To many, the color pink represents love, softness, and happiness, most often found in nature in the form of sunsets, flowers, and gemstones. But there are also some incredible animals that rock that rosy hue in unexpected ways. Check out these quirky creatures that will have you seeing pink in a totally new light!

FOREVER YOUNG

Axolotls are a rare species of salamander that retain their amphibious features and live in water their entire lives rather than metamorphose into land-dwelling adults! Though abundant in home aquariums and science labs, less than a thousand axolotls are left in their native waters of Mexico City's Xochimilco district. A popular variation for pet owners, but even rarer in the wild, are pink axolotls, which are actually leucistic and have no melanin to darken their skin.

ROSY REPTILE

While roughly 30 iguana species exist worldwide, one type can be found only on Wolf Volcano in the Galápagos Islands—and it's pink! The appropriately named Galápagos pink land iguana was first described as a species in 2009, and scientists didn't spot their hatchlings until 2022! With only a few hundred of these rosy reptiles in existence, this discovery offers new hope for saving the species.

WHAT'S IN A NAME?

The pink hairy squat lobster, or fairy crab, is neither a lobster nor a true crab—but it *is* pink, hairy, and squat! This fierce fuchsia crustacean uses its long hairs to catch food that's floating by and then combs it out using two small claws hidden under its shell. Despite its unique look, the fairy crab is hard to spot. It mostly lives on giant barrel sponges in the western Indo-Pacific and is only 0.5 inches (1.3 cm) long!

BORN THIS GRAY

Roseate spoonbills don't come out of the egg looking this fabulous! Like flamingos, they hatch with gray feathers and turn pink after snacking on copious amounts of shrimp, crabs, and crawfish. To catch its hue-changing prey, the birds move their spoon-shaped bills through the water from side to side. Once they feel something touch their highly sensitive beak, they snatch it up!

BLUSHING BURROWER

At only 6 inches (15.2 cm) long, the title for smallest armadillo in the world goes to central Argentina's pink fairies! These furballs have thin pink shells, the color of which is caused by the blood vessels underneath. It's incredibly rare to spot a pink fairy armadillo, as they are nocturnal creatures and spend a lot of their time burrowing underground.

TINY BUT MIGHTY

The shocking pink dragon millipede—yes, that's its real name— is a small but dangerous arthropod whose hot pink hue tells predators to stay away. Get too close to this thumb-sized creature and you may notice the smell of almonds in the air. Don't be fooled though, it's actually the odor of highly poisonous cyanide gas they expel as a defense mechanism!

SALMON SCALES

Coachwhips are nonvenomous snakes that can grow 3 to 8 feet (0.9 to 2.4 m) long and live throughout the southern U.S. and Mexico, where they vary greatly in color in order to blend into their surroundings. Even in places like western Texas, where clay gives the area a distinctly pink landscape, you'll find a coachwhip to match—if you look hard enough!

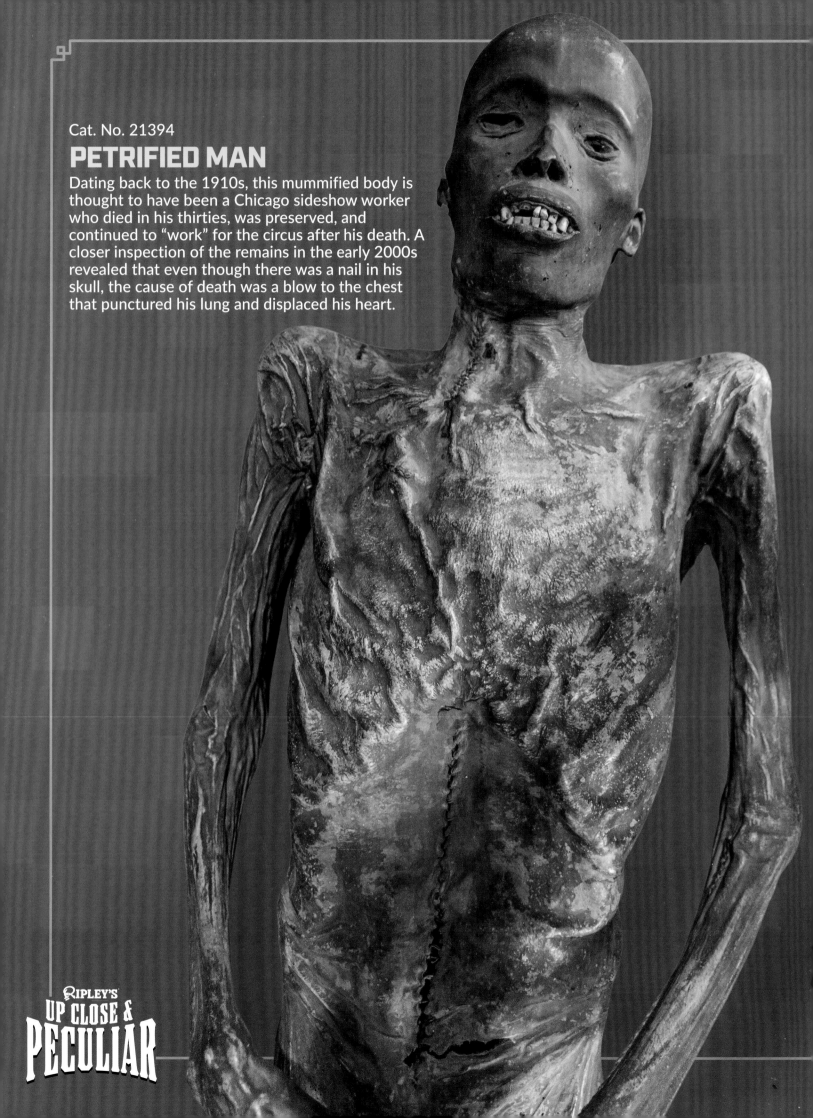

Cat. No. 21394

PETRIFIED MAN

Dating back to the 1910s, this mummified body is thought to have been a Chicago sideshow worker who died in his thirties, was preserved, and continued to "work" for the circus after his death. A closer inspection of the remains in the early 2000s revealed that even though there was a nail in his skull, the cause of death was a blow to the chest that punctured his lung and displaced his heart.

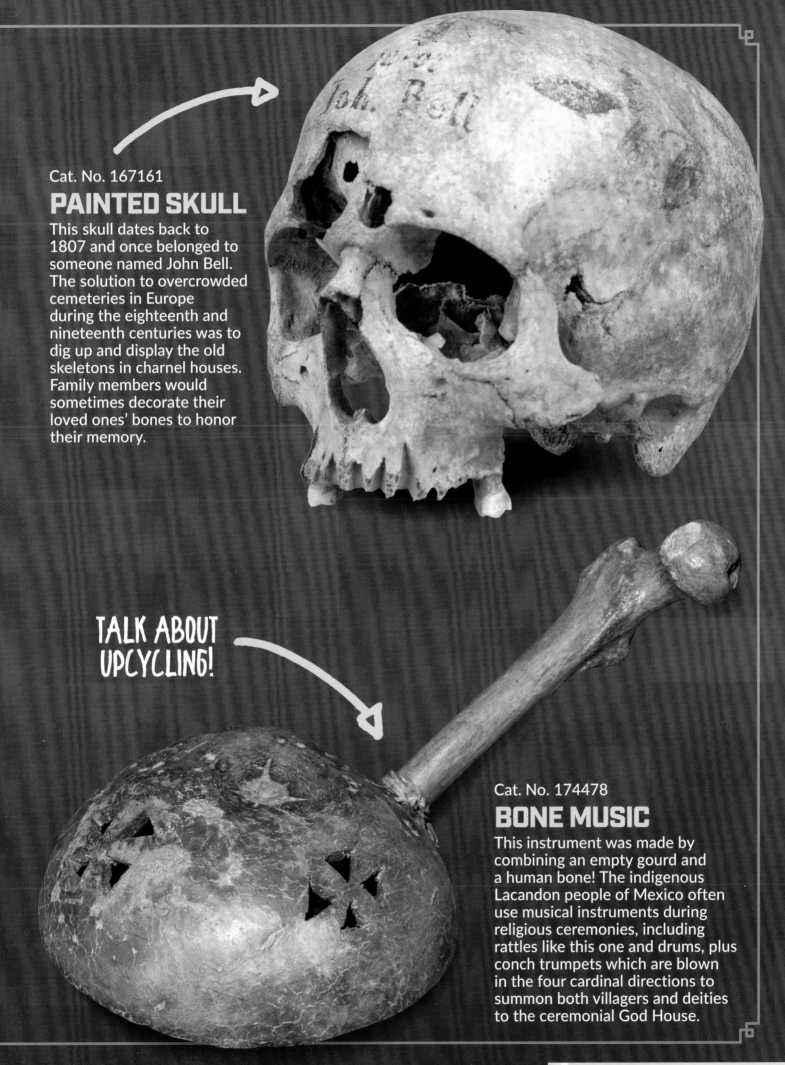

Cat. No. 167161

PAINTED SKULL

This skull dates back to 1807 and once belonged to someone named John Bell. The solution to overcrowded cemeteries in Europe during the eighteenth and nineteenth centuries was to dig up and display the old skeletons in charnel houses. Family members would sometimes decorate their loved ones' bones to honor their memory.

TALK ABOUT UPCYCLING!

Cat. No. 174478

BONE MUSIC

This instrument was made by combining an empty gourd and a human bone! The indigenous Lacandon people of Mexico often use musical instruments during religious ceremonies, including rattles like this one and drums, plus conch trumpets which are blown in the four cardinal directions to summon both villagers and deities to the ceremonial God House.

GASSY SNAKE

The western hook-nosed snake, which lives in the deserts of the U.S. and Mexico, uses farts to deter predators! When threatened, the serpent expels gas audibly from its cloaca—the opening reptiles and birds use for excretion—and this alarms the predator long enough for the snake to escape. The accompanying sound can travel over a distance of 6.5 feet (2 m) and is propelled with such force that the snake often lifts itself off the ground.

EGGSHELL GLOBE

The oldest known globe to depict the Americas dates back to 1504. It is constructed out of the bottom halves of two ostrich eggshells joined together, has a diameter of 4.5 inches (11.2 cm), and weighs just 4.7 ounces (134 g). A calcium counterweight was placed inside the bottom shell and glued in place with egg white to keep the globe upright. Some believe the globe was created by none other than Leonardo da Vinci.

SOLO VOYAGE

Dave Bell, from Dorset, England, rowed solo and unsupported across the Atlantic Ocean from New York to the UK despite having a fear of open water. During his 119-day voyage he frequently had to dive overboard to remove barnacles from his boat and he survived a number of jellyfish stings. Battling 10-foot-high (3-m) waves, he also ended up rowing about 4,600 miles (7,360 km)—1,600 miles (2,560 km) more than anticipated—due to storms.

> Reality TV star Stephanie Matto, from Derby, Connecticut, sold her own farts in a jar for $1,000 apiece and claimed she made up to $50,000 a week. But she ended up in the hospital with chest pains after eating too many beans and eggs in an attempt to boost her output.

TREE COW

In the wake of Hurricane Ida, a cow had to be rescued after it was found wedged in a tree above the floodwaters in St. Bernard Parish, Louisiana.

POOP EATERS

Rabbits will eat their own poop immediately after passing it—a practice called coprophagy. They do this in order to extract all the nutrients they need from their original meal because the grass and weeds that they eat are not easy to fully digest in one go.

PROLIFIC VINE

The Great Vine of Hampton Court Palace in London, England, was planted in 1768 but still yields as many as 700 bunches of black grapes every year. It takes the vine keeper three weeks to harvest the entire crop.

MARILYN MONROES

Every February, hundreds of Marilyn Monroe impersonators, wearing white swimsuits, sunglasses, and blonde wigs, gather at Brighton beach in Adelaide, South Australia, for an annual jetty swim.

CONSTANT COMPANION

Francesco Morosini, who ruled Venice from 1688 to 1694, never went into battle without his beloved cat Nini by his side. When Nini died, he had her embalmed with a mouse between her paws.

HONEYBEE HOME

When Sara Weaver and her husband purchased a farmhouse in Skippack, Pennsylvania, in 2020, they had to pay to have 450,000 honeybees removed from inside the walls.

Dead Weight

Locals to Portugal's Barril Beach have turned its sandy shores into a graveyard of hundreds of rusty anchors! While nobody knows who placed the first anchor, the unconventional cemetery was created and is maintained in honor of the area's history as a tuna fishing community until the 1960s, when the once flourishing bluefin tuna population declined. Interestingly, the anchors on display were not used to keep boats from floating away but were instead used to weigh down nets for catching the fish, a technique unique to Barril Beach.

GRAVE SITUATION

The Hallstatt Charnel House in Austria is home to more than 600 hand-painted human skulls!

The Austrian town of Hallstatt is known for its beautiful mountain scenery, commonly associated with *The Sound of Music*—well, the first half of the movie, anyway. While village's hills may be alive, the 1,200-plus skulls found in its charnel house certainly are not. As it turns out, the town is so beautiful that people have been dying to spend eternity there for centuries.

In the 1700s, burial plots at St. Michael's Chapel were so in demand that the church began digging up corpses to make room for the more recently departed. By 1720, villagers were exhuming their relatives' bones on their own before bleaching and painting them to be put on display. While the tradition ended when cremation became popular in the 1960s, the last painted skull wasn't added until 1995.

DON'T LOOK DOWN

Emirates Airlines took advertising to new heights with a marketing stunt that saw an airplane soaring behind a woman standing atop the Burj Khalifa—the tallest building in the world!

The January 2022 campaign provided a spectacular bird's-eye view of Dubai's iconic skyline from the perspective of a flight attendant, played by stuntwoman Nicole Smith-Ludvik, perched at the tip of the sky-high building. The messaging was loud and clear, with Nicole waving to the pilot of a passing A380 aircraft while encouraging viewers to book a flight to explore "the world's greatest show," the Dubai Expo. While the end result appears effortless, it took 11 attempts and careful choreography to fly the massive plane at only 145 knots at the exact height of the building's peak.

I'M STILL HERE!

Nicole's "I'm still here!" sign is a joke in reference to an Emirates ad from months prior, in which she first stood atop the Burj Khalifa.

BURJ KHALIFA BREAKDOWN

At **2,716.5 feet (828 m) tall**, the Burj Khalifa is the **tallest building in the world!**

If you lined up all of the steel bars used to construct the Burj Khalifa, they'd make it **one-fourth of the way across the entire planet!**

The Burj Khalifa's spire can be seen from **60 miles (95 km) away.**

Construction required the use of **11.6 million cubic feet (330,000 cubic m)** of concrete—weighing about the same as **100,000 elephants!**

The building has three outdoor observation decks, the one on the **148th floor being the highest in the world.**

The amount of aluminum used on the Burj Khalifa would be enough **to build five A380 airplanes**, the same kind flown in the Emirates ad.

It only takes **one minute** for the Burj Khalifa elevator to reach the observation deck on the **124th floor.**

It took **12,000 workers** and **22 million man-hours** to construct the Burj Khalifa over the course of six years, from January 2004 to January 2010.

ANGRY BULL

Three riders competing in the 2022 Bianchi Rock Cobbler, an 80-mile (128-km) off-road bicycle race near Bakersfield, California, were attacked by an angry bull at around the halfway mark. The bull charged Tony Inderbitzin, knocked him from his bike, and tossed him into the air, leaving him badly bruised and unable to continue riding. Inderbitzin said when he saw the animal ahead, he mistook it for a harmless cow. The two other riders who were attacked managed to finish the race.

SOLAR COOKING

On sunny days, the restaurant at the Machanents cultural center in Yerevan, Armenia, cooks food not in an oven but outside in satellite dishes covered with small mirrors. The cooks use glass pans to allow the sunlight to penetrate. By adjusting the satellite to point directly at the Sun, meals can be cooked in less than 10 minutes! During hot Armenian summers, the temperature in the pans can reach 1,292°F (700°C). The satellite dishes are not used when the weather is cloudy.

LOBSTER LADY

In 2022, Virginia Oliver was still working as a lobster fisher off Rockland, Maine, at age 102. She started trapping lobsters in 1928 when she was just eight. The boat she uses, the *Virginia*, belonged to her late husband and she works alongside her 79-year-old son Max.

COAST RIDE

In 2021, 72-year-old retired schoolteacher Lynnea Salvo, from McLean, Virginia, cycled the length of the U.S. from north to south in 43 days. Setting off from Peace Arch on the border with Canada, she completed her 2,083-mile (3,333-km) journey down the Pacific Coast in San Ysidro, California. In 2016, she cycled 3,163 miles (5,061 km) across the U.S. from California to Delaware and in 2018 she crossed Canada by bicycle from British Columbia to Nova Scotia, a distance of 3,836 miles (6,138 km).

MINI REPUBLIC

Kevin Baugh created his very own micronation called the Republic of Molossia—complete with its own navy, bank, and railroad—in 1.28 acres (0.5 hectares) of rural land near Dayton, Nevada. He wears a military uniform and proudly calls himself "His Excellency President Grand Admiral Colonel Doctor Kevin Baugh." Molossia has its own national anthem, its own currency linked to the price of cookie dough, and its own flag, although its sovereignty is not recognized by the state of Nevada.

ROCK BOTTOMS

Finnish recluse Veijo Rönkkönen spent decades sculpting hundreds of statues of people, some of which emit music or voices from internal speakers or have real human teeth!

Born in 1944, the Parikkala native began working at a local paper mill when he was 16. Despite never having taken an art class, Veijo used his first paycheck to purchase a bag of concrete to begin building his life's work. Though he rarely spoke to people, he spent the next 50 years connecting with the world through his art. By the time he passed away in 2010, his garden was filled with somewhere around 550 human figures representing all walks of life, including yogis, nuns, gardeners, and musicians. The spectacular sculpture park attracts more than 25,000 visitors a year.

FISHING FOR GOLD

There's no flushing this fish down the toilet! Andy Hackett of Worcestershire, England, reeled in a big one while fishing in the northeast region of Champagne, France, in November 2022. How big? Try a 66-pound (30-kg) goldfish, to be exact! Despite the fish being one of the largest ever recorded, it managed to evade anglers for two decades until finding the end of the line on Andy's hook. Dubbed "The Carrot," the leather carp and koi carp hybrid was released back into the lake for future generations to admire.

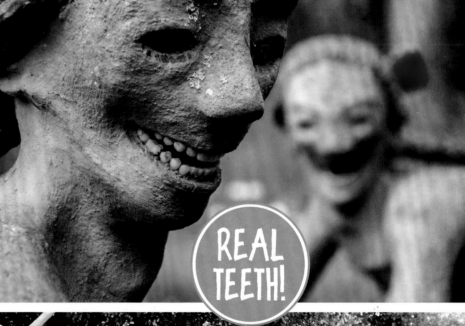

REAL TEETH!

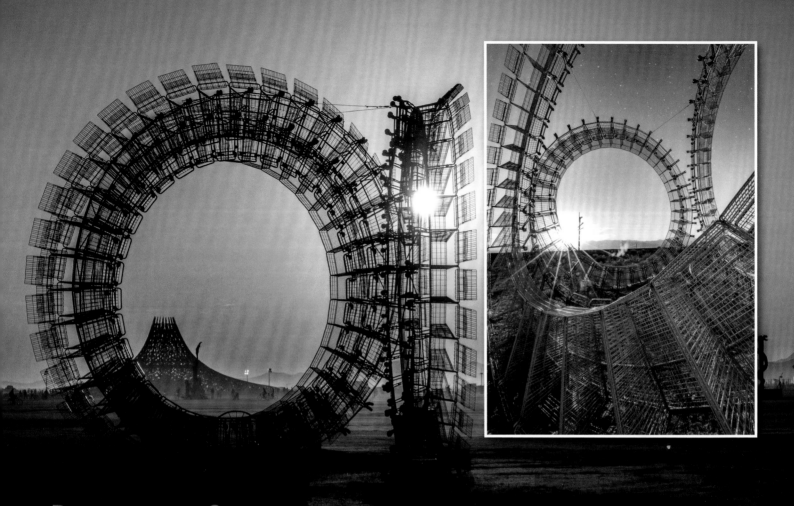

Perpetual Consumption

To create his *Perpetual Consumption* installation, Australian artist Clayton Blake welded more than 100 shopping carts together into three large 26-foot (8-m) rings. Made for 2018 Burning Man, where attendees climbed the sculpture like a playground, the art piece highlights the unending cycle of materialism. Clayton hopes *Perpetual Consumption* encourages people to be more aware of their spending habits and inspires them to reuse and recycle products more often.

BLADE RUNNER
South-African born amputee Jacky Hunt-Broersma ran 104 marathons in 104 days in 2022, covering a total of 2,724.8 miles (4,385 km). Hunt-Broersma, who lives in Gilbert, Arizona, lost her left leg below the knee in 2001 and competes with the help of a $10,000 running blade.

NO HANDS
Mike Jack, a vegan speed eater from London, Ontario, Canada, can peel and eat an entire banana in just 37.7 seconds—without using his hands. Instead, he uses his teeth to peel the fruit. He can also drink 34 ounces (1 liter) of tomato sauce in 1 minute 32.5 seconds through a straw.

SPEEDY CARROT
Jordan Maddocks, of Draper, Utah, completed the 26.2-mile (42-km) 2022 Rock 'n' Roll Arizona Marathon in Phoenix in 2 hours 44 minutes 12 seconds while dressed as a carrot. He finished the same race in 2020 in 2 hours 41 minutes 27 seconds while wearing a banana costume.

OBVIOUS CHOICE
From 1998 to 2003, the coach of German professional soccer club VfL Wolfsburg was Wolfgang Wolf.

TANK TAXI
Merlin Batchelor, of Norwich, England, charges customers about $1,000 for a journey to a wedding or even a funeral in a heavy armored personnel carrier. He bought the 1967 military vehicle, which looks like a tank, for $25,000 online. The 17-foot-long (5.2-m) monster has room for nine passengers and its interior has been fitted out with comfortable seats, a TV, a sound system, and a foldaway cooking area.

EXTREME SITTING
Robert Silk, from Denver, Colorado, once spent 14 hours 27 minutes sitting in a chair in California's Joshua Tree National Park, where the desert temperature reached 102°F (39°C). He is the founder of the new competitive sport of extreme sitting in which participants sit for long periods (usually in a chair) in challenging environments. He has also sat on a beach in Antarctica, where it was so cold that icicles formed on his chair.

BRAVE ASCENT
Albie-Junior Thomas, of Holywell, Wales, had his left foot amputated when he was 15 months old after being born with fibular hemimelia, a condition that stopped his lower left leg and foot from developing properly. But wearing an artificial leg, four-year-old Albie battled snow and wind to climb to the summit of the 3,560-foot-tall (1,085-m) Mount Snowdon, the highest mountain in Wales.

HUGE HUMMER

The Hummer H1 X3 is a custom-built vehicle that is three times the size of a regular Hummer H1!

It measures 21.6 feet (6.6 m) tall, 46 feet (14 m) long, and 20 feet (6 m) wide. Inside there are two stories connected by a staircase, plus a sink and toilet. But all of that mass comes with a price. Despite being powered by four diesel engines, it only has a top speed of 20 mph (32 kmph). The monster truck was commissioned by Sheikh Hamad bin Hamdan Al Nahyan of the United Arab Emirates, who added it to his collection of more than 700 four-wheel-drive vehicles!

RAINBOW MOUNTAIN

Rainbow Mountain near Cusco, Peru, has quickly become a viral tourist attraction thanks to the vibrant hues that color its slopes.

Its namesake stripes of reds, greens, blues, and yellows were created by layers of different minerals deposited over thousands of years—and make for the ultimate FOMO-inducing social media post. Located in the Andes mountain range, the vibrant peak was originally known as Vinicunca and is considered a holy site by many. Believe it or not, the mountain's characteristic colors were only just discovered in 2015 after snow melt exposed its natural beauty to the world!

LOW MOUNTAIN

Mount Tenpō is recognized as a mountain by the Geographical Survey Institute of Japan even though its summit is only 14.8 feet (4.5 m) above sea level. It was built near Osaka in the nineteenth century as a landmark to help ships find port. Today visitors can buy a certificate which states that they have climbed to the summit!

SCORPION POSE

Yoga instructor Yash Mansukhbhai Moradiya, a 21-year-old Indian living in Dubai, held the difficult scorpion pose (where the legs are arched above the body like a striking scorpion) for 29 minutes 4 seconds.

QUINTUPLETS PUSH

Chad Kempel of Idaho ran the 13.1-mile-long (21-km) 2022 Oakland Half-Marathon in California in 2 hours 19 minutes while pushing a stroller holding his four-year-old quintuplets the entire distance.

EINSTEIN NOTES

Albert Einstein's handwritten preliminary notes and calculations from around 1913 that led up to his general theory of relativity sold at auction in 2021 for $18.2 million.

BIG BOOT

The Golden Gumboot in Tully, Queensland, Australia, is a 26-foot-tall (8-m) fiberglass sculpture of a rubber boot with a green tree frog climbing up the side. A spiral staircase inside the oversized footwear allows visitors a view over the town, which is one of the wettest places in Australia. Erected in 2003, the boot was repainted in 2017 after frequent rains dulled its finish. Each year, Tully and the neighboring towns of Babinda and Innisfail take part in the Golden Gumboot contest for which town receives the most rainfall, the winner receiving a rubber boot.

ROBOT BEETLE

Néstor O. Pérez-Arancibia, an associate professor of engineering at Washington State University, created the Robeetle, a crawling robot that is only the same size as a real beetle. The methanol-powered robot weighs just 0.003 ounces (88 mg), about the same as three grains of rice.

They may look cranky, but wolf eels are known to be very friendly with divers.

[FISH-TAKEN IDENTITY]

Wolf eels are creatures of many contradictions, starting with the fact that they're not eels at all!

Despite their slender appearance and tendency to hide in the cracks of rocky reefs, wolf eels are, in fact, fish! While their massive jaws used for crushing sea urchins and crab shells may be intimidating, the species is actually known to be very friendly with divers. Born a bright orange color with purple spots, these magnificent marine creatures begin to look a bit irritable as they grow, developing a face only a mother could love—or their soulmate. While there may be plenty of fish in the sea, wolf eels are monogamous and stick with one mate for life!

Let 'em Rip

On March 24, 2022, Ripley's Aquariums made history with the world's first successful birth by artificial insemination of a sand tiger shark! Named "Rip" after company founder Robert Ripley, the pup marks a major step for its species. Globally, sand tiger sharks are listed as a vulnerable species, and in some areas of the world, they are considered endangered. Rip's historic birth helps pave the way for the continued survival of these fascinating creatures!

IT'S A BOY!

ROTATING HOUSE
Vojin Kusic used electric motors and the wheels of an old military transport vehicle to create a rotating house in Srbac, Bosnia. Mounted on a concrete platform, the house turns full circle so that his wife, Ljubica, can enjoy different views from the same window. It can make a complete rotation in 22 seconds or 24 hours, depending on the speed setting.

ORIGAMI SHIRTS
Jude Coram, of Exeter, England, spent three months folding 4,036 sheets of paper into miniature origami shirts.

MEAGER DIET
When he was struggling to find work in the 1940s, German-American author Charles Bukowski used to survive on nothing more than one candy bar a day. It cost him a nickel.

PRIEST STRANGLERS
Strangolapreti, small Italian bread and spinach dumplings, translates as "priest stranglers" because in the sixteenth century priests and other clergy used to eat so many at church meetings that they choked.

TUSKLESS ELEPHANTS
Some African elephants are evolving without tusks, reducing their risk of being killed by poachers who value their ivory. Normally no more than 4 percent of female African elephants would be tuskless, but about one-third of all female elephants born in Mozambique over the last 30 years did not develop tusks.

GARDEN LIFE
Over the course of 26 years, zoologist Jennifer Owens recorded 2,673 different species living in her small suburban garden in Leicester, England, including 1,997 species of insects.

> While walking along the beach on the Isle of Palms in South Carolina, Lori McGee picked up a whelk shell and found an octopus living inside.

HOME HEIST
Thieves stole an entire 336-square-foot (31.2-sq-m) wooden cabin from a site in Cold Springs Township, Michigan. Five weeks later, the cabin was found 17 miles (27 km) away.

PIZZA DANGER
In 2020, 2,899 Americans went to the emergency room to be treated for pizza-related injuries.

COOL APE
After visitor Lolita Testu's sunglasses fell into an enclosure at a zoo in West Java, Indonesia, a female orangutan picked them up and wore them on her face for 15 minutes.

MOUTH MOLD
Bros', a restaurant in Lecce, Italy, serves a dish of citrus foam inside a plaster mold of the open mouth of chef Floriano Pellegrino.

River Romp

A group of pink Bolivian river dolphins baffled biologists when the elusive creatures were spotted playing with an unlikely toy—a Beni anaconda! Researchers from the Noel Kempff Mercado Museum of Natural History were exploring near the Tijamuchi River when they noticed a pair of dolphins peeking out from the murky water with the apex predator in their mouths. Except for one incident of cannibalism among the anacondas, there have been no recordings of one ever being killed by another animal, leading researchers to believe the playful dolphins found it already deceased and decided to have a bit of fun!

Worms Like a Charm

Snake charming may be alluring, but what about charming the rings off a worm? Worm charming competitions have become increasingly popular in recent years, with dedicated contestants doing whatever it takes to lure wiggling worms out of the ground, including playing music, simulating rain, and making the soil vibrate. Some might argue it's harder to charm a worm than a snake, as evidenced by the 2022 Falmouth Worm Charming Championships in England, where, despite many creative efforts, just one worm rose to the occasion.

Keep It Up

The classic childhood challenge of seeing how long one can keep a party balloon from touching the ground has been elevated to an official World Cup event. Two at a time, players will run, jump, and dive as they do whatever it takes to keep the balloon afloat during their turn. If a player fails to do so, their opponent scores a point. The event is set up as a fully furnished living room, except with clear walls so fans can watch the action. Teams from 32 countries took part in the first-ever Balloon World Cup in October 2021, with 18-year-old Francesco De La Cruz taking home the win for Peru.

SSSTROLLING Snakes

Inventor Allen Pan created a robotic suit with legs to help snakes go from slithering to strutting!

Allen's idea to engineer some limbs for his scaly friends came from his sympathy for the creatures slowly losing their legs to millions of years of evolution, as well as from a desire to prove how much he loves the animals! To get snakes back on their feet again, Allen connected robotic legs to a large tube that serpents could enter and exit voluntarily. He then studied how lizards walk and used what he learned to program the legs' movements. The outcome? The first snake to use the prosthetic slithered comfortably into the tube and, as Allen remotely directed the robot around a room, even appeared to enjoy her first-ever "walk." Success!

WOW! A SNAKE WITH LEGS!

LEVEL UP
SEE PAGE 7!

SCAN AND PLAY!

Look BOTH WAYS

The width of a stalk-eyed fly's namesake eye stalks can be wider than the entire length of the insect's body!

Commonly seen on mollusks and crustaceans such as snails and crabs, eye stalks are long appendages that help extend a creature's field of vision by having the eyes further away from the body. But when it comes to flies, eye stalks are relatively rare and appear to have another important function—showing off! When it comes to choosing a mate, a female is more likely to pick the fly guy with the widest eye stalks. Believe it or not, when stalk-eyed flies hatch from their pupal shells, they have short eye stalks and must "inflate" them using their body fluids!

Tree Stumped

The potoo bird is nearly impossible to spot in the wild! These masters of camouflage have feathers that blend seamlessly with tree bark. To complete the illusion of being a branch, the potoo will sit perfectly still with its head tilted up and eyes almost completely closed. It then waits for insects to fly by so it can snatch them out of the air with its massive mouth!

When they aren't imitating tree stumps, potoo birds look more like cartoon characters!

ODD GOD

The Romans had a goddess of door hinges and handles! Her name was Cardea, and her role was to prevent evil spirits from crossing the thresholds of homes.

TWIN BIRTHS

Identical twin sisters Jill Justiniani and Erin Cheplak, of Yorba Linda, California, both gave birth to baby boys at the same hospital, the Kaiser Permanente in Anaheim, on the same day, May 5, 2022. Both babies weighed 7.2 pounds (3.2 kg) and measured 20 inches (50 cm) long at birth.

PERSONAL TOILET

North Korean dictator Kim Jong-un has his own personal, portable toilet that he takes with him everywhere—even on travels abroad—because he is worried that any left-behind feces could contain vital information about his health. Anyone caught using his toilet without his permission is liable to face the death penalty.

TV DRAMAS

Each year, around 4,600 people in the U.S. require treatment from a hospital emergency department after being injured by falling TV sets.

SPITTING FIRE

Russian mechanic Vahan Mikaelyan converted a regular Lada 1600 automobile into "The Dragon"—a customized vehicle that shoots 20-foot-long (6-m) flames out of its headlights. His previous creations have included a car that, instead of moving on wheels, has eight giant spider-like legs that it glides on.

BAFFLING CASE

Identical twins were arrested for a heist at a jewelry store in Berlin, Germany. DNA evidence showed that at least one of the twins was at the crime scene but since it was impossible to prove which one, both were released.

TIMELY BIRTH

Judah Grace Spear was born in the Alamance Regional Medical Center in Burlington, North Carolina, at 2:22 a.m. on 2/22/22 in delivery room 2.

BABY BOOM

In a 24-hour period in March 2022, three firefighters at Fort Belvoir Army Base, Virginia—Kyle Dean, Kyle Frederick, and Michael Irvine—became fathers to new babies at the same hospital in Spotsylvania.

ROBOT STUDENT

When seven-year-old Joshua Martinangeli was too sick to go to school in Berlin, Germany, but still wanted to interact with his teacher and classmates, a robot was sent in his place. The sleek white head-and-torso combo sat on his desk and sent a blinking signal to indicate when Joshua had something to say.

ESCAPE ARTIST

Professional illusionist Jackson Rayne completed 300 straitjacket escapes in eight hours at Wild Adventures Theme Park in Valdosta, Georgia. He began to study escape artistry at age 11 and received his first straitjacket as a Christmas present when he was 17.

PERFECT SCORE

In 2021, Jake Goldberg, from Bucks County, Pennsylvania, achieved a perfect score in the classic video game *Pac-Man*—making him only the eleventh person in the world to do so. He completed all 256 levels in 4 hours 12 minutes, racking up a maximum score of 3,333,360 points.

TRIBAL TATTOO

Whang-od Oggay works as a tribal tattoo artist in the Philippine village of Buscalan at age 105. Her needle is a citrus thorn, and her ink is a mixture of charcoal and water. She creates the design by tapping the inked thorn into the person's skin with a 12-inch (30-cm) bamboo hammer.

SMALL CINEMA

The Little Prince Micro-Cinema in Stratford, Ontario, Canada, seats only 12 people.

GOLD COINS

On his first walk, Adam Clark and Kim Mcguire's new Lagotto Romagnolo puppy Ollie dug up 15 gold sovereign pieces from the nineteenth century near Blackpool, England. The coins are valued at over $7,000.

BAG COLLECTOR

Angela Clarke, from Aberdare, Wales, has a collection of more than 10,000 plastic shopping bags, some dating back to the 1950s. Her collection, which she started in 1976 when she was 11, includes a bag signed by actor David Soul and another that once held the shoes of former UK talk show host Michael Parkinson. The bags are now considered historical artefacts, and rare ones can sell for hundreds of dollars.

PANCAKE FEAST

At the 2021 Pancake Day festival in Centerville, Iowa, about 100 volunteers served up 14,280 pancakes in four hours.

BASKETBALL BOUNCE

Sean Daly, of Skibbereen, Ireland, bounced two basketballs—one in each hand—729 times in 60 seconds. He has also bounced two balls simultaneously for 2 hours 6 minutes while blindfolded.

Burning Time

Prior to the widespread use of mechanical clocks, people would use candles and incense to track time! One of the simplest fire-fueled methods involved adding incremental lines to a candle, and the melted wax would show how long the candle had been burning. An alarm clock could easily be made by pushing a nail into the wax, so when it melted, the nail would fall and give a little "ding!"

Perhaps more appealing to the senses were the incense clocks that used different scents to mark the hours, allowing people to tell time with a sniff! If a change in smell wasn't a powerful enough alert, there were also alarm clocks that burned incense below a series of strings attached to metal balls; when the hot incense reached a thread and made it snap, the balls would drop into a pan and make a loud sound.

ANCIENT ALARM CLOCK!

BANNER LADIES

You know those commercials that seem completely unrelated to the products they're selling? The Victorian era had something very similar!

During the late 1800s, many businesses in the U.S. used photographs—a relatively new invention at the time—to advertise their goods and services. But rather than display their product in a way that shows how it's used, companies would instead hire "banner ladies" to cover themselves from head to toe in merchandise! The businesses that used this kind of advertisement ranged wildly, leaving us with some curious relics from the era. Believe it or not, it wasn't uncommon to see a banner lady wearing a dress decorated with horseshoes, lightbulbs, or even pretzels! The look was often completed with an ornate hat, plus a banner with the company's name.

PERMANENT SOLUTIONS

Manchester, England–based tattoo artist Dean Gunther gives his clients realistic ink to help solve life's little annoyances, like having to buy new shoes or work out to get abs!

The artist's method for solving everyday problems with tattoos is unconventional, but he loves the challenge nonetheless. Dean spent eight hours tattooing tired shopper Blazej Arkadiusz Ambrozak's favorite pair of Nike sneakers onto his feet, resulting in a pair of shoes that will last! Dean has also proved that abs aren't always made in the kitchen or the gym; they can be made in a tattoo parlor, too! After failing to tone his abs on his own, a client came to Dean looking for a fast fix for a beach-ready bod. Although the client, Seb, thought he couldn't take anymore after an hour of tattooing, Dean convinced him to push through, and after two days he had a full six-pack to show off!

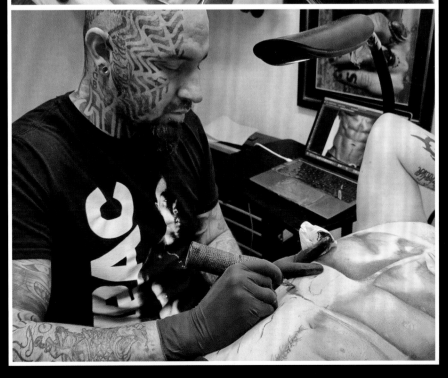

ALL CHALKED UP

While many chalk drawings can be found carved into the British hillsides, none have stood the test of time like the White Horse of Uffington, a 3,000-year-old marvel the size of a football field!

Carved into the ground using the area's natural landscape, the White Horse of Uffington is one of 16 white chalk horses still existing in the south England countryside, with the others only dating back 250 years max. It takes a village— or a *neigh*-borhood—to keep the pride of Oxfordshire in tip-top shape. Every 20–30 years for the past few millennia, the town has hosted "chalking days," when volunteers get on hand and knee, moving inch-by-inch to smash the chalk into a paste, whitening the horse's stony pathway until it looks brand new once again.

SERBIAN HERMIT

Panta Petrovic has lived as a hermit in Serbia for more than 16 years, and among his pets is a 440-pound (200-kg) wild boar named Mara. Petrovic shuns civilization, spending half the year in a riverside cave and the rest in a remote treehouse.

PET RAVEN

Nineteenth-century English author Charles Dickens kept a pet raven named Grip and used to read to his children at night with the bird perched on his shoulder. When it died, Dickens had it stuffed and mounted in his study.

SPACE MISSION

Former *Star Trek* actor William Shatner was launched into space from a site in Texas at age 90. He spent 10 minutes in space aboard the *New Shepard* rocket, which reached an altitude of 66 miles (106 km) and a speed of over 2,000 mph (3,200 kmph).

BUG TATTOOS

After starting with a red ant queen inked on his forearm when he was 21, Michael Amoia from New York City now has 889 insect and arachnid tattoos on his body—including, flies, moths, centipedes, scorpions, and spiders—even though he hates bugs.

HIDDEN MEAL

While renovating their Crystal Lake, Illinois, home, Rob and Grace Jones discovered the remains of a McDonald's meal that had been hidden inside their wall for more than 60 years. The bag contained two burger wrappers and some half-eaten, remarkably well-preserved fries.

SMALL AUDIENCE

Early in R.E.M.'s career they played in front of only five people at a venue in Detroit, Michigan. When the audience demanded an encore, the band took them out to dinner instead.

BOREDOM TO BAYEUX

It's been more than five years since former teacher Mia Hansson began stitching a replica of the famous eleventh-century Bayeux Tapestry out of sheer boredom—and she's only halfway done! Though the UK-based embroiderer is generally disinterested in history, she was inspired to copy the original 223-foot-long (68-m) artwork depicting William the Conqueror's 1066 invasion of England due to its massive size. Mia works on the project for up to 10 hours a day, paying meticulous attention to her stitching to ensure the replica's detailing is exact. The original artwork can be found in Normandy, France, at the Musée de la Tapisserie de Bayeux.

DUNE AND GLOOM

The Skeleton Coast earned its name thanks to the hundreds of shipwrecks left behind in its sands.

It's been more than a century since the *Eduard Bohlen* wrecked into Southern Africa's Skeleton Coast, but the vessel can still be seen today—only now it's in the middle of the Namib Desert!

On September 5, 1909, the 310-foot-long (94.5-m) cargo ship was making its way to Table Bay, South Africa, until a thick fog caused it to run aground. Over the years, the dunes shifted so much that the *Eduard Bohlen* now sits 1,000 feet (305 m) away from the shore where it met its demise, giving the appearance that it was purposefully dropped into the middle of the desert! Named for its unforgiving ways, the Skeleton Coast has devoured many ships in its time, becoming a graveyard of sorts with numerous doomed vessels buried in the sand surrounding the *Eduard Bohlen*.

MAC SABBATH

Los Angeles music group Mac Sabbath is part-tribute band, part-social commentary, and all rock!

Like french fries dipped in a milkshake, Mac Sabbath is an unexpected pairing that works surprisingly well. But instead of mixing salty and sweet flavors, they combine the music of Black Sabbath with lyrics about the dangers of unhealthy fast food! The self-described "Drive Thru Metal" band enhances their live performances with elaborate costumes and stage props, such as front man Ronald Osbourne's giant soda cup that doubles as a microphone stand. Believe it or not, just three years after the band formed in 2014, they played a private show for Black Sabbath lead singer Ozzy Osbourne—who loved it!

MEAT THE BAND!

THE CATBURGLAR

RONALD OSBOURNE

GRIMALICE

SLAYER MACCHEEZE

CROC AMBUSH

Alexander Chimedza survived an attack by at least three crocodiles while fishing in Lake Kariba, Zimbabwe. One croc tried to grab his left hand while another bit his right hand and pulled him into the water. Then he felt the jaws of a third crocodile snap around his foot. He managed to fight off one reptile by shoving his hand into its mouth before his friends succeeded in driving the crocs away. He had metallic plates surgically implanted in his body to help his broken bones to heal but was readmitted to the hospital two months after the attack when a crocodile tooth was found still lodged in his leg.

LARGE ORDER

Brittani Curtis, a McDonald's employee in Perry, Georgia, had just four hours to prepare a 6,400-item order that included 1,600 McChicken sandwiches, 1,600 McDoubles, and 3,200 chocolate chip cookies. The $7,400 order was placed by a local prison.

DUMPSTER RAIDERS

Wild cockatoos in Sydney, Australia, have learned how to lift the lids of trash cans to find food and have been seen raiding dumpsters in more than 40 of the city's suburbs.

FAST PRODUCTION

Rubber Chicken Theatre in Dunblane, Scotland, staged a musical, *Return to the Forbidden Planet*, just 9 hours 59 minutes 3 seconds after opening the box of scripts. In that short time the company had to learn lines, songs, and choreography as well as organize costumes, lighting, sound, sets, and props.

8,000 MEALS

David R. Chan, from Los Angeles, California, has dined at around 8,000 Chinese restaurants in the U.S. over a period of 40 years, with each visit detailed in a spreadsheet. He also keeps thousands of restaurant business cards and menus from his travels.

VINTAGE TINS

Yvette Dardenne, from Grand-Hallet, Belgium, has collected nearly 60,000 vintage tin boxes that used to contain such items as chocolates, tobacco, coffee, and shoe polish. She started her collection about 30 years ago and it is now so big that it occupies four houses.

SKI QUEST

Kyle Kelly and Brad Dykstra of Michigan traveled 763 miles (1,221 km) across the state to ski at 22 resorts in 24 hours. They began at noon on February 26, 2022, and continued through the night, Kelly on skis and Dykstra on a snowboard.

LEGO BEACHES

Pieces of LEGO still wash up on beaches in Cornwall, England, more than 25 years after a container filled with millions of LEGO bricks fell into the sea in 1997.

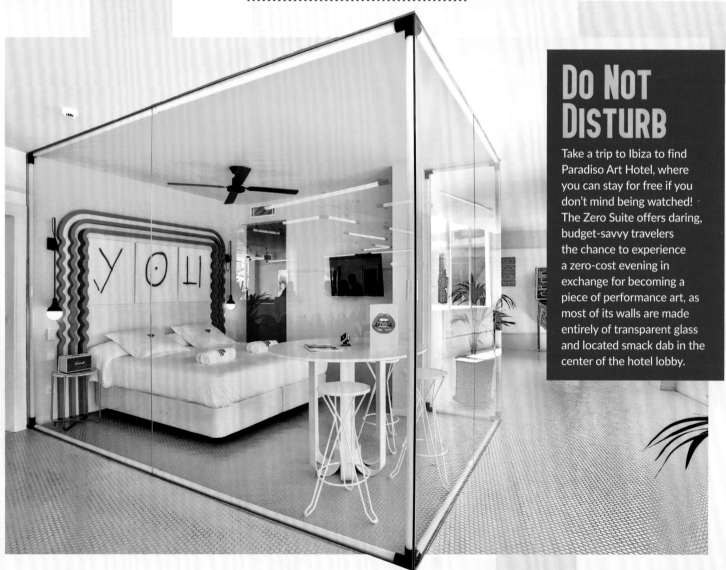

DO NOT DISTURB

Take a trip to Ibiza to find Paradiso Art Hotel, where you can stay for free if you don't mind being watched! The Zero Suite offers daring, budget-savvy travelers the chance to experience a zero-cost evening in exchange for becoming a piece of performance art, as most of its walls are made entirely of transparent glass and located smack dab in the center of the hotel lobby.

OUT OF THIS WORLD

Ripley's Believe It or Not! Orlando is more far out than ever, with the all-new Out of This World gallery!

Here, you can blast off into outer space and touch an actual piece of Mars, marvel at the original Star Wars® Lightsaber® used by Luke Skywalker™, and even slip into a pair of gloves to work in a vacuum, as an astronaut would in space. Front and center is a 16-foot-tall (4.9-m) interactive video wall that also live streams rocket launches! Here's a glimpse at some of the astronomical wonders on display at Ripley's Orlando!

Cat. No. 166300

NANTAN METEORITE

Found in Nantan, China, in 1958, this meteorite is believed to have fallen to Earth on June 11, 1529, during the Ming Dynasty. Composed of 92% iron, the extraterrestrial origin of this 3,197-pound (1,450-kg) "rock" was first discovered when farmers tried, but failed, to melt it down to make steel.

Cat. No. 167978

BUZZ ALDRIN JUMPSUIT

Signed by astronaut Edwin "Buzz" Aldrin, this is the actual jumpsuit he wore during his time at the U.S. Air Force Aerospace Research Pilot School. As part of the Apollo 11 mission with Neil Armstrong and Michael Collins in July 1969, Buzz was the second person to ever walk on the Moon!

Cat. No. 174267

APOLLO TAPES

Ripley's owns the only surviving first-generation reels of the Apollo 11 moonwalk, once thought to be "erased and reused" by NASA. The 2 hours 24 minutes of footage features a solar wind experiment, the moment Armstrong and Aldrin planted the American flag on the Moon, as well as a long-distance phone call with President Richard Nixon!

SEEN in SPACE

Have you ever looked at the sky and noticed an elephant in the clouds? Or perhaps you've toasted a piece of bread only to find a face staring back at you. If so, you've experienced *pareidolia*, a psychological phenomenon where we see familiar shapes in unlikely places. One of the most famous pareidolic sightings is that of the "man in the Moon," but that's only the beginning of intergalactic sightings that make you do a double take.

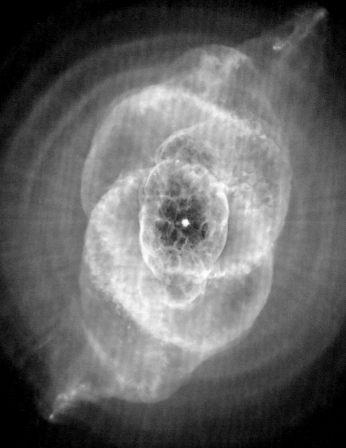

EYE SIGHT

It's not often that you stare into space and space stares back, but such was the case when the Hubble Space Telescope spotted NGC 6543, or the Cat's Eye Nebula. It's easy to see how this dying star got its name—its spherical rings of dust resemble a kitty's purr-fectly round peepers, while intricate gas shells form a vertical pupil just like a feline's.

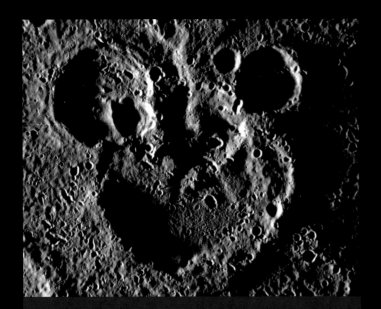

MERCURY MOUSE

Disney's reach goes far and wide here on Earth, but how about in space? In June 2012, NASA released a photo of a cluster of craters on Mercury that form the familiar three-circle shape of Mickey Mouse's head. Captured by the *MESSENGER* space probe, Mercury Mickey's shadowy form consists of a 65-mile-wide (105-km) face topped by two ear-shaped impacts that made scientists say, "Oh boy!"

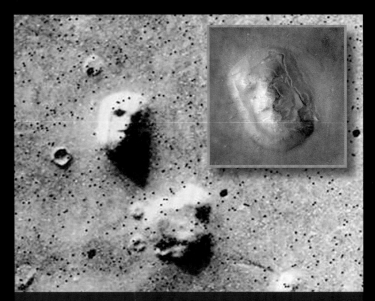

SPACE FACE

Miraculous sightings on Mars are nothing new. In 1976, NASA's *Viking 1* spacecraft spotted something scary on the surface—a person's face! The enormous head, which measured almost 2 miles (3.2 km) from hairline to chin, seemed to be gazing directly at the cameras. The sighting spurred all kinds of conspiracy theories until 1998, when new images of "the Face of Mars" confirmed that it was merely a massive rock formation.

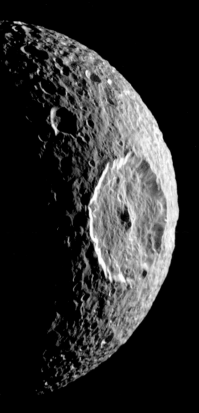

DEATH STAR DOUBLE

Despite the similarities between the Death Star and Saturn's moon Mimas, any resemblance is completely coincidental. The Star Wars® weapon first appeared on movie screens in 1977, and we didn't have clear pictures of Mimas until the *Voyager 1* spacecraft zoomed by in 1980. Rest assured, Mimas will not be blowing up any planets any time soon!

STAR SMILE

In October 2022, NASA's space-based Solar Dynamics Observatory captured an unbelievable photo of the Sun that makes it look as though the star is smiling! The dark splotches that make up the face are known as coronal holes and are less hot and dense than their surrounding areas. When imaged through ultraviolet light, the coronal holes appear as black patches, and in this case gave the star a friendly face!

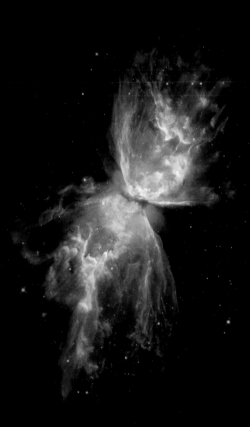

UNIVERSAL UTENSIL

An optical illusion stirred up a frenzy after being spotted on Mars by NASA's *Curiosity* rover in 2015. The photo depicted what appeared to be a clearly formed spoon floating above Martian rocks, complete with a shadow below. Unfortunately, the spoon was not an actual utensil left behind by aliens sipping on soup, but rather a rock sculpted by millions of years of wind and erosion.

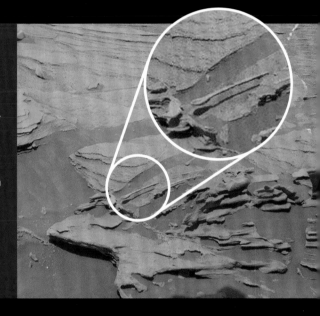

BEARY CUTE

Scientists were in for a grizzly surprise in December 2022 when NASA's *Mars Reconnaissance Orbiter* captured an image of a bear on the planet's surface. It shows two beady eyed craters situated above a hill with a "v-shaped collapse structure" that has an uncanny resemblance to a bear snout. While the combination could resemble many animals, a circular fracture surrounding the formations gives it a distinctly cub-like appearance.

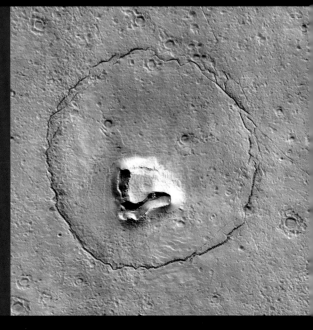

WINGED WONDER

Sometimes when a star dies, a beautiful butterfly is born. In 2009, the Hubble Space Telescope captured the aftermath of such an event in the form of NGC 6302, a butterfly-shaped nebula stretching across three light-years. At the center of this celestial beauty is a dying central star that measures a scalding 450,000°F (250,000°C), surrounded by wings made from gas traveling 590,000 mph (950,000 kmph)!

The invention of the telescope in the early 1600s changed the way we understand Earth's place in the universe.

Humankind's never-ending curiosity has spurred the technological advances that propelled us from a handheld spyglass that barely revealed the craters of the Moon to massive observatories in space able to see galaxies billions of light-years away from Earth. Explore this timeline to see just how far telescopes have advanced throughout history!

CLOSER TO THE COSMOS

1609

GALILEO LOOKS UP

In 1609, Italian physicist and astronomer Galileo Galilei heard about a new Dutch invention that made distant objects appear closer and decided to make his own version. Galileo's first attempt at a telescope had just 3-times magnification, but he quickly made some adjustments and soon had an instrument that could magnify views up to 23 times. He turned the tool to the skies and became the first known person to observe the mountains and craters of the Moon, as well as Jupiter's largest moons.

Galileo presenting his telescope to the leader of Venice in 1609.

A sketch of the Moon from Galileo's 1610 book on his telescope observations, *Sidereus Nuncius*, or *Starry Message*.

1897

BIGGER IS BETTER

The further people saw into space, the more they wanted to see. This meant building bigger telescopes and observatories to house them. Yerkes Observatory in Williams Bay, Wisconsin, opened in 1897 and features a 64-foot-long (19.5-m) movable telescope that weighs 6 tons! With its 40-inch-diameter (102-cm) lens, it remains the world's largest refracting telescope. The observatory floor can be raised or lowered so astronomers can reach the eyepiece no matter where the telescope is pointed. The high-tech laboratory is often considered the birthplace of astrophysics.

1668

MAJOR MIRROR BREAKTHROUGH

Up until this point, magnification was mainly achieved using curved lenses. An unfortunate side effect of this design was a glitch-like distortion of colors called "chromatic aberration." The issue could be fixed with a longer focal length, but this led to absurdly long telescopes with added complications. During the mid-1660s, British scientist Sir Isaac Newton set out to eliminate the problem using mirrors. While Newton wasn't the first to consider the idea, in late 1668, he became the first to build a working model of a reflecting telescope. This improvement was a significant stepping stone to building more efficient and powerful telescopes.

A replica of Isaac Newton's first reflecting telescope.

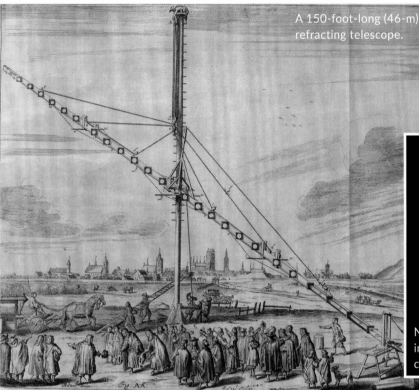

A 150-foot-long (46-m) refracting telescope.

Newton's telescope design produced clearer images by reducing image distortions like chromatic aberration, seen here.

1968

NEW DESTINATIONS

During the 300 years between Newton's breakthrough and this point in our timeline, scientists continued to improve telescopes in size, power, precision, and other uncountable ways. But they were all still limited by interference from Earth's atmosphere. Then came the Orbiting Astronomical Observatory 2, or OAO 2— the first successful space-based telescope. Launched on December 7, 1968, it opened a new chapter in astronomy, allowing scientists to gather information that was previously unattainable from Earth-based telescopes.

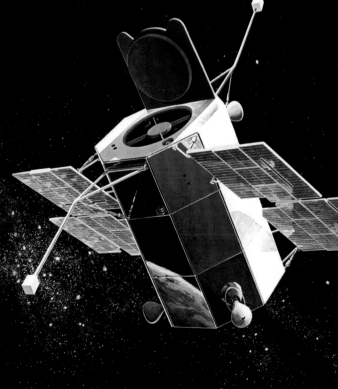

1995

LET'S GET DEEP

Since its launch on April 24, 1990, the Hubble Space Telescope has orbited the Earth, gathering images and data that have revolutionized the way we understand our universe. But perhaps its most iconic contributions have been its "Deep Field" images. The first Hubble Deep Field was captured over the course of 10 days in December 1995, during which the telescope was pointed at a single black spot in space. The resulting image revealed more than 3,000 galaxies, each containing possibly billions of stars and planets! If you want to feel even smaller, the Hubble Ultra Deep Field captured in 2004 includes more than 10,000 galaxies!

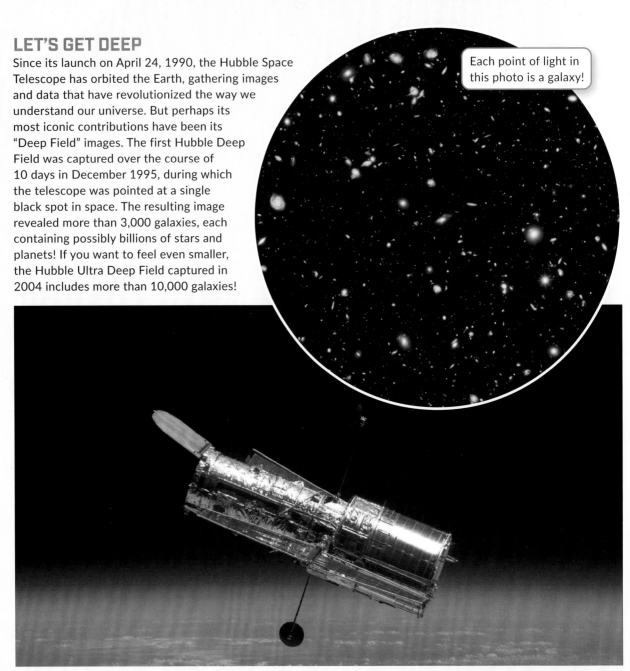

Each point of light in this photo is a galaxy!

2019

NEW HORIZONS

Often called an "Earth-sized" telescope, the Event Horizon Telescope (EHT) is actually a collection of ground-based radio telescopes around the world, designed specifically to capture images of a black hole. In April 2017, EHT pointed its collective eyes at the supermassive black hole at the center of the Messier 87 galaxy and gathered data for two weeks straight. After two years of calibrating and collecting the information, the first-ever image of a black hole was released to the public. Three years later in May 2022, EHT astronomers revealed an image of the black hole in the center of our very own Milky Way galaxy.

The Atacama Large Millimeter/ Submillimeter Array (ALMA) in Chile, shown here, is one of the radio observatories part of the Event Horizon Telescope.

Black holes are so dense that not even light can escape their gravitational pull; this point of no return is called the *event horizon*.

TO THE BEGINNING AND BEYOND

As soon as the Hubble Space Telescope made orbit, NASA began working on an even larger, more powerful telescope to follow it into the great unknown. After 30 years and $10 billion dollars spent, the James Webb Space Telescope launched on December 25, 2021, settling into orbit 1 million miles (1,609,344 km) away from Earth a month later.

Getting the telescope to space was no easy feat due to the sheer complexity of its construction, which features technologies never before used in outer space, a tennis court–sized sun shield, and a powerful infrared optical system. At 21.3 feet (6.5 m), its mirror is three times the size of the Hubble's, and the entire contraption had to be folded like origami to fit onto the rocket!

The hexagonal shape of JWST's mirrors causes the iconic six-spiked stars in the telescope's images, like the ones in the above Deep Field image.

LEVEL UP
SEE PAGE 7!

SCAN AND PLAY!

The funky yet functional Bee Brick is made by UK company Green&Blue.

BUILD A BUZZ

City planners in Brighton, England, caused a bit of buzz by introducing a law stating that all new buildings must include special bricks that provide nests for bees!

The Brighton and Hove Council aims to address biodiversity concerns caused by years of neglect of natural ecosystems. Solitary bees don't live in hives, and they account for around 90 percent of Britain's 270 bee species. To make up for losses in natural habitat, Brighton's law stipulates that any new building above 16.4 feet (5 m) tall must include bricks with narrow openings where solitary bees can build their nests.

SAVE *THESE* BEES!

Not all bees are black and yellow; some are **blue, white, purple, or even green!**

There are more than **20,000 types of bees** on Earth, and every continent **except Antarctica** has its own native species.

While honeybees are important when it comes to agriculture, **native bees play a much larger role** when it comes to the health of local ecosystems!

Some plants **can only be pollinated** by native bees and would **go extinct without them** (and vice versa)!

Sadly, many native bees are at a **high risk of extinction** due to **loss of habitat,** often caused by **intensive farming** practices.

ROOM FOR ONE, PLEASE!

You can help native bees by growing native plants or giving them a place to live, like a **solitary bug hotel!**

DOWN TOWN

2ND-FLOOR DOOR!

Now known for its eclectic architecture, the first-ever Starbucks, and the iconic Space Needle, Seattle's earliest buildings can still be found in tunnels beneath the city's busy sidewalks!

When the Emerald City was initially built in the 1850s, its location right next to Elliott Bay created major problems when high tide rolled in, often flooding the settlement—and its sewage system! Horses would get stuck in muddy streets, and a poorly timed flush by any of the city's residents could result in a fountain of sewage.

On June 6, 1889, the Great Seattle Fire burned down most of the city and provided a unique opportunity to rebuild and elevate the streets above sea level. Rather than wait for the roads to be built, impatient developers constructed buildings with two entrances—one at ground level and another one story above. Once the streets were raised, the first floor of the buildings ended up underground—including their storefronts and sidewalks, still accessible by tunnel today!

Once underground, the first floors were mainly used for storage or illegal activity. Today, guided tours are available for the curious traveler.

FINGERPRINT ISLAND

The oval-shaped island of Baljenac off the coast of Croatia is known as "fingerprint island." It is covered by a 14.3-mile-long (23-km) network of around 1,000 stone walls, which were used to protect crops from strong winds. When viewed from above, the walls make the island look like a human fingerprint!

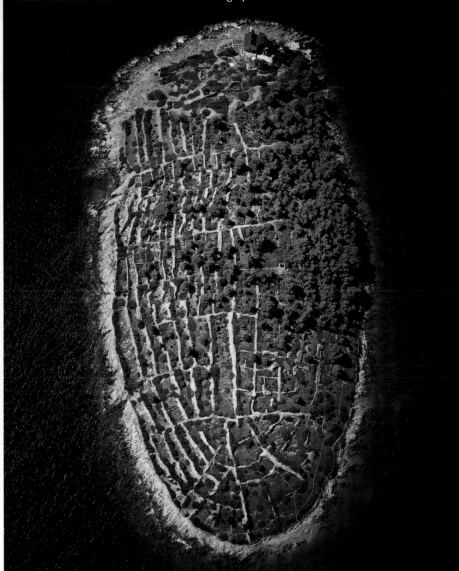

LONG OVERDUE

A library book returned to Boise Public Library, Idaho, in 2021 was 110 years overdue. *New Chronicles of Rebecca* by Kate Wiggin had been checked out of Boise's now-defunct Carnegie Library on November 8, 1911, and would have accrued an $800 late return fee under rules in operation at the time.

REAL BAT

During a March 2022 screening of *The Batman* in Austin, Texas, a real bat was seen swooping around inside the movie theater. The film was put on hold while animal control officers tried in vain to capture the bat. Customers were offered their money back but most decided to watch the rest of the film, complete with the unscheduled special effects.

CLONED FERRET

To help save the endangered black-footed ferret species, scientists successfully cloned one using cells from a female ferret named Willa who had died 30 years earlier. Willa's cells had been preserved on ice since the 1980s at the Frozen Zoo, a program run by San Diego Zoo Global. The clone was born on December 10, 2020, and was named Elizabeth Ann.

DRILL DRAMA

While having a tooth filled at the dentist, Tom Jozsi, a maintenance worker from Illinois, accidentally inhaled a 0.8-inch-long (2-cm) metal drill bit. It remained lodged near the bottom of his right lung for four days before doctors in Kenosha, Wisconsin, removed it in a 90-minute surgery. Jozsi keeps the drill bit on a shelf at his home as a souvenir.

CROWN OF BONES

This regal headwear was crafted by Christina Wong of Orlando, Florida, who started making crowns out of ethically sourced bones after recovering from brain surgery in 2017. Post-operation, Christina was searching for an art form that satisfied her urge to create when she found a bag of crystals. She felt they deserved an elegant treatment, and thus began her accessories brand: The Royal Realm. She soon started selling her crowns in an oddities shop, whose owners challenged her to use some unusual materials—animal bones! She quickly found her niche and now makes custom bone crowns for weddings, celebrations, cosplays, and more. Some customers have even asked her to incorporate their baby teeth into a design!

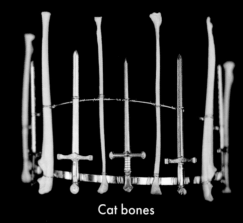
Cat bones

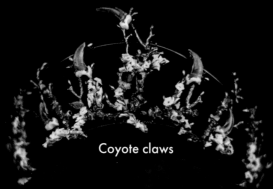
Coyote claws

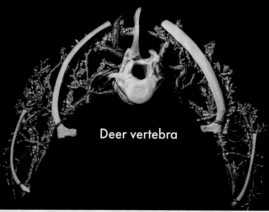
Deer vertebra

VORACIOUS EATER

The common pipistrelle bat is only 1.6 inches (4 cm) long, but it can eat 3,000 insects in a single night!

HIGH FIVES

British skydivers Emily Aucutt and Josh Carratt completed 32 high and low fives in just over 60 seconds while plunging in freefall toward the ground before landing safely in Nottinghamshire, England.

SMELL TESTERS

Nissan employs a team of "smellmasters" whose job is to make sure that the smell of the company's new cars' interiors is up to standard. On the day before testing, they carefully avoid eating foods with strong odors, such as garlic, in case it impairs their sense of smell.

BLOOD TATTOOS

The 5,300-year-old body of Ötzi the Iceman was discovered frozen on the border of Italy and Austria in 1991. He was so well preserved that his 61 ancient tattoos, achieved by rubbing charcoal into cuts on his skin, were still visible. In 2012 and 2016, artist Nicole Wilson had the tattoos copied onto herself, using her own blood as temporary ink.

SNOW GLOBES

Wendy Suen has more than 4,200 snow globes, collected over a period of 20 years. She has spent about $165,000 on her collection, the most expensive of which is a Louis Vuitton–designed globe that cost her nearly $10,000. She keeps them in a special room at her home in Hong Kong and cleans them all once a year—a job that takes her an entire week.

ALIEN LOOK-ALIKE

Anthony Loffredo, a body modification enthusiast from Montpellier, France, had two of the fingers on his left hand cut off so that it would look more like an alien claw. As part of his mission to resemble an extraterrestrial, he also had his tongue split and part of his nose and top lip removed. His entire body is covered in tattoos, even his eyeballs.

STOMACH BUG

There are certain things doctors expect to see when performing a colonoscopy—a live ladybug is not one of them. Gastroenterologists in Columbia, Missouri, were shocked when a different kind of stomach bug made a cameo in a human colon while they were scoping out the intestines of a 59-year-old man. While a bug typically wouldn't survive a journey through the digestive system, it is believed that the pre-procedure cleanse helped the ladybug stay alive until the very rear end. Talk about a lucky lady!

PIE-ABOLICAL

Believe it or not, every part of this blood-curdling pie is edible, right down to the stringy hair and puss-filled boils!

When you think about a delicious dessert, the words "creepy," "blood," and "gore" probably don't cross your mind—at least not until you have met Andrew Fuller of Des Moines, Iowa. Andrew is a baker and horror fan who has found a way to combine his two passions into terrifyingly tasty desserts! He was inspired to create this creepy sweet after seeing similar, but inedible, versions created by special effects artist Ashley Newman. Just don't ask Andrew what he used for the realistic hair, who jokes, "If I told you, I'd have to end you."

FLEXIBLE FIREFIGHTERS

Hashigo-nori is a centuries-old Japanese style of acrobatics performed on ladders and based on ancient firefighting techniques.

Modern-day Tokyo was once known as Edo, an ancient city with a fire problem. Made up of wooden buildings during a time when all cooking, lighting, and heating required open flames, the city was plagued with frequent house fires that would rapidly consume entire neighborhoods. Naturally this kept local firefighters busy, racing to the scene as soon as they heard "kaji" (fire)!

Edo was a compact city filled with tight corners and narrow alleys that made getting a bird's-eye view the best for beating a fire. One firefighter would climb up a bamboo ladder to scope out the situation, twisting and turning his body to relay a message to the rest of the team below. These movements evolved into the art form known as "hashigo-nori," which is still performed today.

20 FEET (6 M) HIGH!

KUMMAKIVI

In the forests of Ruokolahti, Finland, there is a bewildering sight—a massive boulder precariously balanced atop a smaller, rounded rock. Known as the Kummakivi—Finnish for "strange rock"—the 23-foot-wide (7-m) stone has left many scratching their heads, prompting the creation of folk tales involving giants, wizards, or trolls to explain the phenomenon. The scientific reasons behind the seemingly impossible oddity are slightly less exciting. The friction between the two stones essentially glues them together. Plus, the top rock's true center of gravity is not in its exact middle, as one would expect. These factors add up to create nature's ultimate balancing act!

PARACHUTE DROP
To tackle a rat infestation in Borneo in 1960, the UK Royal Airforce loaded 23 cats into crates and dropped them into the region by parachute.

OLD ASH
Strong northwesterly winds in Alaska on November 17, 2021, whipped up volcanic ash from an eruption that took place more than 100 years earlier. The Novarupta volcano in Katmai National Park erupted in 1912, depositing ash up to 700 feet (210 m) deep in what is now known as the Valley of Ten Thousand Smokes, and 109 years later gusts of wind turned some of that debris into an ash cloud that headed 100 miles (160 km) toward Kodiak Island.

SHEEP SHAPE
Ben Jackson carefully scattered grain on his farm in Guyra, New South Wales, Australia, so that hundreds of sheep feeding on it formed a giant heart shape in memory of his late aunt.

POGO PUZZLER
Sixteen-year-old Saul Hafting, of Annapolis Royal, Nova Scotia, Canada, solved 211 Rubik's Cubes in 1 hour 12 minutes while hopping on a pogo stick.

ROCK FOOD
The Rock Food Table at the East Texas Gem and Mineral Society features nearly 400 realistic-looking food items made from inedible materials. These include a ham made of petrified wood, blueberries made from azurite, and an oatmeal cookie that is a chunk of fossilized shark bone. The collection also features a pepper shaker filled with ash from the 1980 eruption of Mount St. Helens and teacups full of black volcanic sand from Hawaii. The display was started in 1983 by rock collectors Bill and Lois Pattillo.

LEGO RACECAR
The organizers of the 2021 Saudi Arabian Formula 1 Grand Prix promoted the event by building a life-size F1 racecar from more than 500,000 green LEGO bricks.

EARS HANG LOW

A baby goat named Simba was born with ears so long they nearly touch the ground!

Bred in Karachi, Pakistan, by Mohammad Hasan Narejo, Simba entered this world in June 2022 with ears measuring 19 inches (48.3 cm) long each. Believe it or not, they grew to 21 inches (53.3 cm) in a matter of days! Mohammad took no time in noticing his goat baby's star potential. In less than two weeks, Simba had already made international news and won a beauty contest! Only time will tell what the future holds for Simba, but in the meantime, Mohammad had custom covers made to protect Simba's famous ears from infection.

BEER DAY
Seth Beer, a rookie for the Arizona Diamondbacks baseball team, hit a game-winning home run against the San Diego Padres on April 7, 2022—National Beer Day.

COASTAL HOP
David Kay, from Blackpool, England, bounced more than 10.5 miles (16.8 km) on top of a hop ball. His ride along the Fylde coast on the large, inflatable ball took him 17 hours. An assistant walked in front of him all the way to clear away any objects that might burst the ball.

HELICOPTER HANG
Roman Sahradyan from Armenia performed 23 pull-ups in one minute while hanging from one of the landing skids of a helicopter that was hovering several feet above the ground.

FEARLESS FOODIE

Koalas can eat 2.2 pounds (1 kg) of eucalyptus leaves a day even though digesting just small amounts would be fatal to most other animals.

RARE CARD
A rare 1998 holographic "Illustrator" Pikachu Pokémon card sold at auction in 2022 for $900,000. The special card was created as part of a promotion for competition winners and fewer than 50 were originally printed.

ELVIS HAIR
A jar of Elvis Presley's hair sold for $72,500 at a Los Angeles auction in 2021. The baseball-sized clump of hair had been collected by Homer Gilleland, Presley's personal barber, over the course of multiple haircuts.

ANTIQUE TOASTER
In 2022, Jimmy James of Northamptonshire, England, was still using a 73-year-old electric toaster every day. The toaster, which was manufactured in 1949, had originally been given to his parents as a wedding present.

42 INCHES (107 CM) OF EARS!

SPARKS FLY

Hummingbirds have some unusual traits, and their mating rituals are no exception. For instance, when a male Anna's hummingbird wants to get a female's attention, he will perform a dance for her in midair. His moves involve swaying from side to side while simultaneously flexing his brightly colored throat patches into a fireworks-like display. This ritual makes for a vibrant performance of mystique and color that is truly mesmerizing to watch!

Animal Crossing

Nutty Narrows Bridge has protected the squirrels of Longview, Washington, since 1963, when builder Amos Peters had enough of seeing the local wildlife risk their lives crossing the street. Amos and Bill Hutch constructed the 60-foot (18.3-m) bridge with aluminum and fire hoses. Soon enough, squirrels were using it regularly, even teaching their babies to use the safe pathway. Since then, the bridge has undergone many repairs and even expanded into a six-bridge system, protecting squirrels citywide!

BODY PLANK

On August 6, 2021, in Adelaide, Australia, Daniel Scali held his body in the plank position for 9 hours 30 minutes, despite the fact he has complex regional pain syndrome, a condition that causes constant pain in his left arm when even the slightest pressure is exerted.

PROSTHETIC HAND

With the help of a 3D printer, 14-year-old Sammy Salvano, of Medford, New Jersey, worked all summer to create a prosthetic hand for his friend Ewan Kirby, who is missing several fingers on his left hand. The false hand allowed Kirby to pick up his mother's car keys for the first time.

LONG SERVE

Following two months of practice, Eric Finkelstein successfully achieved a legal table tennis serve of 51.1 feet (15.5 m) at the Westchester Table Tennis Center in Pleasantville, New York.

MELTING HONEY

A 2022 heatwave caused honey to melt from an old beehive in the closed chimney of Diana Gomes' house in Perth, Western Australia. After thick, sticky honey began to leak from the wall, she had it opened and found a 222-pound (101-kg) mass of hive and honey in the old fireplace.

TASTY TV

Japanese professor Homei Miyashita developed a lickable TV screen with 10 different food flavors, including chocolate and pizza. The selected flavor is sprayed onto the screen from a canister so that the viewer can taste it.

WHITE NOISE

In 2014, eight seconds of white noise from Taylor Swift's upcoming album *1989* were accidentally released on iTunes. But fans thought it was a real song, and it quickly went to number one on the Canadian iTunes chart.

COFFEE PAINTING

Sixteen-year-old Adipudi Devisri, from Ongole, India, created a painting of Mahatma Gandhi from coffee powder that covered an area of 1,684 square feet (156.5 sq m)—more than half the size of a tennis court.

BABY COMFORT

Baby elephants suck on their trunks the way human babies suck on their thumbs or on a pacifier.

1,300 LEGS

Eumillipes persephone, a newly discovered subterranean millipede found 200 feet (60 m) underground in Western Australia, has more than 1,300 legs—more than any other known animal.

USE YOUR HEAD!

Knock, knock! Who's there? A stubborn soldier ant using its head as a door to protect its colony!

After millions of years of evolution, door head ants have developed flat, round noggins that perfectly fit the entrance of their colonies' nests. With few other ways to defend their family, the passive-aggressive ants use their heads to plug the entrance hole when danger is near. Having an entire colony's safety on your shoulders is a full-time job, but there is some work-life balance for the worker ants, as they are so in tune with their senses that many can smell an approaching invader and launch right back into door mode before it's too late.

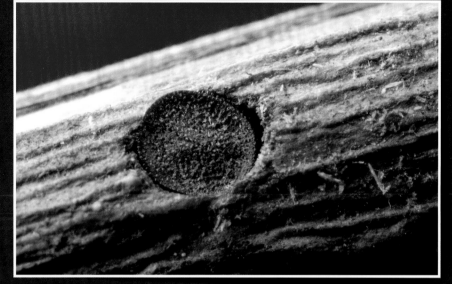

DEEP BREATH

Croatian free diver Vitomir Maricic walked a distance of 351 feet (107 m) along the bottom of a swimming pool on a single breath lasting 3 minutes 6 seconds.

HANGER COLLECTION

Oscar-winning Spanish actress Penelope Cruz collects coat hangers and has more than 500 nonwire coat hangers in her collection.

PI NUMBER

To mark Pi Day in 2022, Switzerland's Thomas Keller led a team of researchers to calculate the value of Pi beyond 62.8 trillion digits. The calculation took them 108 days with the help of a supercomputer. Pi Day is celebrated annually on March 14 because 3.14 are the first three digits of Pi, a number that represents the ratio of the circumference of a circle to its diameter.

ICE ENDURANCE

Valerjan Romanovski from Poland spent more than three hours submerged up to his neck inside a glass container filled with ice cubes in the main square of Vilnius, Lithuania.

WHEELCHAIR CROSSING

Para-athlete Ahmed Al-Shahrani completed the 125-mile (200-km) crossing of Qatar in 41 hours 55 minutes in a wheelchair.

The city of Minneapolis, Minnesota, employs a small group of mussels to test water quality. If they detect contaminants in the water, they close their shells, thereby alerting officials.

MOUNTAIN ROUTE

Josh Quigley of Livingston, Scotland, cycled 2,179 miles (3,486 km) in one week on a route around Aberdeen and the Cairngorm Mountains. He covered the final 637 miles (1,019 km) in one go, finishing at 4:00 a.m.

DAILY VIGIL

A faithful dog visits the same beach in Punta Negra, Peru, every day to wait in vain for his owner, a fisherman who died at sea several years ago. The dog, Vaguito, stares at the ocean for a few hours before wandering off to his new home nearby but always returns to the beach the next day.

SINGING LEMUR

The indri, a large lemur from Madagascar, is the only known nonhuman mammal to possess musical rhythm. The indri's song, which can last for more than three minutes, features a 1:2 pattern of notes, a form of rhythm previously thought to be reserved for people and birds.

Shroom Room

Completely covered with giant colorful fungi, the Yixing Mushroom Outdoor Luxury Hotel lives up to its name! Guests of the magical retreat are sure to feel as if they've been transported into a fairy tale as they walk among the towering toadstools. If you're looking for a trip that's truffles of fun, make your way to the city of Xingyi in China's Guizhou Province, where this one-of-a-kind resort has sprouted up.

HOT STUFF

2462°F (1350°C)!

In February 2022, diners gathered under the stars in an ancient desert canyon in AlUla, Saudi Arabia, to enjoy a meal cooked over molten hot lava!

Titled "Forces of Nature," the dining event was organized by multisensory experience designers Bompas & Parr. Upon arrival, guests were led by torchlight to a sound and light installation, where pitmasters were at the ready to prepare the food. Once the diners were seated, lava technicians poured a 2,462°F (1,350°C) stream of melted rocks into a special basin, above which local ingredients were seared to perfection in a matter of seconds.

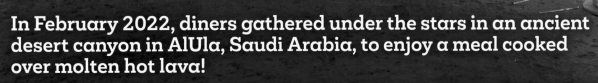

FROZEN FACES

Artist David Popa created his "Fractured" art series by drawing giant portraits onto floating ice off the coast of Finland!

Sketching portraits on paper is a talent on its own, but what happens when your surface isn't so reliable? David Popa decided to find out by using iron oxide and charcoal to draw faces into ice as it floated around the waters of Southern Finland, reassessing his decision each time the ice migrated, fractured, and melted.

The New York City–born artist welcomed the unpredictability of his natural canvas, inspired by the seemingly broken state of the world at the time. While the portraits appeared shattered and chaotic when seen up close, you'd never know it from the view above, a notion David hopes will inspire viewers to question how we can transform our seemingly broken reality into something new and beautiful.

ARTIST AT WORK!

PLAYING DIRTY

Every four years, bachelors of Van, Vietnam, get down and dirty in an ancient mud-wrestling event dating back hundreds of years.

The messy match is part of the Khanh Ha Festival, celebrating the legendary tale of four brothers who defeated a group of demons in a similar sport. Before dusting off the old wooden ball used in the event, local women ensure the yard of the historic Chua Van Temple is nice and muddy by filling it with water carried from a nearby river. From there, two teams of eight bachelors each compete in a three-hour match, attempting to push the ball into their goal at the end of the field. It is believed that the more the teams are able to steal the ball from one another, the better the harvest will be for rice farmers in the upcoming season.

Life of the Party

Frozen Dead Guy Days (FDGD) is a weekend-long celebration in Nederland, Colorado, honoring the town's coolest resident—a cryogenically frozen grandpa! After Bredo Morstoel died while cross-country skiing in his native Norway in 1989, his grandson had the 89-year-old's body preserved on ice. The grandson, Trygve Bauge, later migrated to the U.S. and took Grandpa with him, keeping him frozen in a shed on his Nederland, Colorado, property. When Trygve was deported in 1993, Grandpa Bredo was left behind, his frozen state maintained by monthly deliveries of dry ice. Every March since 2002, Grandpa Bredo's fans have gathered for FDGD, participating in Grandpa look-alike contests, coffin races, snow sculpting competitions, and guided tours to his final resting place.

Grandpa Bredo's chilly final resting place.

PEAK FITNESS

Will Renwick ran up all 189 mountain peaks in Wales that are more than 2,000 feet (600 m) high in less than a month, covering more than 500 miles (800 km) in total.

BUS PULL

Using ropes tied around his waist, bodybuilder Majeed Yehya pulled a double-decker bus, which had 15 passengers on board, a distance of 169 feet (51.5 m) along a street in Erbil, Kurdistan, Iraq.

HIDDEN CAT

A family in Denver, Colorado, accidentally donated their cat to a thrift store along with an old recliner chair. Staff at the store found the orange tabby named Montequilla hiding inside the chair and returned the pet to the family.

TALLER VOLCANO

Mount Etna, an active volcano on the Italian island of Sicily, erupted more than 50 times in six months during 2021, causing it to grow about 100 feet (30 m) in height.

BACK HOME

Juan Carrito, a two-year-old Marsican brown bear, was banned from the Italian town of Roccaraso in 2022 after breaking into a bakery and eating its supply of cookies. He was captured and released in the remote Apennine Mountains, but three weeks later he was back in Roccaraso, having completed an 18-day, 100-mile (160-km) walk.

TOYOTA MONOPOLY

More than 90 percent of all new cars sold in Yemen are Toyotas.

DONUT FAN

Every week David Bosselait makes a 12-mile (19-km) round trip on his horse Jackson to the Dunkin' Donuts drive-through restaurant in LaBelle, Florida. Bosselait orders a coffee for himself and a donut for Jackson.

BEE HAVEN
Around 500 different species of bees live within just over 6 square miles (15.5 sq km) of the San Bernardino Valley on the border of Arizona and Mexico.

DOG NATIVITY
Gellionnen Chapel in Swansea, Wales, staged a Christmas nativity play in which all the characters were played by dogs, including a pug–Jack Russell cross puppy as the baby Jesus, admired by three wise whippets.

HOSE BRIDGES
Endangered langur monkeys are able to cross busy roads on Penang Island, Malaysia, by crawling along recycled fire hoses that have been stretched 40 feet (13 m) above ground to form bridges.

BLOOD DONOR
Woodie, a greyhound owned by Wendy Gray from Melton Mowbray, England, donated his blood 22 times in six years and helped save 88 other dogs with his rare blood type.

SATURDAY RELEASE
New versions of the video game *Dragon Quest* are only ever released on Saturdays in Japan because otherwise children would skip school and adults would report in sick to work just so that they could play it.

SOUND EFFECT
The sound effect of the TIE fighters in *Star Wars* was created by combining an elephant call with the noise of a car driving on a wet surface.

The Shimada Denki Seisakusho elevator button factory in Tokyo, Japan, has a wall test display of 1,000 different elevator buttons that light up when visitors press them.

BORDER COURSE
On the sixth hole at the Tornio golf course, which straddles the border of Finland and Sweden, players tee off in Sweden and hole out on the green in Finland just over one hour later because the countries operate on different time zones. So, technically, on that hole a ball can stay in the air for about 1 hour 5 seconds!

PUPPY LOVE
When Grga Brkic fell 500 feet (150 m) down a ravine and injured himself while climbing in the Croatian mountains on New Year's Day 2022, his cousin's eight-month-old Alaskan malamute dog North, who was accompanying him on the hike, saved his life by lying on top of him for 13 hours to keep him warm until help arrived.

STICKY SKIN
Abolfazl Saber Mokhtari from Iran balanced 85 spoons on his upper body—his shoulders, chest, and back—simultaneously. He has been balancing spoons on his body since he was a child and says that he can make all types of materials stick to his skin, including plastic, glass, fruit, and stone.

JENGA TRICK
In one minute, 16-year-old Nate McEvoy, of Wausau, Wisconsin, removed 32 blocks from a Jenga tower and placed them on top of the tower without it toppling.

CHOCOLATE FALLS
Resembling the chocolate river in Willy Wonka's factory, the Grand Falls in Arizona are a muddy sight to marvel! Powered by snowmelt and rain from the White Mountains, the waterfall only flows during specific times throughout the year. Otherwise, the cliff is about as dry as a chocolate bar in the winter. Believe it or not, at 181 feet (55.2 m) tall, Grand Falls is slightly taller than Niagara Falls!

GROUND BAKING

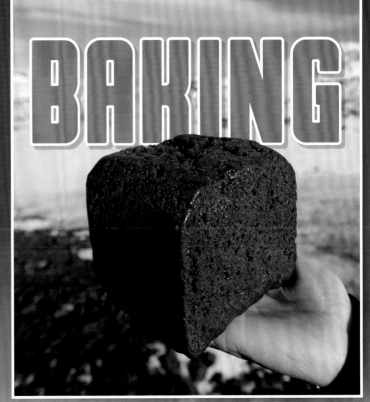

The water in some of Iceland's springs gets so hot that their sandy shores can be used to bake bread!

While foodies flock to Iceland for adventurous eats like sheep's head and fermented shark, one of the country's hottest dishes can be found baking underground next to Lake Laugarvatn, where sands can reach more than 200°F (93°C)! Home to around 130 volcanos and 45 hot springs, it's no surprise the country is a pioneer in geothermal energy. For more than 100 years, Icelandic bakers have gone against the grain, placing rye bread dough into metal containers before burying it in the steamy shore to bake for about 24 hours. The result is *rúgbrauð* (also known as lava, volcanic, or hot spring bread), a dense yet perfectly spongy bread best served hot with a bit of butter.

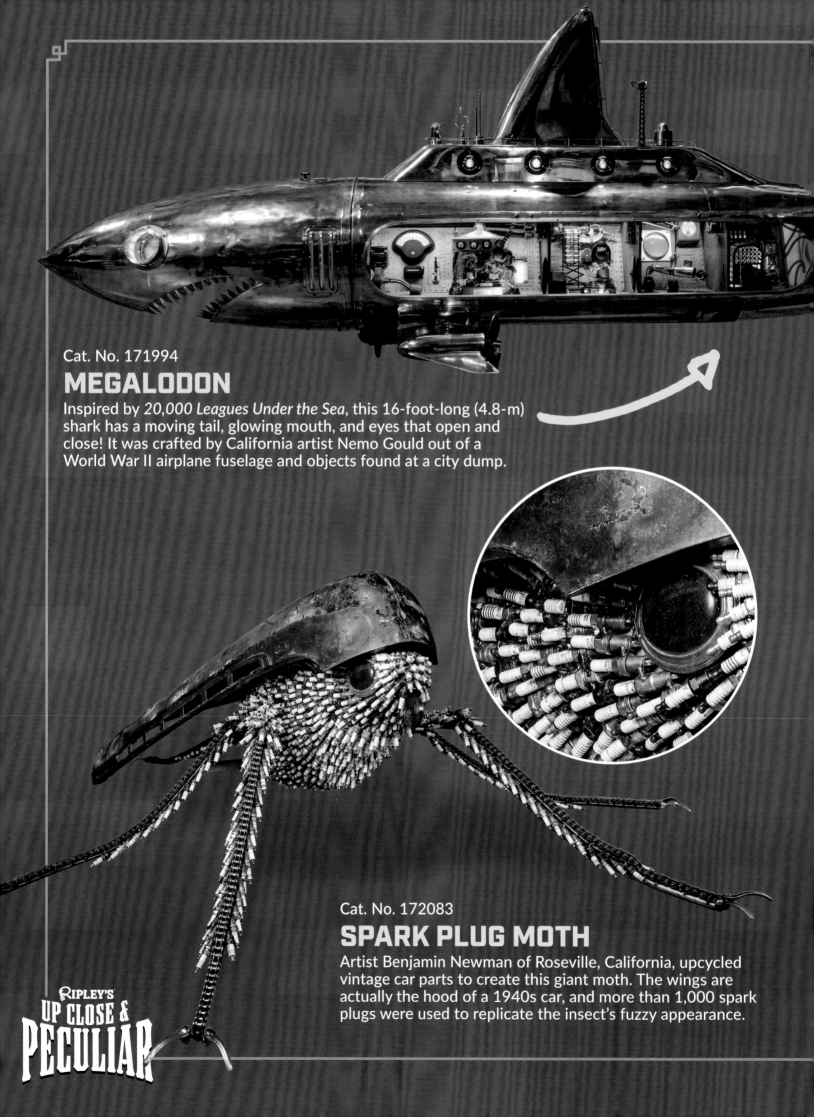

Cat. No. 171994

MEGALODON

Inspired by *20,000 Leagues Under the Sea*, this 16-foot-long (4.8-m) shark has a moving tail, glowing mouth, and eyes that open and close! It was crafted by California artist Nemo Gould out of a World War II airplane fuselage and objects found at a city dump.

Cat. No. 172083

SPARK PLUG MOTH

Artist Benjamin Newman of Roseville, California, upcycled vintage car parts to create this giant moth. The wings are actually the hood of a 1940s car, and more than 1,000 spark plugs were used to replicate the insect's fuzzy appearance.

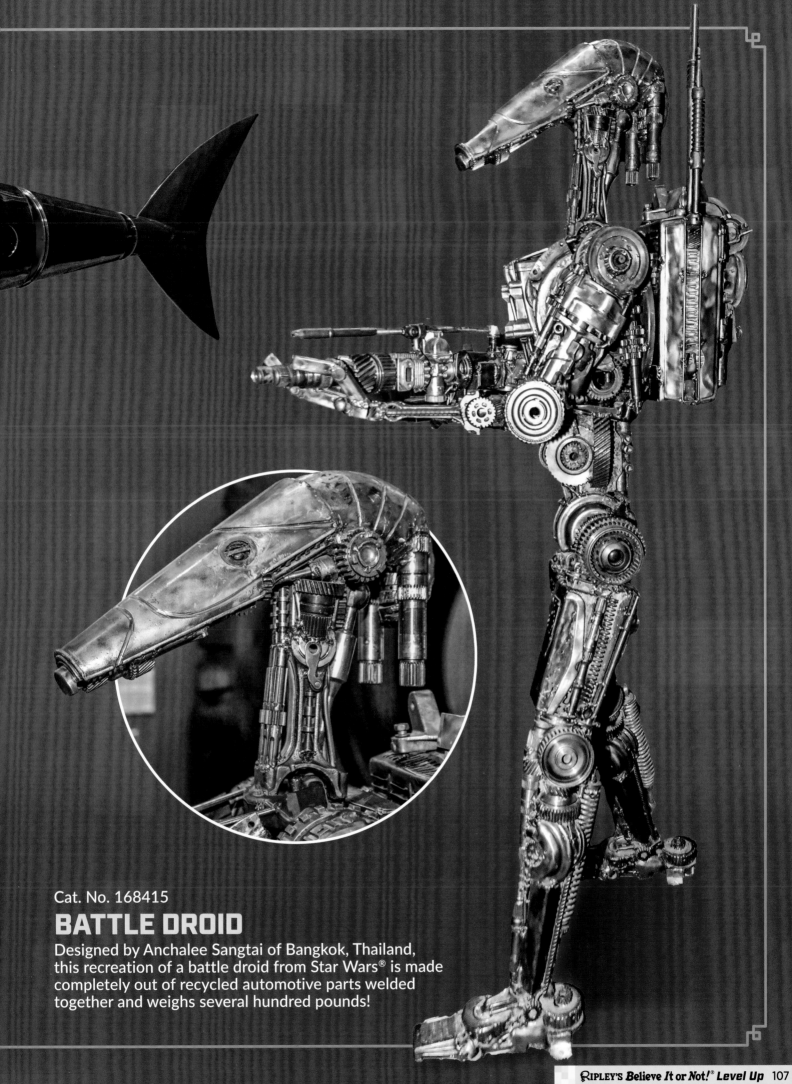

Cat. No. 168415

BATTLE DROID

Designed by Anchalee Sangtai of Bangkok, Thailand, this recreation of a battle droid from Star Wars® is made completely out of recycled automotive parts welded together and weighs several hundred pounds!

Cut It Out!

Mark Langan of Brunswick, Ohio, creates incredible works of art out of corrugated cardboard!

One day, Mark was dismantling boxes to put in the trash when he caught a glimpse of the wavy material found in between the cardboard's paper exterior. Inspired, he collected more boxes from neighbors and began experimenting with the pieces, slicing each layer apart before turning the scraps into surprisingly detailed artworks!

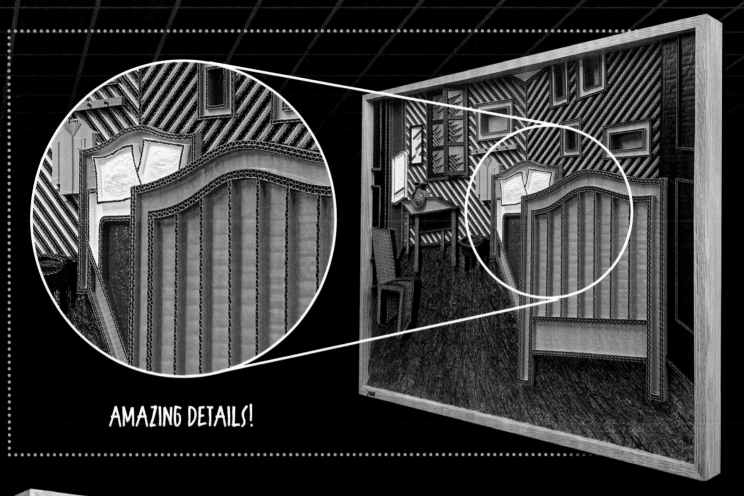

AMAZING DETAILS!

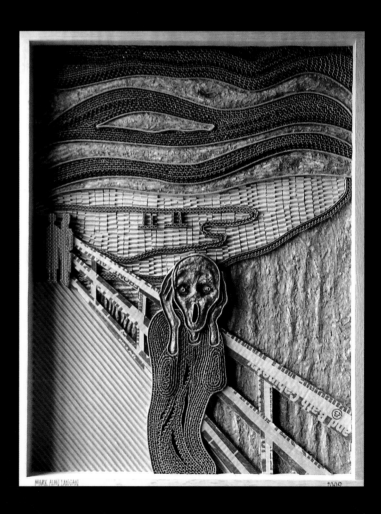

MARK ALAN LANGAN

FAKE FIGHT

A bear cub attacked and wrestled a giant inflatable Christmas reindeer in the front yard of a house in Monrovia, California. Grabbing the 6-foot-tall (1.8-m) fake reindeer by its neck, the cub temporarily brought the lawn decoration to its knees while the mother bear watched the fight from a few yards away.

ATLANTIC VOYAGE

Rye Riptides, a miniature 6-foot-long (1.8-m) boat built by Rye Junior High School students in New Hampshire, was launched into the Atlantic Ocean in October 2020, and on January 30, 2022, it washed ashore in Norway, having traveled 8,300 miles (13,358 km) in 462 days.

VAMPIRE BIRD

The hood mockingbird, which lives on the Galápagos Islands off the coast of Ecuador, uses its sharp, curved beak to drink the blood of young seabirds while they sit on their nests. It also drinks blood from injuries on living sea lions and sometimes even from wounds on the legs of humans!

CLAW POWER

The claws of a coconut crab are so powerful they can cut through the metal shaft of a golf club.

VOLCANIC NATIVITY

Volcanic ash and lumps of lava from the Cumbre Vieja volcano, which erupted on the Spanish island of La Palma in 2021, were incorporated into a Christmas nativity scene at the nearby church in Tajuya. The cradle for the baby Jesus was placed on chunks of black lava, and volcanic ash was scattered around the three wise men.

TINY CHURCH

On his farm in Semmes, Alabama, Gary Smith constructed a wooden church that measures about 4 feet (1.2 m) wide, 5 feet (1.5 m) deep, and 19 feet (5.8 m) tall from the ground to the top of the steeple. His Chapel des Champs has room for just three people and is modeled on the design of Alabama churches from 150 years ago.

WRITING CAFÉ

The Manuscript Writing Café in Tokyo, Japan, is for the exclusive use of writers who are struggling to meet tight deadlines. Before being served, customers must tell reception the number of words they need to write and how much time they have. After that, a staff member checks on their progress every hour and offers encouragement.

FAN FEED

TOOTHPICK TALENT

This amazing work of art was sent to us by the builder himself, Bob Morehead, who crafts his intricate structures using only toothpicks, glue, and raw talent! Born in Naples, Italy, Bob began constructing his masterpiece in 1983 after being inspired by a toothpick art exhibit at a Ripley's Believe It or Not! museum. What started as a series of small buildings has transformed over the years into a bustling metropolis made up of 425,000 toothpicks, with a new section in the works that will bring it up to over half a million!

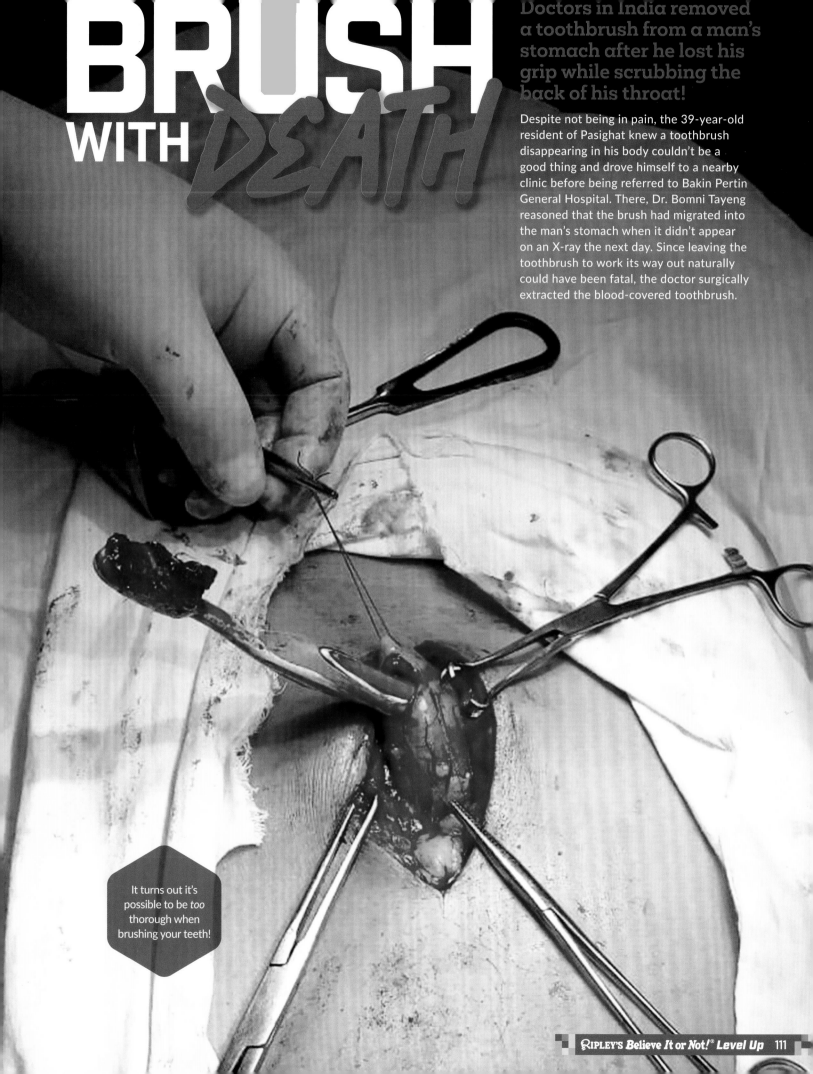

BRUSH
WITH *DEATH*

Doctors in India removed a toothbrush from a man's stomach after he lost his grip while scrubbing the back of his throat!

Despite not being in pain, the 39-year-old resident of Pasighat knew a toothbrush disappearing in his body couldn't be a good thing and drove himself to a nearby clinic before being referred to Bakin Pertin General Hospital. There, Dr. Bomni Tayeng reasoned that the brush had migrated into the man's stomach when it didn't appear on an X-ray the next day. Since leaving the toothbrush to work its way out naturally could have been fatal, the doctor surgically extracted the blood-covered toothbrush.

It turns out it's possible to be *too* thorough when brushing your teeth!

TUG-OF-WOAH!

The annual Naha Tug-of-War Festival held in Okinawa, Japan, takes the schoolyard game to new heights— or should we say lengths!

Before the competition begins, the crowd must connect two ropes into one, locking the looped ends together with a giant wooden pole. The ropes get rebuilt every year and can measure up to an astounding 656 feet (200 m) in length and weigh more than 40 tons! Hundreds of smaller ropes branch out from the sides to allow for thousands of competitors to participate. The first team to pull the rope to a specific point or whichever team pulls the rope the furthest in 30 minutes is the winner!

It is customary to cut off small strands of the rope after the event to take as a memento.

NATURAL GRAFFITI
Brazilian street artist Fábio Gomes Trindade cleverly incorporates nature into his graffiti artworks. He chooses a location with a wall beneath an overhanging tree or shrub, then paints a detailed face on the wall and uses the branches or flowers as the hair.

SLOW BURNER
UK band Glass Animals' song "Heat Waves" finally topped the Billboard Hot 100 in March 2022 after spending 59 weeks on the chart. It was released as a single in June 2020 and entered the U.S. chart at number 100 in January 2021.

LONG SHOT
Using a high-zoom camera, Spanish photographer Mark Bret Gumá once took a picture of the Pic Gaspard mountain in the French Alps from a peak in the Spanish Pyrenees 275 miles (443 km) away.

LITTLE SLEEP

Daisuke Hori from Japan claims to have slept only 30 minutes a day for the last 12 years but insists that he never feels tired! He says he trained his mind and body to function on a small amount of sleep.

HAIRY TONGUE
Cameron Newsom, of Colorado Springs, Colorado, had nearly half of her tongue removed in essential surgery. It was replaced with skin and muscle taken from her thigh, and occasionally this new tongue starts growing leg hair.

TRASH TRAVEL
A blue metal trash barrel from Myrtle Beach, South Carolina, washed up in 2021 more than 3,500 miles (5,600 km) away in County Mayo, Ireland. The barrel's Atlantic crossing left it encrusted with barnacle shells.

SMALL WORLD
In May 2022, while on a speaking tour of the U.S, former Polish president Lech Walesa had a flat tire on his SUV in Tolland, Connecticut. By coincidence the state trooper who went to his aid was also Polish—Trooper Lukasz Lipert.

MADE THE CUT

Red Hill Cutlery in Radcliff, Kentucky, is home to a 34.5-foot-long (10.5-m) pocketknife that actually functions! Having grown up in a family with a long history in cutlery, Jason Basham added to the legacy by crafting the largest pocketknife in the world! After six months of construction and up to $75,000 spent, the giant knife debuted outside the family shop on January 9, 2019. Jason hopes the display, which includes a 1,500-pound (680.4-kg) blade, will attract tourist traffic and drive business to his community.

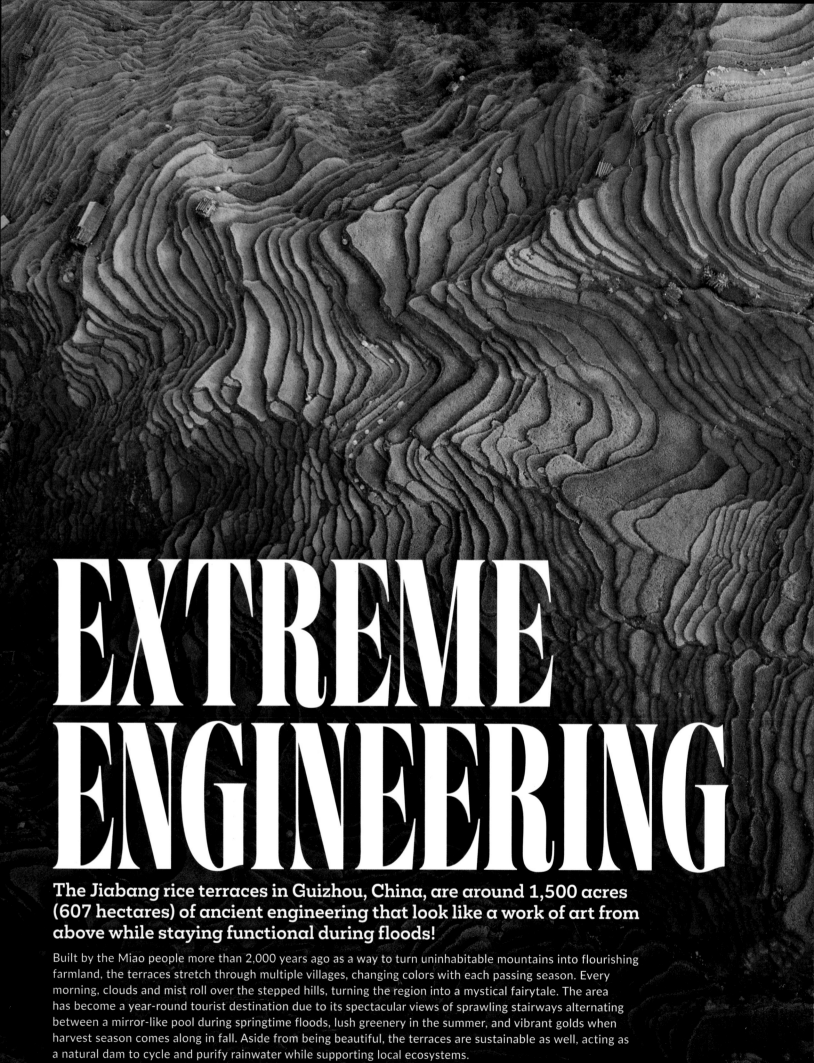

EXTREME ENGINEERING

The Jiabang rice terraces in Guizhou, China, are around 1,500 acres (607 hectares) of ancient engineering that look like a work of art from above while staying functional during floods!

Built by the Miao people more than 2,000 years ago as a way to turn uninhabitable mountains into flourishing farmland, the terraces stretch through multiple villages, changing colors with each passing season. Every morning, clouds and mist roll over the stepped hills, turning the region into a mystical fairytale. The area has become a year-round tourist destination due to its spectacular views of sprawling stairways alternating between a mirror-like pool during springtime floods, lush greenery in the summer, and vibrant golds when harvest season comes along in fall. Aside from being beautiful, the terraces are sustainable as well, acting as a natural dam to cycle and purify rainwater while supporting local ecosystems.

Rice fields are intentionally flooded to help control pests and prepare the soil for the next season.

BIRD BOX

Coal miners of the early 1900s would put their canary companions in special boxes to protect them from carbon monoxide poisoning!

Why would miners carry canaries with them? To warn them when the air was becoming dangerous to inhale! Carbon monoxide gas is deadly in large amounts, but difficult to detect, as it is invisible and has no odor. Because the small birds breathe very quickly, the carbon monoxide would affect them sooner than the miners. If the canary stopped singing and passed out, the miners knew it was time to leave!

Naturally, many miners became attached to their canary companions and protected them with a special cage. As soon as the bird showed signs of poisoning, the miner would close the cage door and open a valve to allow oxygen to flow from an attached tank, saving its life. Thankfully, by the 1980s electronic sensors were used in mines instead of canaries, although many miners were sad to no longer have their feathered friends by their side.

CROC ATTACK

Banjo, a five-year-old Staffordshire bull terrier owned by Tom Cummins, survived an attack by a 10-foot-long (3-m) saltwater crocodile on Casuarina Beach in Darwin, Australia. Banjo had gone for a dip in shallow water when the croc snatched him, but the feisty little dog bit back and escaped!

SPIDER TERROR

Spiders can have arachnophobia, the fear of spiders! When faced with a much larger spider that poses a threat, jumping spiders will instinctively freeze and back away very slowly.

ZOMBIE SHARK

Despite missing half of its body after being savagely attacked by a group of bull sharks, a blacktip shark continued to hunt for 20 minutes off the coast of Mozambique. The zombie shark kept swimming even with a huge chunk bitten out of its side.

SCHOOL VISITOR

An owl flew into a classroom at Central Park Elementary School in Plantation, Florida—where the school mascot is also an owl! Appropriately, the bird landed on a book titled *Nature's Show-Offs*.

METAL MUNCHER

After being taken to Klaipeda University Hospital in Lithuania with severe abdominal pain, a man had more than 2.2 pounds (1 kg) of metal nails, screws, nuts, and knives removed from his stomach. Some of the objects he had swallowed were 4 inches (10 cm) long!

CRAB BOT

Engineers at Northwestern University created a side-shuffling robotic crab tiny enough to fit through the eye of a needle! At only 0.02 inches (0.5 mm) wide, it is the world's smallest remote-controlled walking robot. While bigger robots typically rely on electricity to help them get around, this crafty crustacean is powered by lasers! When heated by a laser, the bot's paper-thin body starts to flatten, but then quickly cools off and contracts back into a 3D shape. By repeatedly flattening and contracting, the robot achieves its crab walk!

World's smallest remote-controlled walking robot!

MEDICINAL BUGS

Some chimpanzees treat open wounds by catching a flying insect, squeezing it between their lips, and then rubbing its body into the cut with their fingers. They even apply the pain-relieving bugs to other chimps in their group.

CRAZY COINCIDENCE

By a one-in-eight-million chance, Kristin Lammert, from Oviedo, Florida, has three daughters, Sophia, Giuliana and Mia, who were all born on August 25—in 2015, 2018, and 2021 respectively.

LEVEL UP
SEE PAGE 7!
SCAN AND PLAY!

HOOFIN' IT

To create automated email responses for vacationing office workers, three Icelandic horses were trained to trot across a gigantic keyboard! The OutHorse Your Email campaign was dreamt up by Iceland's tourism office as a way to remind travelers to unplug from work while on vacation. Anyone who signed up for the service received a message typed by the horse of their choosing to use as their automated out-of-office reply, such as "Qwsdcfrtgb fdfg jhlsajf vdpföð lkdsjahg bksdð adæfbnaqerbvui< i98oimdJVJ <0lÐ." Horses have such a way with words, don't they?

GOTTA CATCH 'EM ALL!

POKÉMON GO!

RARE RIDE!

Grace Klich of Richmond, Virginia, has a remarkable Pokémon collection filled with ultra-rare and vintage items—including Pikachu- and Lugia-themed cars!

Grace has been collecting Pokémon for 13 years, and while she may not have the largest collection, she makes up for it with the quality of the items she finds. Her main focus is on vintage American products released from 1998 to 2004, including food packaging, licensed merchandise, and plush toys.

While each item is cherished, two of them hold a special place in Grace's collection: her prized VW "Pikabug" and the even rarer Luiga PT Cruiser. Both cars were originally owned by Nintendo and used to promote the Pokémon franchise. There were 20 Pikabugs made in total, with around seven remaining today. As for the PT Cruiser, only five were ever produced, and Grace's is the only one left!

PLUSHES GALORE!

CHILDHOOD BESTIES!

POKÉMON-THEMED FOOD!

GAME ON

The average gamer spends about **8.5 hours each week** playing video games.

Video games make more money annually than the **film and music industries combined!**

Gamers have collectively spent more than **six million years** playing *World of Warcraft*!

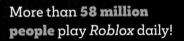

The first video game was created in 1958 by physicist **William Higinbotham,** who also helped build the **first nuclear bomb!**

More than **58 million people** play *Roblox* daily!

Released in 2000, Sony's **PlayStation 2** is the best-selling video game console of all time, with more than **157 million units sold worldwide!**

MELTY MUSHROOMS

The magpie inkcap is one of several mushroom species that spread their spores by decomposing into a slimy black liquid that can actually be used as ink! Named after the black-and-white magpie bird, the gooey fungus is reported to be incredibly poisonous. But on the flip side, it also contains chemicals that could someday be used to treat cancer and neurological disorders. If you look very carefully, you can spot these inedible multipurpose shrooms in European and North American forests with acidic soil.

BOOKSTORE ATTRACTION

As well as displaying hundreds of books, Mon Chat Pitre, a bookstore in Aix-en-Provence, France, is home to six rescue cats that interact with customers. The cats have their own special room at the back of the store with beds and litter trays but still venture into the main part of the shop to lie on books and be stroked.

AMAZING MEMORY

Li Jingwei was reunited with his biological mother after drawing from memory a detailed map of his home village in Yunan Province, China—a place he had last seen 33 years earlier when he was only four years old. In the intervening years, he had been taken to live with another family 1,250 miles (2,000 km) away in Henan Province.

In the 1930s, British botanist Edward Salisbury managed to grow more than 300 plants, including 20 different species of weeds, just from the debris he had collected in the cuffs of his pants while out walking in the countryside.

MODERN VIKING

Stipe Pleić from Tomislavgrad, Bosnia, was so intrigued by a TV series about the Vikings that he decided to adopt their culture. He began calling himself Ragnar Kavurson and dressing like a Viking. He built a working, flat-bottomed traditional Viking boat and sells axes and shields that he makes by hand.

COOL NAME

When Kieran White married Tilly Christmas in Bath, England, they combined their surnames as White-Christmas.

DANGEROUS POTATO

As 100,000 potatoes passed along a conveyor belt at a French fries factory in Auckland, New Zealand, in 2022, workers spotted what appeared to be an extremely muddy potato—but on closer inspection it turned out to be an inert World War II hand grenade.

FROZEN ASSETS

A man in South Korea purchased a used refrigerator online and discovered $130,000 in cash taped to the bottom.

PUCKER UP

Believe it or not, this isn't a rock wearing lipstick! It's actually a lips plant, or *Conophytum pageae*. The small succulent is native to South Africa and Namibia, where it grows on rocky surfaces in clusters only about 1 inch (2.5 cm) tall. Interestingly enough, when it blooms, a daisy-like flower emerges from the "lips" and makes the plant look like it's blowing into a party favor!

BLOOMING BEAUTY

On the grounds of Woolbeding Gardens in West Sussex, England, is a kinetic greenhouse that can unfold just like a blooming flower!

The design team at Heatherwick Studios took inspiration from Victorian ornamental terrariums, which were used to transport plants from all over the world to Europe. The elaborate glass arboretum is part of the estate's Silk Route Garden, created to highlight the Silk Road's influence on British horticulture. On warm days, the diamond-shaped greenhouse can fully open its "petals" in just four minutes to provide the subtropical plants inside with sunshine and fresh air.

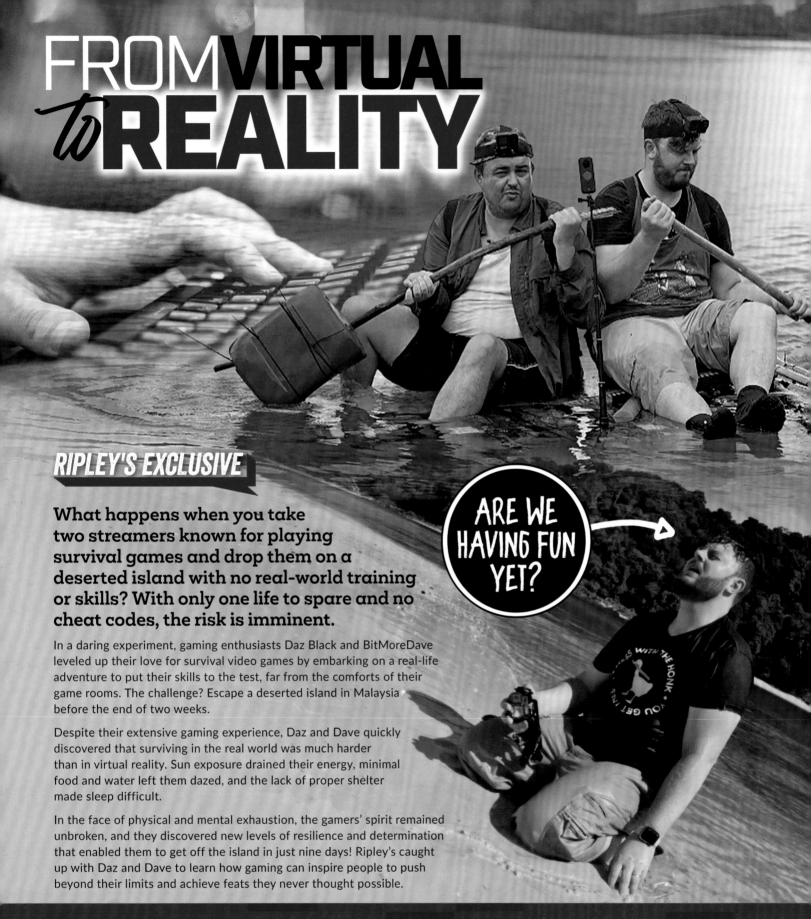

FROM VIRTUAL *to* REALITY

RIPLEY'S EXCLUSIVE

ARE WE HAVING FUN YET?

What happens when you take two streamers known for playing survival games and drop them on a deserted island with no real-world training or skills? With only one life to spare and no cheat codes, the risk is imminent.

In a daring experiment, gaming enthusiasts Daz Black and BitMoreDave leveled up their love for survival video games by embarking on a real-life adventure to put their skills to the test, far from the comforts of their game rooms. The challenge? Escape a deserted island in Malaysia before the end of two weeks.

Despite their extensive gaming experience, Daz and Dave quickly discovered that surviving in the real world was much harder than in virtual reality. Sun exposure drained their energy, minimal food and water left them dazed, and the lack of proper shelter made sleep difficult.

In the face of physical and mental exhaustion, the gamers' spirit remained unbroken, and they discovered new levels of resilience and determination that enabled them to get off the island in just nine days! Ripley's caught up with Daz and Dave to learn how gaming can inspire people to push beyond their limits and achieve feats they never thought possible.

Q: When did you start playing survival games?

Dave: I started playing survival games with Daz around eight years ago, kicking off with *ARK: Survival Evolved*. It doesn't matter what game we play together; Daz and I can make any of them fun!

Q: What made you want to take survival games into the real world?

Dave: Surviving on an island is something we played around with for ages, especially when we would make fun of mechanics in a game, like hitting a coconut with a rock and it magically splitting open. We always knew it was going to be a little tougher in real life, but I think we wanted to know how much tougher it really was.

Q: How was life on the island?

Daz: It was harder than I expected! Every day we faced different weather, we had to find shelter, we needed food—every day presented a new challenge. However, survival games did come in handy.

To get off the island, Daz and Dave built a raft out of natural materials and plastic that had washed up onto the beach (which they later recycled).

" *Thanks to gameplay, we knew how to make water catchers, start fires, craft spears, and open coconuts!* –Daz

Daz and Dave wore cameras on their heads to give their videos a first-person perspective, resulting in clips resembling the survival games that inspired the duo!

REAL SURVIVAL GAME!

Q: What was the most dangerous moment of this experience?

Daz: We woke up in our hammocks one morning and there was a 7-foot-long (2.1-m) monitor lizard underneath us. A bite from those things can seriously hurt you!

Q: What was the biggest shock for you going from streaming to surviving?

Dave: When you are streaming, you are always thinking about how to make it entertaining. In the real world—on the island—we were just thinking, "How can I make it?"

Q: What did you learn about yourself while on the island?

Daz: I learned that when pushed, I'm capable of more than I realized. I never thought I'd be able to physically do the trip and make it back to land, but I learned new coping mechanisms under unique pressures and really proved myself.

SPECTACULAR SEABIRDS

Birds may not immediately come to mind when you think of the world's waters, but there are some pretty spectacular seabirds dipping and diving around our oceans. Learn some fascinating facts about these feathered animals!

BLUE-FOOTED BOOBY

The blue-footed booby gets its name from the Spanish word "bobo," meaning "foolish"—a reference to their clumsy nature on land. The seabird is much more adept in the water, into which it dives at high speeds to catch fish. The brightness of a booby's feet indicates how healthy the bird is—bluer is better—a helpful tool for females choosing a mate!

CRESTED AUKLET

The crested auklet attracts a mate by emitting a chemical that smells like tangerines! The scent is so strong that it is possible to smell a flock before seeing it. While plenty of birds follow their noses to find food, crested auklets were the first confirmed to use odor to communicate.

Scientists measuring the wingspan of a wandering albatross.

WANDERING ALBATROSS

The wandering albatross has the largest wingspan of all living birds, measuring up to a mind-boggling 11.5 feet (3.5 m) wide! These awesome aviators are extremely efficient and spend most of their lives in flight, able to glide more than 500 miles (805 km) in a single day with just a few flaps of their wings.

NORTHERN GANNET

The northern gannet hunts by "plunge-diving" from 100 feet (30.5 m) above the water before torpedoing into the surface at up to 60 mph (96.6 kmph)! Fortunately, these bad birds are built for impact with a reinforced skull, no external nostrils, adapted neck muscles, and a bone plate at the base of their bills to soften the blow.

Northern gannets have air sacs under their skin, making them buoyant so they pop right back to the surface after a dive.

GREAT FRIGATEBIRD

The great frigatebird can remain airborne for two months without landing! Unlike most seabirds, its feathers are not waterproof and it could drown if it landed in water. Frigatebirds make up for this with incredible feats of flight, hitching rides on updrafts that take them more than 13,000 feet (4,000 m) above the sea's surface!

AFRICAN PENGUIN

African penguins prefer sunny beaches over chilly icebergs! The pink patches around their eyes are an adaptation to the warm weather of their natural evironment and fill with blood to help keep them cool. They're also strong swimmers and can dive up to 400 feet (121.9 m) deep, using a third eyelid to keep water from blurring their vision.

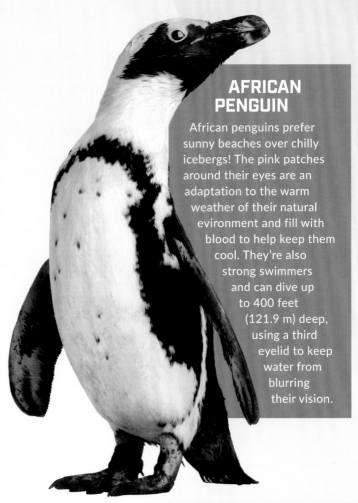

PELICAN

Often seen swooping along the shoreline on the hunt for tasty fish, the pelican is known for its gular pouch, a stretchy pocket of skin that can hold up to 3 gallons (13.6 l) or 24 pounds (10.9 kg)! Pelicans can use this versatile wobble to catch fish, hold food for their chicks, and even cool themselves off.

IDEAL PALACE

In 1879, French postman Ferdinand Cheval encountered a rock along his delivery route so strange it inspired him to devote 33 years to building a dream palace made of stones!

Constructed in the middle of Postman Cheval's vegetable garden in Hauterives, France, the Ideal Palace is made up of rocks collected during his daily 18-mile (29-km) walks. Inspired by literature, nature, and postcards, the monument features carvings of mythological creatures, ancient architecture, and various historic emblems. In 1912, Cheval's dream was complete. Left feeling alone and misunderstood in his endeavor, the unlikely artist inscribed his palace with "the work of a single man." Today, many consider the Palace one of the most incredible artworks of all time.

The stone that started it all!

Postman Cheval gathering his building material.

RIP 'N Slide

What happens when a professional wakeboarder has a water park all to themself? If you're Pedro Caldas, you bring your board along for a ride down an 82-foot (25-m) water slide!

Pedro lived out every kid's dream when Brazil's Beach Park, one of the largest water parks in Latin America, let the watersport powerhouse rip through its wave pools and seamlessly drop in on giant slides. A winch was used to pull Pedro through most of the park's attractions, including Vaikuntudo, a massive slide that plunges thrill-seekers into a giant funnel at up to 43 mph (69 kmph) and then spits them out 82 feet (25 m) below. Overall, the entire adventure required three months of planning!

DOWN A HUGE SLIDE!

AROUND A GIANT FUNNEL!

DOWN A LAZY RIVER!

SHIRT INJURY

Cleveland Indians pitcher Zach Plesac fractured his right thumb when ripping off his undershirt too vigorously after being taken out of a 2021 game against the Minnesota Twins and getting his thumb caught on a chair at his locker.

RING RETURNED

When Donald MacPhee of Benbecula, Scotland, took up metal detecting as a hobby, he found the wedding ring that his neighbor Peggy MacSween had lost while gathering potatoes more than 50 years earlier.

COW MAILBOX

A mailbox in the shape of a cow was stolen from Trina Zammit's property in Kynuna, Queensland, Australia. The bovine box, named Bessie, was found several days later over 435 miles (700 km) away by the side of a road in Emerald.

FALLING SNAKES

The scenes in the movie *Lara Croft: Tomb Raider* where Lara drives her Land Rover through the Cambodian jungle had to be reshot several times because snakes and other creatures kept falling through the vehicle's open roof, much to the discomfort of Angelina Jolie, who played Lara.

HOVER CROSSING

Rob Wylie and his 19-year-old son Morgan crossed the 23-mile (37-km) English Channel nonstop from Cap Gris Nez, France, to Folkestone, Kent, on eFoil boards—hi-tech, electric-powered hydrofoil boards that hover about 3 feet (0.9 m) above the water. Traveling at speeds of up to 20 mph (32 kmph), the crossing took them 1 hour 44 minutes.

APOLOGETIC BURGLAR

When homeowners disturbed a burglar at their house in Santa Fe, New Mexico, he apologized and gave them $200 to cover the costs of the window he had broken to gain entry.

ALPHABETICAL NAME

A boy in South Sumatra, Indonesia, has the name ABCDEF GHIJK Zuzu because his father loves the English alphabet and crossword puzzles. The boy goes by the name of Adef because it is easier to pronounce.

SHARED BIRTHDAY

Katie Chisholm, of Omaha, Nebraska, her mother, Mary Adams, and Katie's daughter Charlotte were all born on March 17. The likelihood of three generations of the same family being born on the same day of the year are estimated to be one in 100,000. Even though they were all born on St. Patrick's Day, Katie is only two percent Irish.

YOUNG DRIVER

Still in bare feet and wearing his pajamas, a four-year-old boy in Utrecht, the Netherlands, picked up his mother's car keys and took her car for a drive early one morning in 2022. His joyride soon ended when he crashed into two parked cars. Luckily, he was unhurt.

A special gel protected the bride and groom from the fire's heat.

Burning Love

Stunt actors Gabe Jessop and Ambyr Mishelle were 2022's hottest newlyweds—literally. The couple turned their Utah wedding into a Hollywood film set by lighting themselves on fire! Gabe and Ambyr actually met while on the job, and the fiery feat was their way of sharing that part of their love story with their guests. Having worked on shows and movies such as *Yellowstone* and *Hereditary*, the stunt double duo was more than qualified to pull off the breathtaking display. Preparation included wearing fire-resistant wedding attire, securing permits, and having emergency help on standby. Thankfully, everything went according to plan and the unconventional send-off ended with the newlyweds doused by fire extinguishers!

At Ripley's, Sultan stopped to pose next to the tallest man to have ever lived, Robert Wadlow (1918–1940) of Alton, Illinois. When last measured in 1940 at age 22, Wadlow was 8 feet 11.1 inches (2.7 m) tall and wore a size 37 shoe!

NEW HEIG

THE WORLD'S TALLEST MAN

HTS

A towering 8 feet 3 inches (2.5 m) tall, world's tallest man Sultan Kösen celebrated a major milestone—his fortieth birthday—at Ripley's Believe It or Not! Orlando in 2022, visiting all the way from Turkey!

Born on December 10, 1982, Sultan didn't start his incredible growth spurt until he was 10 years old. His unique stature is the result of a tumor on his pituitary gland causing an over-production of growth hormone, a condition known as "pituitary gigantism."

Believe it or not, there are only ten reliable cases in history of a person reaching 8 feet (2.4 m) or more. In 2009, Sultan Kösen became the first man over 8 feet (2.4 m) to be measured by Guinness World Records in more than 20 years. Gaining international recognition for his lofty stature, Sultan has visited 127 countries.

As he celebrated another year and blew out his birthday candles at Ripley's Orlando, he wished to "travel the remaining countries which I have not visited so far," then jokingly added, "and to keep my record title. I hope there will be no one taller than me."

Sultan also holds the record for largest hands on a living person, each one measuring 11.22 inches (28.5 cm) from the wrist to the tip of the middle finger!

NICE MOHAWK!

Hear Her Roar

An 18-year-old female lion at Kansas' Topeka Zoo and Conservation Center is ready to take her place as leader of the pack after sprouting a mane! While male lions are famous for their long and luscious locks, females usually have short sandy fur all over. Zuri became one of these extremely rare maned lionesses after Avus, the only male of her three-lion pride, passed away in 2020. Unlike her male counterparts, Zuri's mane is short and less full, with a fuzzy mohawk showcasing her dominance.

CALENDAR LAKE
Africa's Lake Malawi is popularly known as the Calendar Lake because it is 365 miles long, 52 miles wide, and fed by 12 main rivers.

MASSIVE PLANT
A single seagrass plant discovered underwater off the coast of Western Australia is over twice the size of Manhattan. The plant covers 77 square miles (200 sq km) and is about 4,500 years old.

CHIP SANDWICHES
Zoe Sadler, from Coventry, England, ate almost nothing but cheese and onion potato chip sandwiches for 23 years—since she was two.

STAIRCASE CHALLENGE
Between 2017 and 2022, Laura Zurowski climbed every one of the 739 public staircases in Pittsburgh, Pennsylvania, taking more than 25,000 steps. Pittsburgh has more public staircases than any other American city.

FINGER LIFT
Martial artist Steve Keeler, from Kent, England, deadlifted 285.5 pounds (129.6 kg)—the weight of a three-seater couch—with just his middle finger.

DEADLY STRIKE
A single lightning strike on August 9, 2021, killed 550 sheep grazing on a mountain pasture in Ninotsminda, southern Georgia.

GOLD HAIR
Mexican rapper Dan Sur had gold and silver metal chains implanted into his head to replace his natural hair. He says the chains are attached to hooks implanted in his skull beneath his skin.

SELFIE DANGER
Around the world, more than 300 people have died while taking selfies since 2011.

MYSTERY CIRCLE
More than 40 toy rocking horses have been arranged in a circle in an open pasture in Lincoln, Massachusetts—a collection that has been named Ponyhenge. The installation was started by local couple Jimmy Pingeon and Elizabeth Graver in 2010 with a single rocking horse, and since then others have mysteriously appeared. Ponyhenge is now so popular that some people have even gotten married at the quirky circle!

WRONG TURN
Alan Todd's racing pigeon, Bob, was meant to fly from Tyneside, England, to the Channel Islands, a distance of 460 miles (736 km). But instead, the bird took a wrong turn on the return journey and ended up 4,000 miles (6,400 km) away in Mexia, Alabama.

SMART CHOPSTICKS
Japanese scientists have developed smart chopsticks that use electrical stimulation to create a mild shock in the mouth that enhances the salty taste of food. This saves people from eating too much unhealthy salt in their diet.

SQUARE TREES
In Panama's El Valle de Anton, formed from the ashes of a vast volcano, stands a group of cottonwood trees with square trunks. Even the tree's rings, which indicate their growth, are square rather than round.

Feathered Dragon

Is it just us, or does the great eared nightjar look like a baby dragon? With ear tufts that look like horns and facial feathers that resemble a snout, this bird is a sight to be seen—if you can spot one! Found across Southeast Asia, the great eared nightjar has impeccable camouflage. They blend in especially well with the forest floor where they nest despite being expert fliers. In fact, this species even eats and drinks while flying!

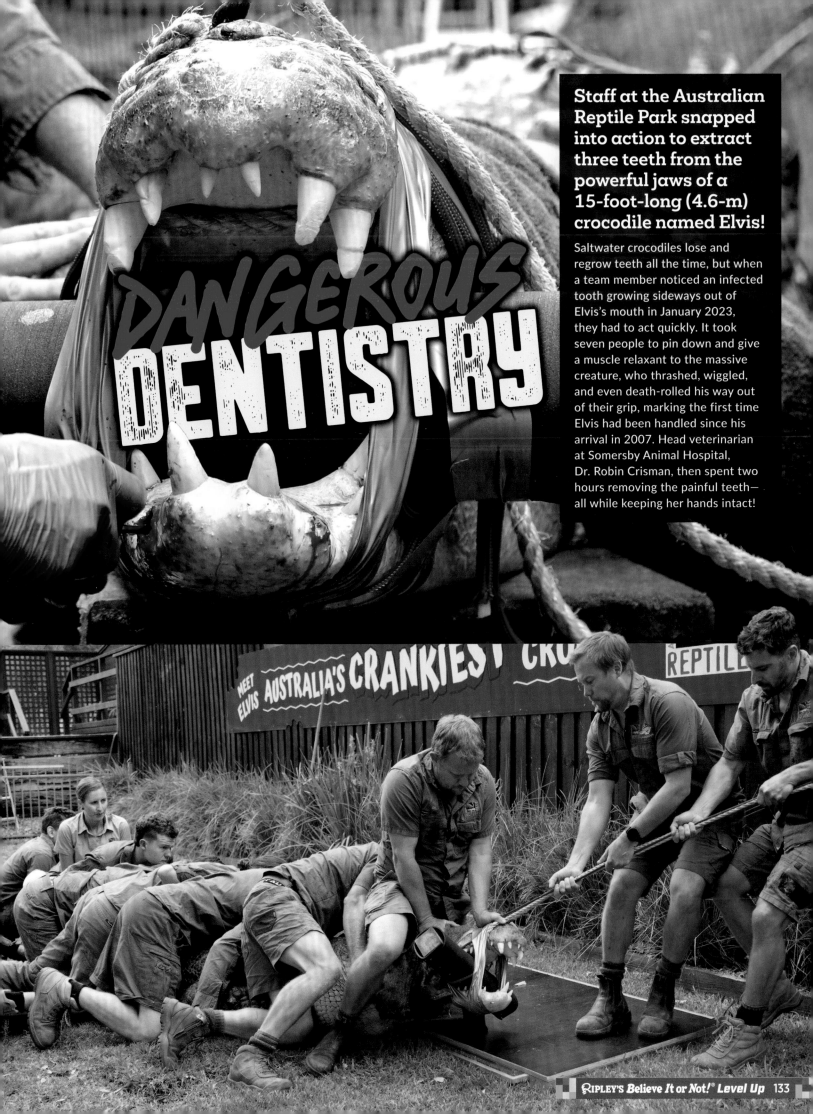

DANGEROUS DENTISTRY

Staff at the Australian Reptile Park snapped into action to extract three teeth from the powerful jaws of a 15-foot-long (4.6-m) crocodile named Elvis!

Saltwater crocodiles lose and regrow teeth all the time, but when a team member noticed an infected tooth growing sideways out of Elvis's mouth in January 2023, they had to act quickly. It took seven people to pin down and give a muscle relaxant to the massive creature, who thrashed, wiggled, and even death-rolled his way out of their grip, marking the first time Elvis had been handled since his arrival in 2007. Head veterinarian at Somersby Animal Hospital, Dr. Robin Crisman, then spent two hours removing the painful teeth— all while keeping her hands intact!

MEET ELVIS AUSTRALIA'S CRANKIEST CRO

REPTILE

Cat. No. 175548

RYAN REYNOLDS ASH PORTRAIT

Hollywood leading man Ryan Reynolds is almost universally considered to be attractive. But whether or not you find him hot, this portrait of him is smokin'—literally! Believe it or not, artist Paulina Saldaña of Mexico City used cigarette ashes to recreate the actor's smoldering visage.

LEVEL UP
SEE PAGE 7!
SCAN AND PLAY!

RIPLEY'S
UP CLOSE &
PECULIAR

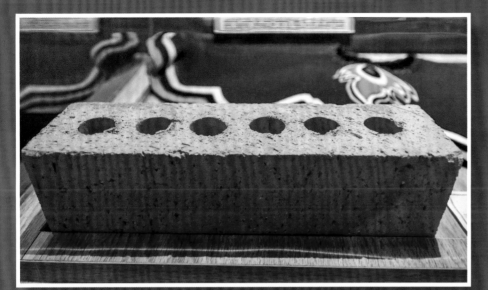

Cat. No. 21917

YELLOW BRICK

When it was released in 1939, *The Wizard of Oz* amazed audiences with its extraordinarily vibrant colors. Many of the film's sets and props remain iconic to this day, such as the Emerald City, Dorothy's ruby slippers, and of course, the yellow brick road.

Cat. No. 175545

FORREST GUMP CHOCOLATES

Signed by Tom Hanks, this prop comes from the 1994 film *Forrest Gump*, in which Hanks's character tells his life story to strangers at a bus stop while holding a box of chocolates. To keep the box from sliding off Hanks's lap during filming, it was filled with about 4 pounds (1.8 kg) of sand and sealed shut!

Cat. No. 175552

DARTH MAUL'S LIGHTSABER®

This double-bladed Lightsaber® was used by actor Ray Park as the character Darth Maul on the set of *Star Wars: Episode I – The Phantom Menace*. The prop was used for dueling scenes and features threaded rods so the "blades" can be securely attached to the hilt.

Barista ART

Your local barista has nothing on Michael Black, an artist who has created more than 20,000 pieces of latte art in the last 10 years!

Widely credited as the pioneer of latte art, Michael decided to expand from topping his coffees with hearts and swirls to crafting elaborate portraits of celebrities, recreations of memes, and even three-dimensional sculptures out of milk foam as a way to express himself with materials that were readily available. It wasn't long after he began posting his creations on his Instagram that the public took notice. Since then, Michael has traveled the world, appeared on national television, and worked with global brands to bring pop culture to life—in a cup.

Timothée Chalamet

Hugh Jackman

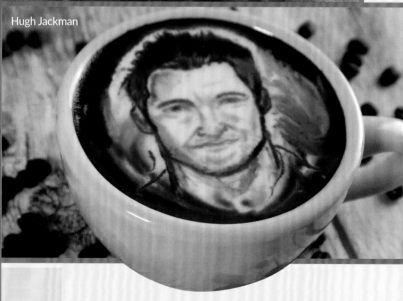

Counting Sheep

Every autumn since 1994, thousands of sheep have flocked to the streets of Madrid, Spain, causing a major traffic ram! Shepherds dressed in traditional black berets and wide black belts lead the way, reenacting the ancient practice of moving livestock to greener pastures for the winter. The stampede comes at the end of the Transhumance Festival, an annual celebration of the now-bustling capital city's history as a stopping point along the migration route. The festivities leading up to the sheep's arrival includes music, dancing, and a speech by the mayor welcoming the flock to town.

DEADLY BIRD

The first bird to be domesticated was not the chicken but the cassowary—a flightless bird that can reach 6 feet (1.8 m) tall, weighs up to 130 pounds (59 kg), and is considered to be the most dangerous bird in the world due to its long, dagger-like toes. Although it can kill a human with its kick, the cassowary was reared by humans in New Guinea about 18,000 years ago—more than 8,000 years before the domestication of chickens.

CHEAP MEALS

An electrical engineer named Dylan used a discount deal to eat 2,000 meals over a period of seven years at Six Flags Magic Mountain in Valencia, California. He paid $150 for unlimited year-round access to the theme park, which included two meals a day. Not only did the money he saved on groceries allow him to pay off his student loan debt, he was also able to save enough to get married and buy a house in Los Angeles.

FACE SLAP

The Arnold Classic, an annual bodybuilding contest founded by Arnold Schwarzenegger and held in Columbus, Ohio, features a slap fighting championship where competitors hit one another in the face with open hands. The fights are staged over three rounds, with each competitor allowed one slap per round. The winner can be determined by knockout or by a participant's failure to proceed within 30 seconds of being slapped.

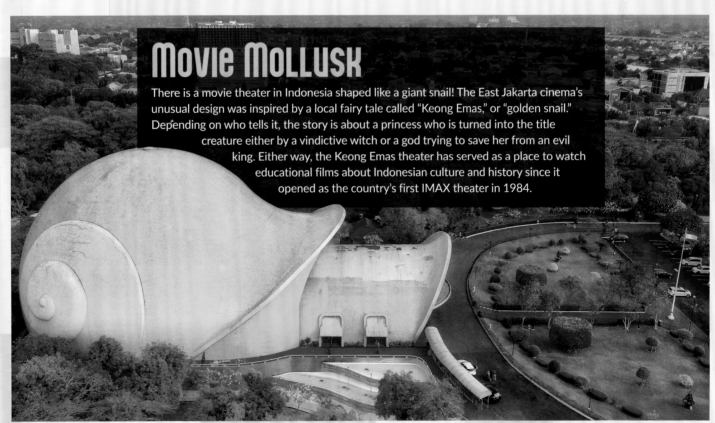

Movie Mollusk

There is a movie theater in Indonesia shaped like a giant snail! The East Jakarta cinema's unusual design was inspired by a local fairy tale called "Keong Emas," or "golden snail." Depending on who tells it, the story is about a princess who is turned into the title creature either by a vindictive witch or a god trying to save her from an evil king. Either way, the Keong Emas theater has served as a place to watch educational films about Indonesian culture and history since it opened as the country's first IMAX theater in 1984.

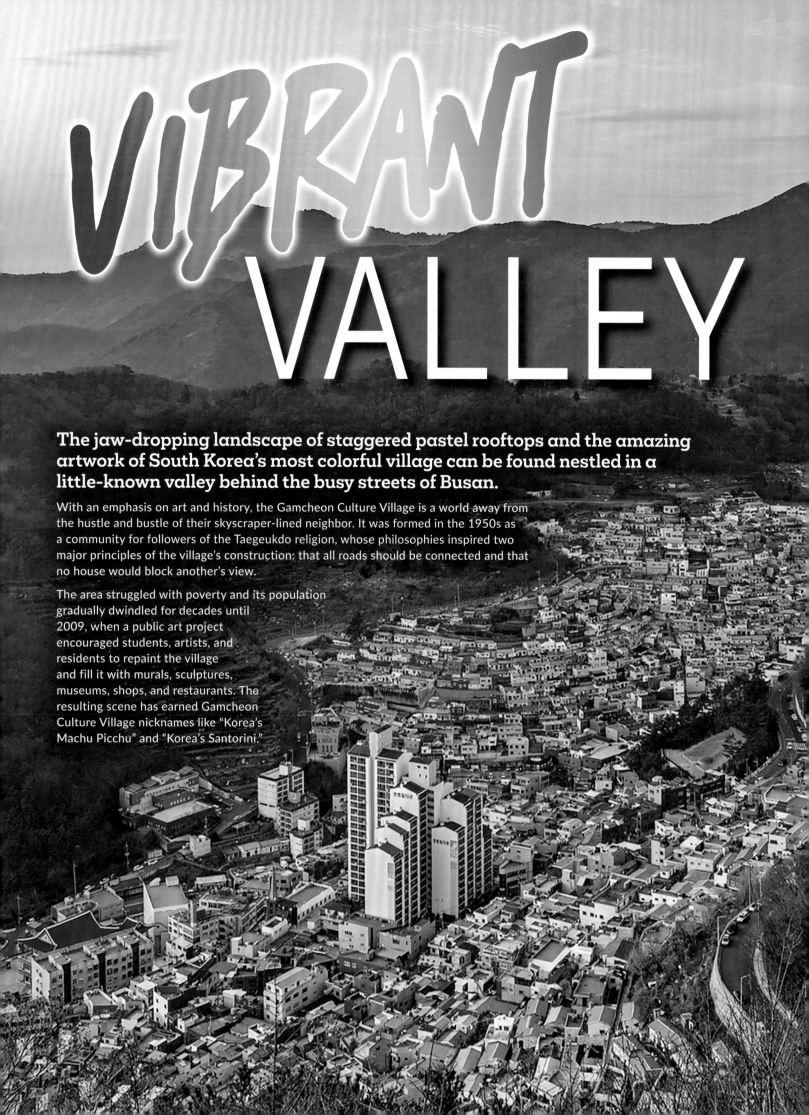

VIBRANT VALLEY

The jaw-dropping landscape of staggered pastel rooftops and the amazing artwork of South Korea's most colorful village can be found nestled in a little-known valley behind the busy streets of Busan.

With an emphasis on art and history, the Gamcheon Culture Village is a world away from the hustle and bustle of their skyscraper-lined neighbor. It was formed in the 1950s as a community for followers of the Taegeukdo religion, whose philosophies inspired two major principles of the village's construction: that all roads should be connected and that no house would block another's view.

The area struggled with poverty and its population gradually dwindled for decades until 2009, when a public art project encouraged students, artists, and residents to repaint the village and fill it with murals, sculptures, museums, shops, and restaurants. The resulting scene has earned Gamcheon Culture Village nicknames like "Korea's Machu Picchu" and "Korea's Santorini."

The village's winding streets and alleys are lined with fish that help point lost tourists in the right direction.

Special Snout

You've probably never seen a nose quite like this one. Partially because saiga antelopes are critically endangered, but mostly due to the fact that few animals have had to adapt to their environment in such a way. The saiga's sniffer is filled with many bones that help sort passageways lined with hairs, glands, and mucus membranes. This complicated setup is thought to help the antelope survive in its native habitat, the Eurasian grasslands, by warming cold air in the winter and filtering out dust in the summer. Talk about efficient!

TRAIL TREK
M. J. "Sunny" Eberhart (a.k.a. Nimblewill Nomad), from Flagg Mountain, Alabama, hiked the 2,193-mile (3,500-km) Appalachian Trail at age 83. He began hiking after retiring as an eye doctor in 1993, and in 1998 he trekked 4,425 miles (7,080 km) from the Florida Keys to northern Quebec in 10 months.

BURGER ORDER
While Kelsey Golden was working on her computer, her two-year-old son Barrett borrowed her unlocked phone and used the DoorDash app to order 31 cheeseburgers from McDonald's to be delivered to their Kingsville, Texas, home. Barrett generously included a $16.50 tip, bringing the total order to $91.70 after fees. He only ate half of one burger, so Kelsey handed out the rest to neighbors.

SKY LIGHTS
An 1859 solar storm known as the Carrington Event was so powerful that the spectacular aurora borealis, usually only visible near the Arctic Circle, were seen in skies as far south as Hawaii.

ANT VOMIT
Ants often communicate and exchange information by vomiting into each other's mouths—an action thought to help them build social bonds.

DIFFERENT CALENDAR
A year in Ethiopia lasts 13 months: 12 months of 30 days and one month of five days (or six days during a leap year). The Ethiopian calendar is also seven years and eight months behind the Western calendar because it calculates the birth year of Jesus Christ differently. So it wasn't until September 11, 2021, that Ethiopia marked the start of 2014.

GIANT WEB
A tiny South American social spider, *Anelosimus eximius*, uses synchronized dance moves to trap prey 700 times its size. The dance allows the 0.2-inch-long (0.5-cm) spider to feel for vibrations from any large insect caught in the massive communal web. Each web can be more than 25 feet (7.6 m) long and may contain 50,000 spiders.

OLYMPIC CHALLENGE
UK couple Charlotte Nichols and Stuart Bates completed all 102 individual Olympic events in 17 days—at the same time as the 2020 Olympic Games in Tokyo. The challenge was created as a way for them to raise money for the Motor Neurone Disease Association in memory of Bates' brother. Their events included shooting, climbing, boxing, diving, skateboarding, cycling, and the marathon. One of Bates' worst moments was when he fell from his horse during the cross-country event; meanwhile, Nichols' fish phobia meant that she nearly had to withdraw from windsurfing when she saw a trout. In the end, they raised more than £155,000 (around $185,000 USD) for the charity.

CANINE INTELLIGENCE
The average dog can learn and understand 89 words and commands, but some can master as many as 250 and can count to five—equivalent to the comprehension level of a two-year-old child.

RAMPANT ROSE

A three-year-old rose bush grown by Stephen and Amy Boucher in their yard in West Hartford, Connecticut, soared to a height of 22.9 feet (7 m).

REAL-LIFE LASSIE
When Lebanon, New Hampshire, police officers responded to a call about a loose dog on the Veterans Memorial Bridge, which spans the border with Vermont, they found a one-year-old Shiloh shepherd named Tinsley behaving in an agitated manner. Refusing to be captured, she led the officers to the top of an embankment, and when they looked down they saw a truck that had veered off the road. The truck had been driven by her owner, Cam Laundry, who was lying injured along with his passenger, Justin Connors.

RACCOON HAVOC
In February 2022, a raccoon suddenly crashed through the ceiling of the crowded dining hall at Louisiana State University in Baton Rouge while students were eating their evening meal. Evading a cook who tried to catch it in a basket, the raccoon ran loose in the building for a while before it was eventually captured and taken outside.

TONGUE TWISTED

The alligator snapping turtle uses a pink, worm-like extension at the end of its tongue to lure prey directly into its mouth!

The prehistoric-looking reptile lives in freshwater habitats throughout the southern United States and can hold its breath for nearly an hour. To hunt, the turtle stays still as a statue while wiggling the blood-filled appendage that looks like a tasty treat to hungry aquatic critters. When a curious creature gets too close—*SNAP!* The statue suddenly comes to life, biting down with enough force to sever a human finger. Weighing up to 200 pounds (90.7 kg), alligator snapping turtles are not picky eaters. While most of their diet consists of fish, they have also been known to chow down on frogs, snails, ducks, other turtles, and even beavers!

TRICK OR TREAT?

Alligator snapping turtles stay so still underwater that algae can grow on their shells!

Known as the Bridge Capital of China, the city of Chongqing is home to more than 14,000 bridges!

BUTT BOUNCE

Athlete Olga Henry bounced from her feet to her bottom and then back up again 25 times in one minute on a slackline at Santa Monica Beach, California—while wearing high-heeled shoes!

MINI MARVEL

Even though he is only 3.3 feet (1 m) tall, Pratik Mohite, from Maharashtra, India, is a competitive bodybuilder. He was born with short arms, short legs, and small hands, but is still able to lift 187 pounds (85 kg). As part of his training, he runs for 30 minutes every day despite being told when he was young that he would never be able to walk.

INCREDIBLE BULK

David Eliuk ran the 13.1-mile (21-km) Hypothermic Half Marathon in Edmonton, Alberta, Canada, while wearing 90 T-shirts. He trained for the challenge for five months, adding 12 T-shirts every two weeks to get used to the extra weight.

STOWAWAY LIZARD

Unpacking her suitcase at her home in Rotherham, England, following a trip to Barbados, Lisa Russell discovered a gecko that had stowed away for the 4,000-mile (6,400-km) journey inside her bra.

EASTER EGG

Hillion Fern from Cardigan, Wales, has kept an unopened chocolate Easter egg for more than 60 years. Her father gave it to her in 1960, and she now pays $100 a month to keep it in cold storage so it won't melt.

SURPRISE AWARD

Rapper Eminem was asleep at home after watching cartoons with his daughter when it was announced that he had won an Oscar for Best Original Song in 2003 with "Lose Yourself." He didn't even watch the awards show on TV because he thought he had no chance of winning.

SPRING LAUNCH

The springtail—a tiny, insect-like creature known as a hexapod—uses a spring-like appendage on its body to launch itself into the air away from danger. This device allows it to complete 470 spins per second—100 times faster than the main rotor of a helicopter.

HIGH LIFE

The colorful village of Linshi in Chongqing, China, is built on a bridge!

Built atop a 1,300-foot-long (400-m) bridge, the quirky community attracts travelers from around the world. The small space is packed tight with a mix of traditional Chinese and Western-style buildings, mostly used as small shops to entertain tourists as they take in the unusual architecture.

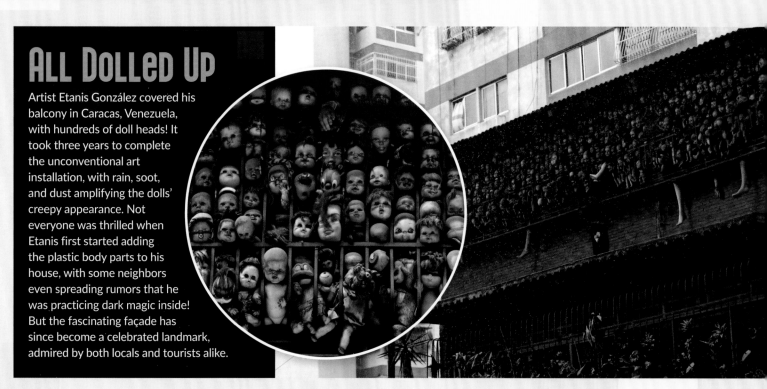

ALL DOLLED UP

Artist Etanis González covered his balcony in Caracas, Venezuela, with hundreds of doll heads! It took three years to complete the unconventional art installation, with rain, soot, and dust amplifying the dolls' creepy appearance. Not everyone was thrilled when Etanis first started adding the plastic body parts to his house, with some neighbors even spreading rumors that he was practicing dark magic inside! But the fascinating façade has since become a celebrated landmark, admired by both locals and tourists alike.

SHAKEN
NOT SHUCKED

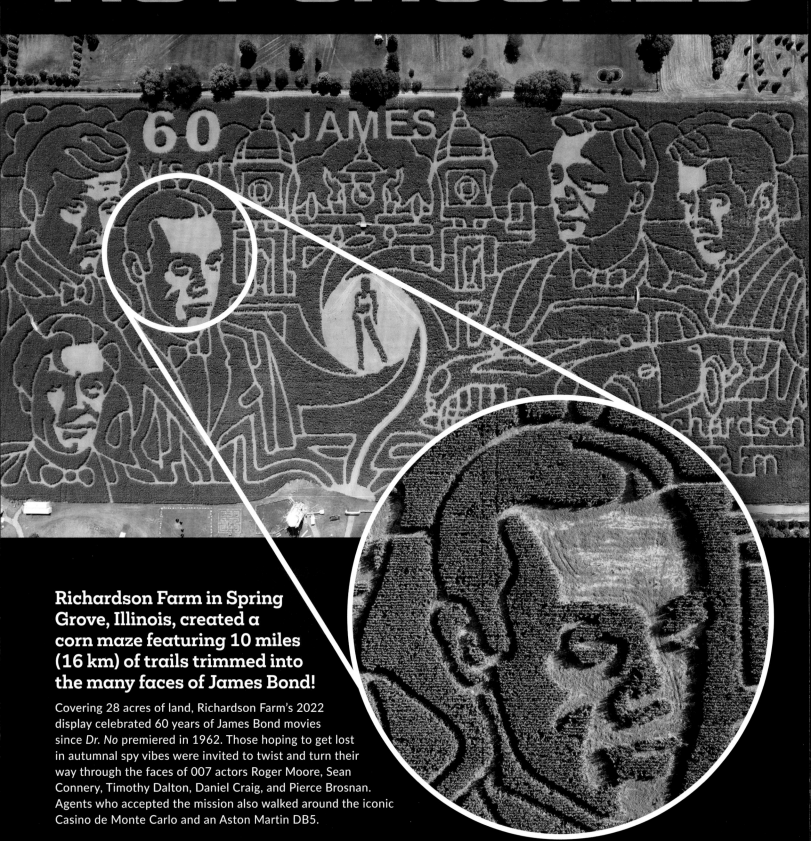

Richardson Farm in Spring Grove, Illinois, created a corn maze featuring 10 miles (16 km) of trails trimmed into the many faces of James Bond!

Covering 28 acres of land, Richardson Farm's 2022 display celebrated 60 years of James Bond movies since *Dr. No* premiered in 1962. Those hoping to get lost in autumnal spy vibes were invited to twist and turn their way through the faces of 007 actors Roger Moore, Sean Connery, Timothy Dalton, Daniel Craig, and Pierce Brosnan. Agents who accepted the mission also walked around the iconic Casino de Monte Carlo and an Aston Martin DB5.

BRAVING THE BRICKS

Playing with LEGO bricks is all fun and games until you step on one of the tiny terrors, but that didn't stand in Jacqueline Jossa's way when it came to raising money for charity. Jacqueline stepped up and braved walking across not one, not two, but 30,000 LEGO bricks to support the UK charity Comic Relief. This wasn't the first LEGO-stomping rodeo for the *EastEnders* star, whose daughters leave their tortuous pieces all over her house. After filming herself taking a brick walk across the toys, Jacqueline encouraged anyone who got a laugh at the relatable experience to contribute to Comic Relief's Red Nose Day, an event dedicated to helping people "live free from poverty, violence and discrimination."

ALL FOURS

Julie McCann, of Vernon, British Columbia, Canada, finished the 100 meters in 22.99 seconds—while running on all fours. She has been running on her hands and feet simultaneously for more than 35 years—since she was three years old. She says she always wanted to be a horse and used to run on all fours as a party trick.

POP ORIGINS

The term "pop" referring to popular music dates back more than 150 years. It was first used by English journalist and author George Eliot (real name Mary Ann Evans) in 1862. She used a male pen name to ensure that her writing would be taken seriously and was also the first person to use the word "lunchtime."

POTATO TRIBUTE

Visitors leave potatoes on the grave of Frederick the Great of Prussia near Berlin, Germany, because he popularized eating potatoes in the eighteenth century.

LEMON BATTERY

The Royal Society of Chemistry in Manchester, England, generated 2,307 volts of electricity from a battery made out of 2,923 lemons. They cut the lemons in half and connected strips of zinc and copper to each end. The lemon juice acts as an electrolyte while the zinc and copper act as electrodes.

BIRTHDAY PRESENT

Josephine Bridges, from Birmingham, England, lost her prosthetic leg while swimming in Lake Windermere—but was reunited with the limb after diver Angus Hosking found it at the bottom of the lake in a matter of minutes the next day, which happened to be Bridges's birthday!

Frozen in Carb-onite

A long time ago, in a bakery far, far away. . . Han Solo's famous carbonite freeze was recreated out of bread! The 6-foot-tall (1.8-m) sculpture dubbed "Pan Solo" was built by mother-and-daughter duo Catherine and Hannalee Pervan, co-owners of One House Bakery in Benicia, California. They started with a plywood base and even used a mask of Harrison Ford, the actor who played Han Solo, to ensure the proportions were correct. The Pervans then sculpted the details out of two types of dough, including a yeastless variety with high sugar content that helped Pan Solo last long enough to be entered in a local scarecrow contest!

HOLY HIVES

Joseph Priestley, marketing officer for Ripon Cathedral and a seventh-generation beekeeper, has taken honey to the heavens by raising bees on the northern England church's rooftop. In only a year, the four holy hives produced so much honey that Joseph was able to tap into his marketing side and branded the sweet product as "The Venerable Bees of Ripon Cathedral," to be sold in the gift shop!

Unlike social honeybees that live and work together in hives, mason bees are solitary insects.

EXTRA PASSENGER

When Kristi and Jared Owens checked in at the Lubbock Preston Smith International Airport in Texas before their flight to Las Vegas, Nevada, they were told their bag was 6 pounds (2.7 kg) overweight. Upon opening the bag, they discovered the cause—their Chihuahua dog Icky had stowed away inside a cowboy boot!

FIRST EDITION

A first edition of Mary Shelley's 1818 novel *Frankenstein* sold for $1.17 million in 2021. It was one of only 500 copies printed in the book's first run.

HUNGRY BADGER

In 2021, a hungry badger searching for food unearthed a haul of 209 Roman coins that had remained hidden in a cave in northern Spain for 1,800 years. The haul is the largest treasure trove of Roman coins ever found in the region.

555 TEETH

A voracious hunter, the Pacific lingcod fish, which is found along the West Coast of North America, has about 555 razor-sharp teeth lining its two sets of jaws. It gains and loses around 20 teeth every day.

LUCKY CALL

Rachel Lawrence, from Essex, England, was reunited with her cat Barnaby eight months after he went missing when she heard his meows during a phone call. While she was on a call with a veterinarian about her other cat, she recognized a noise in the background. Rachel was told it was a stray cat, but when she described Barnaby to the vet, the stray matched the description.

HOUSE FLOOD

Whiskey, a Labrador–Great Dane mix, caused $5,000 in water damage to a UK house after he turned on the kitchen tap while his owners were out.

BOTOX BAN

In 2021, 43 camels were disqualified from the annual beauty contest at the King Abdulaziz Camel Festival in Saudi Arabia for receiving Botox injections, facelifts, and other cosmetic procedures.

TAKING SHELL-TER

Watch your step! Mason bees are an important part of the ecosystem. Be careful not to harm their nests.

Red-tailed mason bees keep their babies safe by turning empty snail shells into tiny bee bunkers!

After searching high and low for the perfect shell to protect her eggs, the mama mason bee moves in. She uses chewed-up leaves, or mastic, to make individual cells for each egg. To ensure her babies are well-fed from the moment they hatch, she leaves a little bit of pollen on each egg. Then, she seals the nest with more mastic and camouflages it with grass, leaves, and pine needles. The fortress allows the eggs to survive the winter as they hatch and grow into pupae before emerging as adults in the spring!

BITING ART

Chinese craftsman Wang Weiting brings new meaning to mindful eating by using thoughtful bites to turn his snacks into celebrity portraits!

Using his teeth as his chisel, the foodie sculptor gets his recommended daily servings of fruits and veggies while chewing the shapes of famous faces into apples, tofu, and more. Once his masterpiece is complete, he shines a light on the edible sculpture to cast a perfect silhouette of his subject on the wall of his Jinhua studio.

MADE FROM ONE SHEET OF PAPER!

FINISHED PIECE!

SURGICAL SCISSORS

Bachena Khatun from Bangladesh unknowingly lived with a pair of surgical scissors lodged in her abdomen for 20 years. She suffered constant pain after undergoing gallstone removal surgery at a clinic in Chuadanga in 2002 until an X-ray finally revealed the presence of the scissors and they were removed.

DIFFERENT DECADES

Kaylie and Brandon DeShane, from Norwood, New York, have triplets who were born not only on different days but also in different decades! Baby Cian was born on December 28, 2019, and was followed by Rowan and Declan on January 2, 2020.

BRAIN MOLD

While on vacation in Costa Rica, Tyson Bottenus, from Providence, Rhode Island, picked up a toxic tropical fungus that led to black mold growing in his brain—a disease so rare that there have only ever been 120 recorded cases in the world. The fungus, which caused him partial facial paralysis and severe migraines, may have been absorbed into his bloodstream through a wound sustained when he grazed his elbow while cycling on a dusty Costa Rican road.

SPACE JUNK

According to NASA, there are 23,000 pieces of debris larger than a softball currently orbiting the Earth, often traveling at speeds up to 17,500 mph (28,000 kmph).

BAND SHIRT

A 1967 yellow T-shirt bearing the name of U.S. rock band The Grateful Dead sold at auction in 2021 for $17,640.

CARS COLLECTOR

Jorge Arias of Mexico City has more than 1,200 pieces of memorabilia related to the 2006 animated movie *Cars*. His collection is so impressive that he even received a visit from Brian Fee, the director of *Cars 3*.

Oversized Origami

Origami enthusiast Chris Conrad spent his senior year of college crafting a life-size person out of a single piece of uncut paper! Titled *Dragon Tamer*, the artwork began as a flat sheet measuring 19 × 19 feet (5.8 × 5.8 m) and took Chris about 45 hours to fold into shape. That time doesn't include how long it took for him to plan the design, which had to be perfectly executed so the warrior and dragon were in different colors. The finished piece was featured alongside 46 other origami creations by Chris in an art exhibit at his school, Haverford College in Pennsylvania.

ON TRACK!

Switzerland celebrated the 175th anniversary of their first railway by launching a record-breaking 1.2-mile-long (1.9-km) passenger train!

Organized by Rhaetian Railway, the extra-long train was made up of 100 cars and existed for just one day in October 2022. Seven drivers and 21 technicians were required to safely navigate the locomotive over 48 bridges and through 22 tunnels on a historic route through the Swiss Alps. However, it was not a speedy trip. In all, it took almost an hour for the train to travel just 15 miles (25 km)—which helps explain why this was a one-time only event!

ONE LONG TRAIN!

THE END!

TICKET to RIDE

One of the **most expensive airport-to-city taxi rides** is Japan's Oita airport, where a ride from the airport to city center will set you back about **$165 on average.**

France hosts about **90 million tourists** per year, making it the **most visited country** in the world

India's trains transport roughly **23 million** passengers each day—nearly the **entire population** of Australia!

Pilots and copilots are advised to **not eat the same food** when on duty to avoid a **double disaster** if something were wrong with the meal!

The air in most airplane cabins is **drier than the Sahara!**

One of the **dirtiest place** on an airplane is an item you're likely to touch—the **tray table!**

INFINITE PASTA-BILITIES

Nothing is im-pasta-ble for Danny Freeman of Beacon, New York, who has an uncanny ability to turn homemade noodles into edible art!

Danny's curious culinary creations range from adorable animals to pop culture icons and nearly everything in between. He uses natural ingredients like vegetables and spices to dye his pasta just about any shade imaginable, allowing him to add complicated patterns to tortellini, create realistic chocolate chip cookie ravioli, and even make over a dozen different Pride flag pastas. After cutting out the shapes he needs from the dough, Danny smooshes all the different-colored scraps into a ball and runs it through his pasta roller in a super #satisfying process that creates tie-dyed dough and leaves no waste.

LEVEL UP
SEE PAGE 7!

SCAN AND PLAY!

INGREDIENTS DANNY USES TO DYE HIS PASTA:

RED: beets, tomatoes
ORANGE: harissa, paprika, carrots
YELLOW: turmeric, egg yolks
GREEN: spinach, matcha
BLUE: spirulina algae, pea flower tea
PURPLE: ube, blueberries
PINK: dragon fruit powder, beets
BLACK: squid ink
BROWN: cocoa powder

FAVORITE TUNE

After escaping from a family's home in Ephrata, Pennsylvania, Lucky the cockatiel was lost for three years before turning up at a church in nearby Lancaster County, where he was identified because he loved the theme song from *The Andy Griffith Show*. A family member suggested seeing if the bird reacted to the theme and he immediately started whistling and dancing when it was played for him.

LEOPARD KIDNAP

After a leopard had snatched her six-year-old son, Rahul, from their home in the village of Badi Jhiriya in India, Kiran Baiga chased the animal for nearly 1 mile (1.6 km) and managed to pry the boy from its jaws. When she hit the leopard with a stick, it attacked her but then ran off when villagers, who had been alerted by her screams, ran to help her.

INLAND SEAL

Instead of living in the ocean, a young harbor seal made his home in freshwater nearly 100 miles (160 km) up the Hudson River near Saugerties Lighthouse in New York.

THREE EYES

When a Holstein Friesian cow with three eyes and two sets of nostrils was born on Neeraj Chandel's farm in Rajnandgaon, India, dozens of villagers brought it gifts in the belief that it was the reincarnation of the Hindu god Shiva, the Lord of Cattle.

MONSTER CROC

Deinosuchus, a prehistoric genus of crocodiles that lived around 80 million years ago, grew up to 35 feet (10.6 m) long and weighed eight times as much as today's crocodiles. Its bite was even more powerful than that of a *Tyrannosaurus rex*, and its name translates as "terrible crocodile."

PIRATE NAME

U.S. singer-songwriter Billie Eilish has "Pirate" as one of her middle names. Her older brother, Finneas, loved pirates as a child and kept referring to his baby sister as "Pirate" before she was born. In the end the name stuck.

17 WHEELS!

Wheely Impressive

Czech unicycle acrobat Pavel Valla Bertini pedaled a distance of 66.6 feet (20.3 m) on a 29.8-foot-tall (9-m) "unicycle" made of 17 wheels stacked atop one another! The fifth-generation circus performer achieved this towering feat at the fourteenth Budapest Circus Festival in Hungary, his head mere feet from the ceiling of the Capital Circus building.

BARGAIN BUY

A drawing bought for $30 at a U.S. yard sale in 2017 was valued at more than $10 million after being identified as *The Virgin and Child with a Flower on a Grassy Bank*, a previously unknown work by sixteenth-century German Renaissance artist Albrecht Dürer.

SOIL SCULPTURE

Since 1977, a room on the second floor at 141 Wooster Street, New York City, has been filled with 140 tons of dirt as a permanent sculpture. *The New York Earth Room* was created by local artist Walter De Maria, and the curators keep it in pristine condition by periodically watering and raking the soil and removing any mushrooms that occasionally appear. About 100 people visit the exhibit every day it is open, but they are forbidden from stepping on it or even touching it.

CAR FIRE

Michael Jackson was so absorbed in writing "Billie Jean" that while traveling down the Ventura Freeway in Southern California during a break in a recording session, he failed to notice that his Rolls-Royce was on fire until a passing motorcyclist alerted him.

DAILY PHOTO

Every day for more than 10 years, artist and hairdresser Samuel Ryde, from London, England, has taken a photograph at exactly 12:34 p.m. It started in 2012 when he got his first smartphone, and since then his pictures have captured the different aspects of everyday London life, ranging from the exciting to the mundane.

YOUNG AUTHOR

Eight-year-old Dillon Helbig, of Boise, Idaho, wrote an 88-page illustrated book, *The Adventures of Dillon Helbig's Crismis*, and secretly placed it on the shelves of his local library. It proved so popular that there was soon a waiting list of more than 100 people hoping to check it out.

RUG PORTRAITS

Tom Quirk, from Gloucestershire, England, uses his vacuum cleaner to draw impressive portraits in the fabric of his rug, including The Joker from *Batman* and guitarist Slash from Guns N' Roses. First, he vacuums the gray rug all over in one direction to create a light image. Then he removes the hose, adds a narrow attachment, and drags the long fibers in the opposite direction to form the darker shades. He can complete a rug portrait in only 20 minutes.

MUSTACHE SUIT

Australian menswear brand Politix teamed up with Melbourne-based visual artist Pamela Kleeman-Passi to create a suit made of men's mustache hair. She collected the hair from barbershops and weaved it with cotton to form a fabric, which was then cut into a single-breasted suit.

RADICAL ROAD

Skateboard, scooter, and BMX enthusiasts flocked to a country road in Wiltshire, England, after a landslide transformed it into the skate park of their dreams!

After a February 2022 landslide caused severe pavement damage to the B4069 country road, authorities were quick to warn locals not to drive their cars on the broken boulevard—but they never expected skateboarders to drop in! Despite warning signs, pleas from officials, and the fact that the ground still moved sometimes, daredevils from across the country continued to arrive at the site, using bent trees, cracks, and barriers to pull off new tricks.

BISHOP CASTLE

Jim Bishop of Rye, Colorado, spent more than 50 years constructing a massive castle with just a pulley, a pickup truck, and his own two hands!

In 1969, Jim began building a simple one-bedroom cabin for him and his wife in the mountains of southern Colorado. He used rocks found nearby as his main building material, prompting visitors and passersby to ask if he was building a castle rather than a cabin. After a few years of hearing the same joke, Jim decided to make it a reality, and in 1972 Bishop Castle was born.

Jim continuously added to the castle over the next five decades. Today it reaches 160 feet (48.8 m) tall and features three stories of interior rooms, a grand ballroom, several towers, a glass roof, wrought iron bridges, and even a fire-breathing dragon made of recycled hospital trays! The spectacle has become one of Colorado's most interesting roadside attractions, free of charge to anyone wishing to see what might be the world's largest one-man project.

WACKY TAXIDERMY

British taxidermist Jack Devaney gives animals a second life by turning them into toasters, pencil cases, and more!

The artist's history with dead animals goes back to his days working in a butcher shop in Manchester. Utilizing skills he learned there, Jack created his first piece of taxidermy art: a rat pencil case with a zipper down its spine and a pencil sharpener in the rear. The one-off project spiraled into a full-time job after his mouse-terpiece went viral online. Today, Jack sells "Animalgamations" through his virtual shop, The World Around Ewe, where quirky art collectors can go for all of their googly-eyed taxidermy needs.

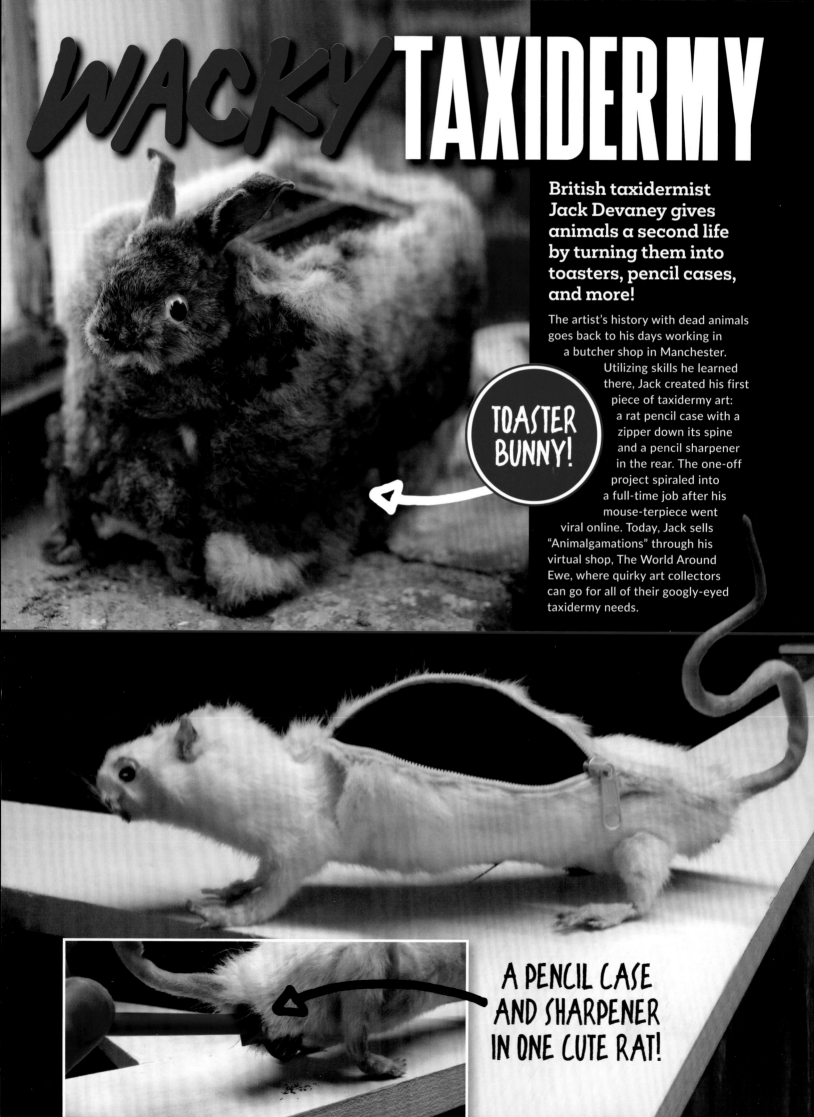

TOASTER BUNNY!

A PENCIL CASE AND SHARPENER IN ONE CUTE RAT!

BUSTED BUSTS

An industrial recycling center in rural Virginia has become a cult tourism destination as travelers flock to walk among the giant decaying busts of 42 U.S. presidents. Each statue measures up to 20 feet (6 m) tall and weighs as much as 20,000 pounds (9,072-kg)! Sculptor David Adickes created them as an exhibit for Presidents Park in Williamsburg, Virginia. Six years after its opening in 2004, the park went bankrupt. Rather than destroy the busts, one of the park's builders, Howard Hankins, moved the sculptures to his property in Croaker, Virginia, where they have lived ever since. It turns out the allure of abandonment is stronger than a squeaky-clean theme park—images of the perishing presidents sparked major interest on social media, resulting in a second term for the sculptures.

BAT FLIGHT

A female Nathusius's pipistrelle bat weighing just 0.25 ounces (7 g) flew more than 1,500 miles (2,400 km) from a nature reserve near Moscow, Russia, to the French Alps.

ANT BOOM

There are around 20 quadrillion ants alive in the world at any one time, compared to just 7 billion humans. That works out to roughly 2.5 million ants per person.

VOLCANIC ERUPTION

Within seven hours of the January 2022 underwater volcanic eruption in Tonga, nearly 400,000 lightning strikes were triggered, including an incredible 200,000 strikes in a one-hour period.

ELEPHANT HOTEL

Lured by a mango tree, herds of elephants regularly wander right through the lobby of Mfuwe Lodge, a safari hotel in Zambia. Some even stop to look in the gift shop.

STATE SPORT

In 1962, jousting became the official state sport of Maryland.

KILLER MONKEY

Mohammad Kurbaan was killed after a monkey threw a brick at him from the second floor of a building in New Delhi, India. The brick hit the 30-year-old man on the head.

APPLE CRUSHER

At 70 years old, Naseem Uddin from Pakistan could crush 21 apples in one minute with his bare hands.

SLAM DUNKS

Molly, a guinea pig owned by Emma Müller from Dombóvár, Hungary, can dunk a 1.7-inch (4.25-cm) ball into a tiny hoop eight times in 30 seconds.

STATES OF THE UNION

The Monument of States in Kissimmee, Florida, contains stones from every U.S. state! Following the attack on Pearl Harbor in 1941, Florida doctor Charles Bressler-Pettis came up with the idea for the landmark as a way to inspire unity among Americans—and it seemed to work! Governors and mayors from across the country sent stones from their states, and even President Roosevelt sent a rock! The resulting 50-foot-tall (15.2-m) monument was unveiled less than two years later on March 28, 1943.

ALL 50 STATES!

WATER SLIDE

A 700-pound (318-kg) cow escaped from a ranch and went for a ride on a slide at a water park in Nova Granada, Brazil. The ranch owner was so impressed that he decided to adopt the cow as a pet and named it Tobogã, which is Portuguese for "slide."

MONSTER MILLIPEDE

The *Arthropleura* genus of millipedes lived in Europe 326 million years ago and grew more than 8 feet (2.4 m) long—the size of a car.

FLAG CATCH

During a Miami Hurricanes college football game at the Hard Rock Stadium in Florida, a stray cat fell from the upper deck after losing its grip but was saved when a group of quick-thinking fans below spread out an American flag and caught it.

Completely Coated

In 1936, Danish clothier Christian Troelstrup covered his entire five-story department store with more than a thousand coats! The city of Copenhagen had condemned the building, forcing Christian to move his store to another location. As a last hoorah for the property that housed his business for more than 20 years, Christian organized the fabulous façade of frocks. It's rumored the stunt attracted so many curious shoppers that local police ordered its removal, but it was too late to matter—all of the coats had already been sold!

Double Trouble

On September 29, 1940, two Australian bomber planes collided and became one in the sky, forcing Leading Aircraftman (LAC) Leonard G. Fuller to pull off a miraculous landing! While 3,000 feet (914 m) in the air during a World War II training flight, Leonard's aircraft crashed directly into the top of that flown by LAC Jack Inglis Hewson, jamming the planes together and blowing Leonard's engine. As everyone else parachuted to safety, Leonard noticed his controls were still intact and flew the conjoined airplanes 5 miles (8 km) before improvising an emergency landing on a farm. Incredibly, everybody survived to tell the tale!

HERBERT & JOE

Dynamic duo Herbert Bell and Joe Garso astounded early twentieth-century crowds with incredible feats of agility despite them having just one leg each!

In January 1921, people of all ages gathered on the streets of Washington, D.C., to watch in awe as Herbert and Joe performed one-legged acrobatic stunts on bicycles and roller skates. Sadly, little else is known about the talented pair beyond the few remaining photographs of that performance. However, based on the men's estimated ages and when the pictures were taken, it is likely that Herbert and Joe were veterans who lost their legs during World War I.

In this photo, one of the men jumps rope while skating on one foot—talk about multitasking!

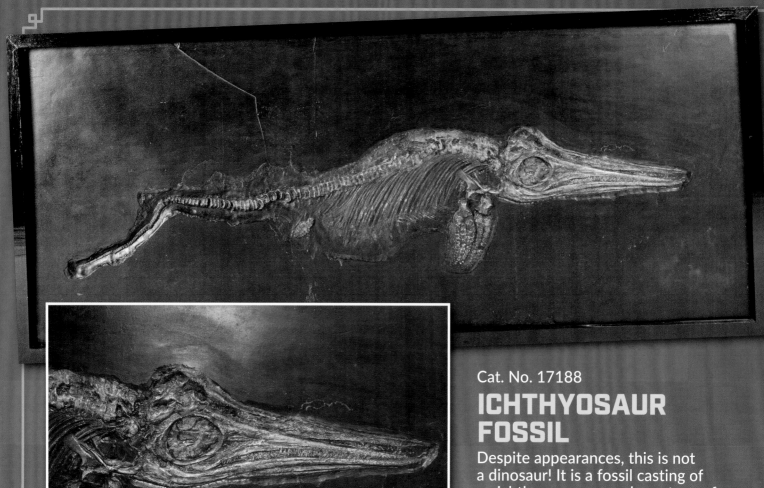

Cat. No. 17188

ICHTHYOSAUR FOSSIL

Despite appearances, this is not a dinosaur! It is a fossil casting of an ichthyosaur, a very large type of extinct marine reptile. Although they lived alongside many dinos during the Triassic, Jurassic, and Cretaceous periods, ichthyosaurs are actually an entirely separate group of species.

Cat. No. 167993

DINO NEST

Found in China in 1993, this nest is up to 100 million years old! The eggs are believed to be the spawn of a *Therizinosaurus*, a bipedal dinosaur that grew up to 33 feet (10 m) long and had huge claws that were likely used to grasp vegetation.

MORE THAN 485 MILLION YEARS OLD!

Cat. No. 17576

TRILOBITE FOSSIL

Found in Millard County, Utah, this fossil dates back to the Cambrian Period between 541–485 million years ago! Trilobites were bottom-dwelling marine creatures, so how did they end up in landlocked Utah? Believe it or not, the state used to be covered by shallow seas!

Cat. No. 11660

STOMACH STONES

Some dinosaurs ate rocks! Known as gastroliths, these stones would sit in the stomach of an herbivorous dinosaur and help grind up the creature's actual food—plants! It must have worked well, because many creatures living today still use gastroliths, including some birds, crocodiles, and even sea lions.

Ichthyosaurs are extinct ocean-dwelling reptiles that lived alongside dinosaurs.

Sea Dragon Discovery

Known as the Rutland Sea Dragon, the 32.8-foot-long (10-meter) remains of a prehistoric aquatic reptile were discovered by complete accident! Considered one of the greatest paleontological finds in British history, this 180-million-year-old ichthyosaur's head alone weighs more than a ton! In February 2021, Joe Davis of the Leicestershire and Rutland Wildlife Trust was doing a routine draining of a lagoon island at the Rutland Water Reservoir when he stumbled upon the massive fossil. The deep-sea stunner is the largest and most complete fossil of its kind ever found in the region.

DRONE DISPLAY

To celebrate the tenth birthday of her dog Doudou, a woman in Changsha, China, paid $16,000 to hire 520 illuminated drones that spelled out "Happy Birthday to Doudou" in the night sky. The flying drones also formed a likeness of the dog, a birthday cake, and a gift box containing a bone.

BURIED CITY

After an earthquake destroyed the Italian city of Conza della Campania in 1980, bulldozers clearing the rubble discovered the hidden remains of another ancient Roman city, Compsa, which had been inhabited more than 2,000 years earlier.

RESILIENT VINE

A grape vine in Maribor, Slovenia, dates back more than 450 years and still produces up to 110 pounds (50 kg) of grapes every year—enough to make 100 bottles of wine. The vine has survived frequent forest fires and also the bombing of the town during World War II.

UNKNOWN ISLAND

The world's northernmost island was discovered by accident in 2021. Scientists from Denmark and Switzerland thought they were on Oodaaq Island, north of Greenland, but in fact they were on another, previously unknown island some 80 miles (128 km) north of Oodaaq. The new island measures about 100 × 200 feet (30 × 61 m).

1,000 MARATHONS

By completing the 2022 Irving Marathon, Angela Tortorice, from Dallas, Texas, finished her 1,000th marathon. She has competed in marathons in all 50 states and in 2013 ran 129 marathons in a single year, averaging one race every three days.

GIANT TONGUE

K Praveen, from Tamil Nadu, India, has a tongue that measures 4.3 inches (10.8 cm) in length—0.9 inches (2.3 cm) longer than the average adult male human tongue. He can touch the tip of his nose and his elbow with it, and he once touched his nose with his tongue 219 times in one minute.

BOTTLE CAPS

Jean Marie Lambert, a graphic designer from Paris, France, creates detailed mosaics by arranging up to 1,500 different colored beer bottle caps. His replica of Leonardo da Vinci's *Mona Lisa* used 485 caps, and his portrait of former Argentine soccer star Diego Maradona used 763 caps. Lambert receives beer cap donations from fans all over the world.

NEAR MISS

Ruth Hamilton was asleep at her home in Golden, British Columbia, Canada, in October 2021 when a 2.8-pound (1.3-kg) meteorite the size of a melon crashed through the roof and landed on her pillow just inches away from her head.

CROC CONGREGATION

This crocodile hangs inside the Sanctuary of the Beata Vergine Maria delle Grazie in Curtatone, Italy.

Among the ornate stained glass, murals, and crucifixes normally found in European churches, you might find a relic more reptilian than religious—ancient crocodiles dangling from the rafters!

Crocodiles dressed in their Sunday best can be found wrapped in chains and warding off evil across Europe. Believe it or not, the resident reptile hanging out in the Sanctuary of Our Lady of Immaculate Tears in Ponte Nossa, Italy, has been there for more than 500 years, making it one of the oldest pieces of taxidermy in existence!

Exactly how these well-preserved reptiles made it from the swamp to the sacrament remains a mystery. While some may be victims of trophy hunting, scholars suspect that others were mistaken for dragons and hung as a reference to Leviathan, a fire-breathing reptilian devil found in the book of Revelations. It's also possible the practice was picked up in Egypt, where there is a long history of hanging stuffed crocodiles above doorways to represent strength or protection.

BOLTING BUFFALO

Thousands of people gather in Chonburi, Thailand, every year to celebrate the beginning of the rice-planting season at Wing Kwai—the buffalo racing festival!

Racers train their buffalo for weeks in preparation for the heart-pounding competitions. One race requires jockeys to balance on top of their buffalo's rear end as they sprint to the finish line. Another event sees racers scrambling to keep up as they hold onto a plough connected to a pair of buffalo charging across a muddy paddy field! The Wing Kwai festival is more than 140 years old and usually begins a day before the October full moon each year, marking the end of the monsoon season in hopes of a prosperous harvest.

Water buffalo can run up to 30 mph (50 kmph), so falling off not only means disqualification but possible injury as well!

OFF TO THE RACES

There's no denying that humans are a competitive bunch—and nothing makes that clearer than a footrace to the finish line! To keep things interesting, people have added twists to the classic contest, and today there seems to be a race for every occasion. Here are just a few modern-day races that represent the strange side of competitive spirit.

HARD DOG RACE

"Six legs, two hearts, one victory." That's the motto for Hard Dog Race, an obstacle course where racers and their furry best friends lap up the competition in the name of canine cooperation. András Púza was climbing trucks with his dog while serving in Afghanistan in 2012 when inspiration struck. After years of planning and testing, HDR's first official event occurred on October 1, 2016, with 180 participants and pups signed up to compete. Since then, HDR has hosted events across Europe, featuring 6k and 12k obstacle courses, a charitable Not Just Run event, and a 2k mud race.

YAKUTIA'S POLE OF COLD MARATHON

While a nip in the air is sure to put some pep in anyone's step, Yakutia's Pole of Cold Marathon pushes runners to the extreme, with frigid temps plummeting as low as −63.4°F (−53°C)! Known as the coldest inhabited place on Earth, Oymyakon, Yakutia, invites chill-seeking runners from far and wide to compete in "the coldest race in the world," with events ranging from full and half marathons to 10ks and 5ks (for those feeling a bit less ambitious). In January 2022, Vasily Lukin of Russia beat out 64 other bundled-up runners, earning his second victory in the event with a finishing time of only 3 hours 22 minutes!

GREAT WALL MARATHON

The Great Wall Marathon is a bucket-list experience in which runners from around the world push themselves to the limit as they traverse up 5,164 steps of one of the world's most recognizable sites! Founded by Søren Rasmussen of Danish-owned travel agency Albatros Travel in 1999, the internationally recognized race has gained traction throughout the years, becoming a sell-out event attracting 2,500 adventurous runners from more than 65 countries each year. While many have participated in the challenge, only one person has finished every race since its inception: Henrik Brandt of Denmark.

ET FULL MOON RACE

Every August, on the weekend of the nearest full moon, hundreds of alien-enthusiast athletes head about two and half hours north of Las Vegas, Nevada, for a marathon of intergalactic proportions. The ET Full Moon Race begins at midnight near Area 51, on a stretch of highway so well-known for its reported alien sightings that it was officially named the "Extraterrestrial Highway" in 1996. While participants are required to wear reflective gear during the nighttime road race, the quirky bunch is also known to show up in full alien garb, including costumes, antennas, and cosmic-inspired outfits—perhaps to inspire a visit from a galaxy far, far away.

CONQUER THE CASTLE

Conquer the Castle is a 2.5-mile-long (4-km) obstacle course created by Red Bull that turns participants into sixteenth-century warriors as they race to be the first to "conquer" Denmark's Rosenholm Castle! Contenders face more than 20 obstacles meant to test their strength, stamina, and cleverness, such as archery, wall climbing, firing catapults, and escaping a torture chamber! All of which must be completed before they can plant the victory flag and declare the castle conquered. The race has proven so popular that it has been duplicated at other castles, including Ireland's Rock of Cashel.

HELLZAPOPPIN

Part rock concert, part circus—Hellzapoppin is a classic sideshow turned up to 11!

Since its first production in 2009, Hellzapoppin has put on more than 3,000 shows around the globe. But it's not all about world travels and jaw-dropping stunts; it's also about following dreams and creating a sideshow family that sticks together! While the show features a rotating cast of about 50 performers, the core crew behind Hellzapoppin is just three people—let's meet them!

The Govna

Bryce "The Govna" Graves is the ringleader, sideshow stuntman extraordinaire, and founder of Hellzapoppin. Known for his long, salt-and-pepper beard and mischievous smile, The Govna runs the show while also performing death-defying acts that include fire eating, sword swallowing, and "the human blockhead," during which he drills a 6-inch (15.2-cm) bit into his nose! When he isn't raising hell on the road with Hellzapoppin, you can find him raising chickens and living the simple life on his Florida farm.

"I wanted to push the boundaries and challenge people's perceptions of what a sideshow could be."
–The Govna

LEVEL UP
SEE PAGE 7!
SCAN AND PLAY!

Short E. Dangerously

Short E. Dangerously is the show's biggest performer despite measuring just 3 feet 3 inches (1 m) tall! In fact, you can find wax figures of the half-man daredevil in Ripley's Believe It or Not! attractions around the world. In Hellzapoppin, Short E. performs glass walking, fire breathing, feats of balance, and more—all on his hands! To celebrate his tenth year with the show, their 2023 tour was dedicated to Short E. and dubbed the "Shortyth Anniversary: Decade of Destruction Tour."

"I am dedicated to making sure sideshow continues to thrive for future generations."
–Short E.

"We are capable of so much more than we realize. . . We truly can live the life of our wildest dreams."
–Willow

Willow Lauren

Previously a dancer and motorcycle stunt rider, Willow Lauren joined Hellzapoppin in 2017, barely a year after learning her first sideshow stunt—fire eating! Since then, she's also picked up sword swallowing, razor blade regurgitating, contortion, and more. But don't let her dangerous side fool you; Willow is a self-proclaimed nerd, spending a lot of her time reading, learning, and growing. The rest is spent raising animals on the farm she shares with The Govna.

In Good Hands

Since 1992, travelers exploring the arid terrain of Chile's Atacama Desert have been met with an unusual sight—a 36-foot-tall (11-m) concrete hand rising out of the sand! *Mano del Desierto*, or "Hand of the Desert," is one of several giant hands artist Mario Irarrázabal has constructed around the world, with others located in Madrid, Venice, and Punto del Este in Uruguay. The massive fingers lifting from the landscape represent Mario's signature style, demonstrating human helplessness and vulnerability.

CABBAGE BEER

Icelandic brewer RVK created a green pea and pickled red cabbage–flavored beer, Ora jólabjór, and it proved so popular that it sold out in just six hours. Master brewer Valgeir Valgeirsson has also made beers from seaweed and dried fish.

LIGHTNING BOLT

A single bolt of lightning on April 29, 2020, extended for 477.2 miles (768 km) and lit up the sky across three states—Mississippi, Louisiana, and Texas. Lightning bolts are rarely more than 10 miles (16 km) in length.

SUNKEN SHIPS

There are an estimated three million shipwrecks lying on the floors of the world's oceans and less than 1 percent of them have been explored. More than 5,000 ships have sunk just in a treacherous stretch of water off the Outer Banks of North Carolina known as the Graveyard of the Atlantic.

RUDE PARROT

The 1845 funeral of U.S. President Andrew Jackson at his home in Nashville, Tennessee, was repeatedly interrupted by the loud squawking and cursing of his African gray parrot named Poll.

HAIRBALL DAY

National Hairball Awareness Day, celebrated annually on the last Friday in April, was founded by Kansas veterinarian Dr. Blake Hawley to encourage cat owners to take steps to prevent their pets from coughing up hairballs.

INTESTINE SOUP

A popular dish in Taiwan is milkfish intestine soup. The milkfish's intestines, which look like a swarm of worms, can also be eaten fried in oil. The fish usually aren't fed for a few days beforehand so that the intestines are clean, making the dish more hygienic.

FLYING PICTURES

A tornado that ripped through Kentucky on December 10, 2021, sucked up Michaela Copeland's wedding photos from her in-laws' home in Mayfield and dumped one of the pictures 140 miles (224 km) away in Breckinridge County.

JUST MY TYPE

London-based artist James Cook creates detailed landscapes and portraits using only a typewriter!

With a sheet of paper loaded into one of his more than 40 typewriters, James types out a variety of numbers, letters, and punctuation marks to form images of everything from buildings and scenery to celebrities and animals! He was inspired to take up the artform in 2014 after learning about Paul Smith, a twentieth-century American typewriter artist with cerebral palsy. Since then, James has created around 200 works of art. They range greatly in scale, from small postcard-sized pieces to possibly the world's largest typewriter drawing—a massive panorama of the London skyline measuring 6.5 feet (2 m) wide!

WHAT'S THE *BUZZ!*

The honey buzzard feeds on the larvae of wasps and bees, picking hives and honeycombs apart all while being swarmed by angry stingers!

The honey buzzard doesn't fear the dreaded bee sting. In fact, it seems like the bird has almost no fear at all! Likely because its body is built for chowing down on insects with stingers! For example, the scales on its legs and feet work like armor while its body is covered in dense, overlapping feathers. And thanks to the honey buzzard's curved beak, it's able to capture prey efficiently as it digs in the dirt and cuts through honeycombs. Just a few reasons why the honey buzzard is truly the bees knees!

5TH WHEELING

Mark and Kelly Tucker of Crazy T Ranch in Russellville, Arizona, sent a story about their calf 5th Wheel, who was born with a little something special on his head—an extra leg! Along with growing in an unexpected place, 5th Wheel's bonus leg had two hooves. The calf lived for more than a year and a half with the extra appendage before it was removed due to having outgrown his body. Despite no longer having hooves on his head, 5th Wheel is still kicking and living life to the fullest on the family's farm.

LOCKED IN

Danish golfer Jeff Winther won the 2021 Mallorca Open in Spain—his first European tour victory—despite getting locked in the bathroom for 45 minutes on the morning of his final round. To escape, he needed the help of his six-year-old daughter, Nora, who went off and found someone to break down the door.

DRANK URINE

Lost, alone, and thirsty after collapsing on a remote sand dune, Glynn Sherris, from Perth, Western Australia, survived by drinking his own urine to prevent dehydration. He then buried himself partly in sand to keep warm through the night. The next morning, he staggered to a beach where he was spotted by a rescue helicopter.

SPORTS DAY

Four of the UK's most successful Olympic sportsmen—rower Steve Redgrave (five gold medals), cyclist Chris Hoy (six gold medals), runner Mo Farah (four gold medals) and cyclist Jason Kenny (seven gold medals)—were all born on March 23.

SLEEPING BUS

A five-hour, 47-mile (75-km) bus journey in Hong Kong is designed specifically for insomniacs. Passengers are given a bag containing an eye mask and ear plugs to help them sleep, and many also bring their own pillows and blankets. Almost 70 percent of Hong Kong residents experience some form of insomnia in the bustling city.

KNITTING BIKE

Souki, a sock manufacturing company in Japan's Nara Prefecture, hosts workshops where people can knit their own socks by pedaling on a stationary bike for about 10 minutes. The bicycle is connected to a knitting machine, and once customers have chosen the size and color of the socks they want, they start pedaling.

PLENTY OF FISH

"There are plenty of fish in the sea" is common phrase heard in the dating world, but a grass puffer fish looking for love will have better luck on land. The curious spawning routine of grass puffers involves dozens of the fish throwing themselves out of the ocean! They wait for the tide to wash them ashore, where they spend an hour or so laying and fertilizing eggs. The bizarre speed-dating event is over when the tide returns and the puffer fish ride it back into the ocean.

FISH
Fest

More than one million people attend the Hwacheon Sancheoneo Ice Festival in Korea each year in hopes of catching a delicious mountain trout—sometimes with their bare hands!

Held in January, the three-week-long festival sees the frozen Hwacheon River dotted with thousands of ice-fishing holes where anglers of all ages, nationalities, and experience levels can drop a line and wait for a bite. Prefer a more active approach? Sign up for the barehanded fishing experience and spend three minutes chasing trout in ice-cold water!

Whichever you decide, be sure to take your catch to one of the on-site kitchens where your fish can be grilled, steamed, or turned into sashimi. Other activities at the festival include ice racing, snow sculpting, zip-lining, ice soccer, sledding, and skating.

WHAT A CATCH!

FISH SHOWER

On December 29, 2021, dozens of dead fish fell from the sky during a storm in Texarkana, Texas. The fish had probably been swept up by waterspouts before falling to the ground at the same time as the rain.

FREE TREAT

A special ice cream served in Hirata, Japan, is liberally sprinkled with habanero pepper powder, making it so hot that anyone who can eat it does not have to pay.

ROOT BRIDGES

The Khasi people of Meghalaya, India, build bridges across rivers by shaping the live roots of Indian rubber trees. They grow the trees on both sides of rivers and then guide the roots to join midway across the water. A living root bridge needs about 15 years of growth before it is ready to carry people. Some structures stretch to 250 feet (80 m) long and are strong enough to bear the weight of 50 people at a time. Each living bridge can last for as long as the tree survives—at least 500 years.

MACABRE FUNGUS

Cordyceps militaris is a parasitic fungus that grows out of the carcasses of dead insect pupae. After infecting the pupa, usually of a butterfly or moth, the parasite mummifies it, keeping it alive just long enough to generate sufficient nutrition to support the fungus, which then emerges above ground from the corpse in the form of a thin, orange mushroom.

CAPITAL ANAGRAM

Tokyo, the current capital of Japan, is an anagram of the country's previous capital, Kyoto.

FAN FEED

GLASS HOUSE

Haley Pastor reached out to share the work of her grandfather, Randy Ruder, who has spent nearly 30 years building magnificent glass sculptures in his spare time. Each creation is made from thousands of hand-cut pieces of glass, can take years to assemble, and are built without any preplanning or measurements! One of Randy's most impressive works is a 27.5-inch-tall (70-cm) lighthouse that took three years to build and includes a spiral staircase, table, and chair inside.

BEYOND A DROUGHT

When a drought caused the water levels of China's Yangtze River to drastically decrease, it unexpectedly revealed 600-year-old Buddhist statues! Located on a previously submerged island near the city of Chongqing, the three statues were built during the Ming and Qing dynasties. The largest of the trio is just over 3 feet (91 cm) tall and depicts a monk sitting on a lotus petal. Although the extreme weather conditions are disturbing to witness, at least now there are a few bright spots of previously undiscovered beauty to admire.

Tunnel Vision

On September 4, 2021, Italian stunt pilot Dario Costa became the first person to ever fly a plane through a tunnel—and he did it twice! Dario piloted his Zivko Edge 540 aircraft 1.4 miles (2.3 km) through the twin Çatalca tunnels along the Northern Marmara Highway near Istanbul, Turkey, flying at an average speed of 153 mph (245 kmph). Accomplishing his years-old dream of completing the Tunnel Pass wasn't easy, even for a pilot with over two decades of experience and more than 5,000 hours logged in the air. Flying through the concrete walls required Dario to react to changes in airflow in less than 250 milliseconds and only move his hands mere millimeters throughout the entire flight!

RENT-A-STRANGER

Shoji Morimoto of Tokyo, Japan, charges $85 to wave goodbye to lonely people at train stations, sit with them while they work, accompany them to shops, or greet them at the end of marathons—even though he doesn't know them. Since he set up business in 2018, he has had over 4,000 assignments hiring himself out to clients who do not want to be alone.

OCEAN CASTAWAYS

Two castaways, Livae Nanjikana and Junior Qoloni, survived 29 days at sea by eating floating coconuts and drinking rainwater collected in a piece of canvas. They were eventually rescued off the coast of Papua New Guinea 280 miles (448 km) from their home in the Solomon Islands after the GPS tracker on their small boat stopped working and they were battered by violent storms.

TREE HUGGING

The town of Levi, Finland, hosts the Tree Hugging World Championships. There are three categories: speed hugging (hugging as many trees as possible in a minute, with each tree hugged for a minimum of five seconds), dedication (showing emotion while hugging a tree), and freestyle (demonstrating imaginative ways to hug a tree). The 2021 winner hugged 11 trees in a minute.

FAN FEED

HELICAMPER

Check out this extreme version of upcycling U.S. Coast Guard helicopter pilots Blake Morris and his wife Maggie shared with Ripley's! When they stumbled on the main body of a 1978 SA 330J Puma helicopter for sale, the couple felt compelled to buy it but were unsure what do with it—that is, until Blake mentioned turning the chopper into a camper and Maggie instantly loved the idea. Thanks to the serial number still visible on the helicopter, the duo was even able to find old photos of the aircraft from its time in the German military police! After months of work, the "helicamper" is now finished and has been successfully used for camping trips!

SKY'S THE LIMIT

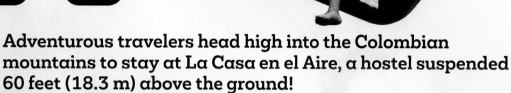

Adventurous travelers head high into the Colombian mountains to stay at La Casa en el Aire, a hostel suspended 60 feet (18.3 m) above the ground!

Located more than 1.5 miles (2.4 km) above sea level in the rural region of Abejorral, Antioquia, the wooden structure clings to the edge of Cerro San Vicente with the help of steel wires and cables. La Casa en el Aire (or "The House in the Air") began as a dream of mountain climber Nilton López, who prides his creation on its eco-friendly features, which include solar power and trash collection. Visitors to the cliffside cabin can expect nonstop thrills, including taking a leap of faith right off the porch on a giant swing or sleeping in hammocks suspended over the hostel!

RELAXING HEIGHTS!

Fabulous FLAPJACKS

Dancakes has flipped the script on fine art, turning pancake batter into edible masterpieces!

Daniel Drake began creating pancake art as a party trick to entertain customers while working at a St. Louis, Missouri, diner in 2009. It wasn't until a video showcasing his creations went viral in 2013 that his flapjacks became famous. His new online following led to TV gigs and an influx of phone calls and emails for Dan to ditch the diner for the big leagues. With the help of his best friend, Hank Gustafson, Dan created the world's first professional pancake art company: Dancakes.

Since then, the company has grown into a collection of pancake artists who post their deliciously detailed creations online and even travel the world doing live events, where they take audience requests for on-the-spot designs. They even have their own line of supplies and equipment for budding batter artists!

Kobe Bryant

Sprigatito, Fuecoco, and Quaxly

Shrek

Lil Nas X

Billie Eilish

Monkey D. Luffy

Taylor Swift

Jimmy Fallon

Mark Maron

Bluey

Holey Site

Every summer, sand martins flock to greener—or rather, grainier—pastures, turning sandy cliffsides into seasonal resorts filled with hundreds of tiny burrows. Sand martins, a.k.a. bank swallows, are social birds that nest together all season long, arriving as early as March to stake their claim on rivers, lakes, and gravel pits. Pairs will dig a tunnel up to 3.3 feet (1 m) deep, laying four to five eggs at the end of the chamber. Once autumn hits, the vacation is over, and the tiny brown and white birds return home to their native Africa to enjoy a warm winter.

CELEBRITY SIGNATURES

Jorge "Funky" Matas, a Venezuelan-born social media influencer based in Florida, has more than 225 celebrity signatures tattooed on his back, including Usain Bolt, Gerard Butler, Mike Tyson, and Michael J. Fox. Matas also once tattooed himself while skydiving.

ALBINO FAMILY

All six siblings of the Parvez-Akhtar family from Coventry, England, were born with albinism, a genetic condition that causes a lack of pigment in the skin, hair, and eyes. Their parents, Aslam and Shameem, also have the condition.

BLIND RACER

On March 31, 2022, Dan Parker of Columbus, Georgia, drove his customized Corvette car at a speed of 211 mph (338 kmph) at Spaceport America, New Mexico, even though he is blind. He lost his sight in a high-speed racecar accident in 2012, which left him in an induced coma for two weeks.

TWIN SUCCESS

Twin brothers Nicolai and Rasmus Højgaard from Denmark won back-to-back professional golf tournaments in 2021. A week after Rasmus had won the European Masters in Switzerland by making a birdie on the final hole, Nicolai won the Italian Open—also by sinking a birdie putt on the last hole!

Tall Tail

The tail feathers of a male Onagadori chicken can grow more than 30 feet (9.1 m) long! The breed dates back hundreds of years and originated on Shikoku island in Japan, where they are considered a Living Cultural Monument of the country. Very few people raise the chicken, and those who do go to great lengths to ensure the fowl's feathers are not damaged by raising them in special coops and regularly grooming them. Under the right conditions, some of an Onagadori's tail feathers will never molt and can grow up to 4.5 feet (1.3 m) in a single year!

IN-FLIGHT EEL

OUCH!

A heron literally lost its lunch when the eel it had swallowed attempted to escape the bird's gullet mid-flight!

Photographer Sam Davis had his lens toward the skies in Delaware when a heron flew by with an unlikely passenger. Sam snapped his photo and carried on with his day thinking a snake or eel had bitten the bird and was hanging on for dear life, even witnessing the heron descending into the water with no signs of stress. Once he got home and enlarged the image, Sam noticed that the eel was actually dangling head-first out of the bird's throat! The fate of either animal remains a mystery.

HOME Sweet HOME

Interior designer Virginia Hoffman and her family turned their home in Salt Lake City, Utah, into a real-life gingerbread house!

After realizing her red brick home resembled the famous holiday treat, Virginia enlisted a few elves (her family) to help turn her vision into a reality. Virginia, her husband (a professional artist), their kids, and even their grandkids spent hours sculpting, molding, insulating, and painting the pieces that would turn their house into a winter wonderland. By Christmas 2019, their holly jolly home was covered in giant gumballs, candy canes, peppermint swirls, and even a resident gingerbread man! Since the display's debut, the family has continued adding to the festive fun, turning foam and insulation into vanilla wafers for 2021's display!

WEIGHTLIFTING GRANNY

Edith Murway-Traina, from Tampa, Florida, was still taking part in powerlifting competitions at age 100. A great-great-grandmother and former dance instructor, she only took up the sport when she was 91 but managed to lift up to 150 pounds (68 kg) in competitions.

CHICKEN LOVER

Ben Boyles, of Bakersfield, California, had lunch at a Chick-fil-A restaurant for 153 days straight, except Sundays when all of the chain's locations are closed.

MULTI-FRUIT TREE

Hussam Saraf, from Shepparton, Victoria, Australia, successfully grafted 10 different varieties of fruit onto a single tree. His tree produces white nectarines, yellow nectarines, white peaches, yellow peaches, apricots, peachcots, almonds, cherries, red plums, and gold plums.

PERFECT HEADSTAND

Tony Helou, from Deux-Montagnes, Quebec, Canada, can still perform a perfect headstand at age 75. When he was younger, he often used to walk around on his hands and to entertain his family he would perform a headstand on a moving bicycle.

SWALLOWED PHONE

Egyptian man Mohamed Ismail Mohamed lived with a cell phone in his stomach for six months. He experienced severe pains before finally undergoing surgery to remove the phone at Aswan University Hospital. He said he had swallowed the phone before to stop it from being confiscated by guards but had always succeeded in pooping it out.

COCKROACH CANVAS

Brenda Delgado, from Manila, the Philippines, paints miniature versions of famous works of art onto the bodies of dead cockroaches. The insects' shiny, smooth wings make an ideal surface for oil paints and allow her to recreate masterpieces such as Vincent van Gogh's *Starry Night* and Johannes Vermeer's *Girl with a Pearl Earring*.

CAT TREATS

For Halloween, Singaporean café Nasty Cookie created cat poop brownies—small, dark, poop-shaped brownies placed on a layer of crumble so that they looked exactly like cat excrement on litter sand.

BEER MEMORABILIA

Since the 1970s, Steve Miner, of Winnebago, Minnesota, has collected more than 4,000 items of Hamm's Beer memorabilia, including one of the brewery's first-ever cans from 1935. He also has Hamm's can coolers, posters, bottle openers, calendars, watches, Christmas decorations, and even piggy banks.

SOCK LINE

The Fresno Mission, a nonprofit charitable organization in California, collected 80,000 socks over a period of six months and arranged them in a line that stretched for 7.4 miles (11.8 km). Afterward, they distributed the socks to people in need.

ADVENTUROUS CAT

Five years after he went missing, Dexter the one-eyed cat was reunited with his owner, Bridie Dorta, in Aberdeenshire, Scotland. Dexter was discovered inside a shipping container that was being loaded onto an offshore oil platform in the North Sea and was promptly flown back to the mainland by helicopter. In his years away from home, the adventurous cat had been a regular visitor to a local prison, where he befriended inmates.

MATH PRODIGY

Eight-year-old Brooke Cressey, from Kent, England, can correctly answer more than 200 math questions in one minute.

FAMILY GRADUATION

On December 11, 2021, 88-year-old Rene Neira graduated from the University of Texas in San Antonio alongside his granddaughter, 23-year-old Melanie Salazar. The pair, who graduated in economics and communications, respectively, enrolled in 2017 and used to carpool to school and study together.

CUNNING DISGUISE

In 1774, botanist Jeanne Baret became the first woman to circumnavigate the world— after disguising herself as a cabin boy with the French Navy. The French Navy did not allow women on its ships, so she had to pretend to be a young man.

HERSHEY'S MOUNDS

Throughout the Bohol province in the Philippines, more than a thousand "Chocolate Hills" rise above the trees as far as the eye can see! Even more bizarre, no trees or shrubs grow on the hills themselves—just grass! The cocoa color appears when the green grass turns brown during the dry season, transforming the view into a chocolatey spectacle that some consider to be an Eighth Wonder of the World. Filipino legend claims the hills were the outcome of a fight between two giants throwing boulders at each other, while the geological theory is that they're simply a result of weathered marine limestone.

Mint CONDITION

LEVEL UP SEE PAGE 7!

SCAN AND PLAY!

Remington Robinson proves that art can be done anywhere by creating portable paintings inside of mint tins!

The Boulder, Colorado, artist began transforming the tiny containers into easels in 2017. Remington attaches small wooden panels inside the lids to use as a canvas, while the bottom half of the tin proves to be the perfect place for his little plops of paint. Once he finishes a scene, Remington lets any unused paint dry inside the container, as he considers it part of the entire artwork.

Despite his chosen art form, Remington rarely eats mints himself! Out of the dozens of paintings he's created, he estimates that only four or five were completed in tins of his own. These mint-condition masterpieces may be small, but they're extremely detailed, with each one taking one to three hours to complete!

EGG EXERCISE
Cuckoos lay their eggs in the nests of other birds. Cuckoo chicks exercise while they are still in the egg so that when they hatch, they will have built up enough strength to kill rival chicks of other species, usually by pushing them out of the nest.

RARE LOBSTER
In November 2021, Maine lobsterman Bill Coppersmith landed an extremely rare "cotton candy" lobster in Casco Bay. Only one in 100 million lobsters have that combination of blue and pink coloring.

DUCKLING DELIVERY
In 2022, a mother duck hatched her eggs in a fenced-in courtyard within the labor and delivery center of a hospital in Jacksonville Beach, Florida. The mother duck and her 10 ducklings were safely escorted through the Baptist Medical Center Beaches maternity unit by staff.

MUCUS BAGS
To protect themselves from predators at night, parrotfish produce their own "sleeping bags" made of mucus that they secrete from glands within their gills.

CRAFTY CROWS
Since a crow's beak cannot break through the hard seashells of limpets and winkles, the bird flies high into the air with the mollusk in its beak and then drops it onto rocks below so that the shell smashes.

MARRIED CAT
In an attempt to stop landlords banning her from keeping a pet, Deborah Hodge married her cat India in a park in London, England. Hodge wore a tuxedo-dress and India was dressed in gold for the civil ceremony, which was led by a legally ordained friend.

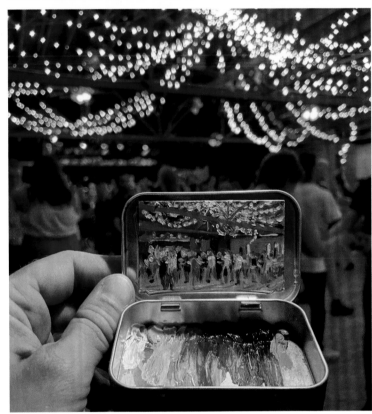

LET THEM WEAR CAKE

Israeli fashion student Tal Maslavi designed a collection of shoes so sweet they'll have you craving dessert! Inspired by a viral internet trend showcasing cakes that look like everyday items, Tal challenged himself to create something wearable that would call reality into question. The outcome is a series of leather shoes that appear to have missing chunks, exposing frosted layers of cake! No matter how you slice it, his design takes the cake for the most surreal footwear on the internet.

↰ Cat. No. 171125
LINT TRIBUTE

This tribute to surrealist artist Salvador Dalí was created entirely out of dryer lint by Heidi Hooper of Tannersville, Pennsylvania. Heidi has made countless artworks with the unusual medium, and much of what she uses is mailed to her by fans. She especially appreciates colorful donations, as she uses no paint and dryer lint cannot be dyed!

Cat. No. 171705
GRAPHITE TAJ MAHAL

Malaysian artist Sirajudeen Kamal Batcha sculpted this tiny Taj Mahal out of graphite he removed from pencils! It took him 72 hours of careful carving with a knife and tiny chisel to complete. His every move had to be precise or else the sculpture would crack!

RIPLEY'S
UP CLOSE &
PECULIAR

Cat. No. 166422

OSTRICH EGG FAIRY

Pat Beason of Carlsbad, New Mexico, carved this fairy's wings out of a single ostrich egg! The design was inspired by the wings of an Eastern tiger swallowtail butterfly. Ostriches lay the largest eggs of all living creatures, with the average egg weighing over 3 pounds (1.4 kg)!

ACTUAL SIZE!

Cat. No. 11838

PAINT BLOCK

Every day for 14 years, artist Pete Peterson, of Washington, D.C., wiped the excess paint from his brush onto the same piece of wood. The result was a 7-inch-thick (17.8-cm) block made up of more than 5,000 multicolored layers of paint!

MONUMENT OF LOVE

Indian businessman Anand Prakash Chouksey spent three years constructing a scaled replica of the Taj Mahal for his wife!

Anand spent 20 million rupees ($260,000) on the home in Burhanpur City in the Indian state of Madhya Pradesh. The structure is one-third the size of the real Taj Mahal and features a 29-foot-tall (8.8-m) dome, four bedrooms, a library, and a meditation room fit for Anand's wife of 27 years, Manjusha. While the building's exterior is an exact replica of its inspiration, the interior is a mix of traditional Islamic and contemporary design. Visitors are not allowed inside the home, but Anand does welcome guests to walk the 50-acre (20.2-hectare) property and take photos of the replica, considering it a gift to the town in addition to his beloved wife.

TAJ MAHAL TIDBITS

The real Taj Mahal was built **to honor Mogul Emperor Shah Jahān's favorite wife, Mumtāz Mahal**, who died during childbirth.

$1 BILLION

Shah Jahān is said to have spent the equivalent of **$1 billion USD** to construct the iconic mausoleum.

To protect the monument from air pollution, cars and buses must stay at least **1,640 feet (500 m)** away from the building.

Legend has it that Shah Jahān planned to build an **all-black version of the Taj Mahal** for himself across the river from the original but died before he could make it a reality.

It took a team of **20,000 workers** and **1,000 elephants** more than **20 years** to build the Taj Mahal, with the elephants providing transport of heavy materials.

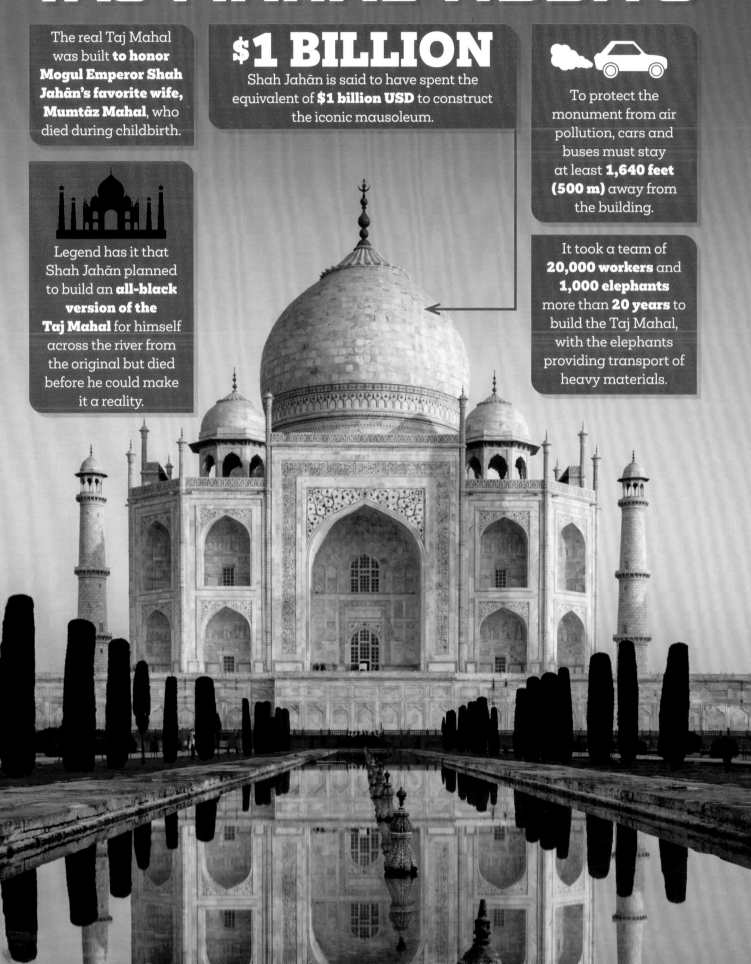

Purple Paradise

In an attempt to attract visitors, the sparsely populated South Korean islands of Banwol and Bakji were painted into a picture-perfect purple paradise! Inspired by the area's native purple bellflowers, the local government planted more than 230,000 square feet (21,300 sq m) of lavender fields, coated over 400 rooftops in lilac, and painted everything from bridges to phonebooths shades of purple, attracting upwards of 500,000 visitors since 2018 alone!

Block Albums

Brooklyn-based artist Adnan Lotia recreates iconic album covers using LEGO bricks! Adnan began toying around with LEGO builds while teaching creative engineering and robotics classes in 2012. After realizing the limitations of his old LEGO collection, he decided to level up and go digital with his designs, turning to BrickLink Studio to access bricks of all shapes and sizes without spending a fortune or taking up physical space. Adnan's first LEGO-fied album was Pink Floyd's *Dark Side of the Moon*, and he's recreated hundreds more since.

TONGUE BRUSH

Forget about brushing your tongue; Multi Awesome Studio wants you to brush *with* a tongue!

Branded as "the only brush you'll ever need," the Austria-based creative studio's Tongue Brush is a fascinating—and slightly unsettling—multipurpose tool made to look, feel, and move like a human tongue. Seeing the silicone brush in action is a surreal experience, as demonstrated in a video in which the organ-on-a-stick is used to lap up paint and butter croissants. Fortunately for the squeamish, the product is conceptual and not for sale.

LOOKS SO REAL!

FAST MOWER
Tony Edwards, from Shropshire, England, rode at a speed of 143 mph (229 kmph) on a lawnmower. His homemade mower is powered with a 1300cc motorbike engine and is still able to cut grass.

CAN COLLECTOR
Gary Feng, from Markham, Ontario, Canada, has a collection of more than 11,300 different Coca-Cola cans from 108 countries. They include a 1955 can that was one of the first to be produced by the company and another that was specially designed for drinking in zero gravity for the 1985 *Challenger* space shuttle mission.

FIRST BOOK
Bella-Jay Dark, from Dorset, England, had her first book published at age five. Her illustrated book, *The Lost Cat*, has sold more than 1,000 copies and she did all the drawings herself apart from one by her older sister.

SAME BARBER
Before landing the part of secret agent James Bond in the 1969 movie *On Her Majesty's Secret Service*, Australian George Lazenby was a car salesman and a model whose only acting experience was in commercials. He won the prized role of Bond partly by wearing one of his predecessor Sean Connery's suits and by going to Connery's barber.

HORROR ACCIDENT
After U.S. horror author Stephen King was involved in a serious accident in Lovell, Maine, in 1999, he purchased the vehicle that hit him for $1,500 to prevent it from being listed on eBay. Bryan Smith, the driver of the van, was found dead the following year—on King's 53rd birthday.

WRONG SHOES
Ethiopian runner Derara Hurisa finished first in the 2021 Vienna City Marathon in Austria—but was then disqualified for wearing the wrong shoes. The soles of his shoes were 0.4 inches (1 cm) thicker than the maximum 1.6 inches (4 cm) allowed.

ROLL PLAYING

WAVE Asian Bistro & Sushi in Mount Dora, Florida, can turn sushi into just about anything—including other foods and cartoon characters!

Sometimes it's hard to decide what kind of food you're in the mood for. But that's not an issue at WAVE, where you can have it all! Pizza, burgers, hot dogs, donuts, tacos, and more—you want it? They've got it—made completely out of sushi, of course! Along with a menu full of maki-fied versions of your favorite foods, this Central Florida spot will roll up some pretty famous faces, including Grogu (a.k.a. Baby Yoda), Pikachu, and *Among Us* crewmates!

SUSHI HOT DOGS!

SUSHI GROGU!

SUSHI DONUTS!

SUSHI
PIKACHU!

SUSHI BURGERS!

SUSHI TACOS!

SUSHI PIZZA!

SUSHI CREWMATES!

Into the FOLD

Although they seem immovable, mountains can actually be folded!

Over the course of millions of years, the rocky layers that make up the Earth's surface have slowly crashed into each other and created what geologists call "folds." One breathtaking example of a fold can be found next to Udziro Lake in the Greater Caucasus mountains of Georgia. Known as Katitsvera Peak, its name is said to translate to "cat's whiskers" and is in reference to the mountain's curved layers.

SKULL POWDER
In seventeenth-century Europe, people were often treated for strokes with a powder containing 5 pounds (2.3 kg) of crushed human skulls mixed in alcohol. The most effective skulls were thought to be from someone who had died a violent death when still young and healthy, so battle or execution victims were ideal. King Charles II of England was given this remedy, which became known as "The King's Drops," although it failed to save his life.

SEAL SAVIOR
When sea urchin diver Scott Thompson, wearing only shorts and a T-shirt, fell from his boat miles from land off the coast of California at night in January 2022, he was helped to safety by a harbor seal. As his boat drifted away, Thompson feared that he would die alone in the cold water, but then the seal swam over to him and kept playfully nudging him. The seal's actions encouraged Thompson to carry on swimming for five hours to the nearest oil platform.

ROBOTIC PEELER
Scientists at the University of Tokyo in Japan have developed a robot that can peel bananas without damaging the fruit inside. The robot can skillfully peel a banana with its mechanical hands in about three minutes.

SUBWAY RIDE
On August 20, 2021, Maya Jonas-Silver visited all 114 Massachusetts Bay Transportation Authority subway stations in Boston in 7 hours 4 minutes 29 seconds.

Group Effort

The Rock Garden in Calhoun, Georgia, is a sprawling town of more than 50 miniature landmarks crafted out of stones, shells, cement, rocks, tires, and beyond! DeWitt "Old Dog" Boyd started building the replicas as a way to teach his children about commerce and community. As his kids grew, so did his passion for the project, leading to the expansion of his tiny town on the land of a local church. Since then, volunteers have joined in, crafting minis inspired by Notre Dame, Bethlehem, the Colosseum, and more!

Petersen's Passion

Between the cities of Redmond and Bend in Oregon you'll find Petersen Rock Garden, a 4-acre (1.6-hectare) folk art museum made of volcanic and river rock, fossils, shells, petrified wood, and semiprecious stones! In 1935, Danish immigrant Rasmus Christian Petersen began working 14-hour days to construct miniature monuments, buildings, bridges, and fountains out of his rock collection. Rasmus continued working on the village until his death in 1952, at which point his passion project had transformed into a full-blown tourist attraction, drawing 120,000 visitors annually!

100TH MARATHON

Born with a broken neck, a broken spine, and two broken feet, El Salvador's Jocelyn Rivas was unable to compete in many sports when she was young. But in 2014, at age 17, she ran her first marathon and over the next seven years she ran 99 more, reaching the 100 mark at the Los Angeles Marathon in November 2021 at the age of 24 years and 292 days. Incredibly, she ran 30 marathons in 2021, twice running 26.2-mile (42-km) races on consecutive days.

UNIQUE TICKET

On October 26, 1984, Northwestern University student Michael Cole attended a basketball game alone, having been unable to persuade anyone to join him and use the extra ticket he had purchased for $8.50. As the game was Michael Jordan's first for the Chicago Bulls, Cole decided to keep the unused spare ticket. It is the only known intact ticket from Jordan's NBA debut, and in 2022 it sold at auction for a colossal $468,000.

STREET RUNNER

Starting in March 2020, Michael Shanks ran along all 6,100 streets in Glasgow, Scotland, in under two years, covering a total distance of more than 1,400 miles (2,240 km).

LUCKY FIND

When Laura Spears, from Oakland County, Michigan, spotted an email in her spam folder informing her that she had won a lottery prize of $3 million, she might have suspected a hoax—but it turned out to be true. She had been checking her junk mail for a missing message but found the days-old Michigan Lottery email instead.

LOOKS FAMILIAR

When Jacob Hansen and his wife went shopping for a casserole dish at a Goodwill store near their home in Denver, Colorado, he glanced up at a painting of sunflowers on display and realized it was one he had done as a high school freshman 21 years earlier. Back in 2000, his teacher had entered the painting in a Jefferson County art show and it had sold for $150 at the time. In 2021, Hansen bought it back for $20.

RICE, RICE BABY

Some new parents in Japan sent bags of rice that weighed the same as their babies to relatives who were unable to visit during the COVID-19 pandemic. The bag of rice featured a picture of the baby on the front so that family members could feel that they were really hugging the newborn.

DELAYED MAIL

In 2021, Susan Nordin, of Duluth, Minnesota, received a letter that had been mailed from Copenhagen, Denmark, 68 years earlier. Through Facebook she was able to identify the intended recipients, the Nelson family, who used to live at her address. The 1953 letter announced the birth of a baby.

TSUNAMI SURVIVOR

When a huge underwater volcanic eruption produced a tsunami that hit the South Pacific archipelago of Tonga in January 2022, 57-year-old Lisala Folau, a retired disabled carpenter, was swept out to sea, where he drifted and swam between islands for 28 hours. He floated from his home island of Atata via two uninhabited islands before finally reaching the main island of Tongatapu, having traveled more than 8 miles (13 km).

FAN FEED

IMPOSSIBLE BOTTLES

This mind-bending creation was crafted by magician and illusionist Zhengis Aitzhanov of Kazakhstan. With a mix of skill and creativity, he is able to insert objects into glass jars, despite the items being larger than the bottle openings! This seemingly unfeasible feat is why these are called "impossible bottles." Items Zhengis has trapped inside glass include Rubik's Cubes, baseballs, padlocks, and decks of cards.

Haka Pei is a traditional Easter Island sport in which competitors wearing little more than a loin cloth race down a volcano on sleds made of tree trunks!

Every February, the island hosts the Tapati Rapa Nui festival, a multiday event celebrating Easter Island culture. While the festival schedule is packed with art, dance, and sports competitions, Haka Pei is a major highlight. An extreme sport like no other, Haka Pei begins with creating a long sled by tying two banana tree trunks together. Contestants then haul their toboggans 984 feet (300 m) up the Maunga Pu'i volcano before lying on top and holding on tight as their teammates launch them down the hill. Reaching speeds of up to 50 mph (80 kmph), competitors reach the bottom in less than 10 seconds flat!

Crashes and injuries are common, with only the bravest attempting this ancient rite of passage!

FAN FEED

UNDER PRESSURE

Shout out to Sam Ward, of New Braunfels, Texas, for introducing us to what might be the most satisfying art form ever—pressure washing! It's not an easy task spraying the perfect likeness of icons like David Bowie and Batman into dirty driveways and sidewalks. To create his masterpieces, Sam alternates through a wide range of nozzles and pressures to ensure the details are accurate—and that he doesn't crack the cement!

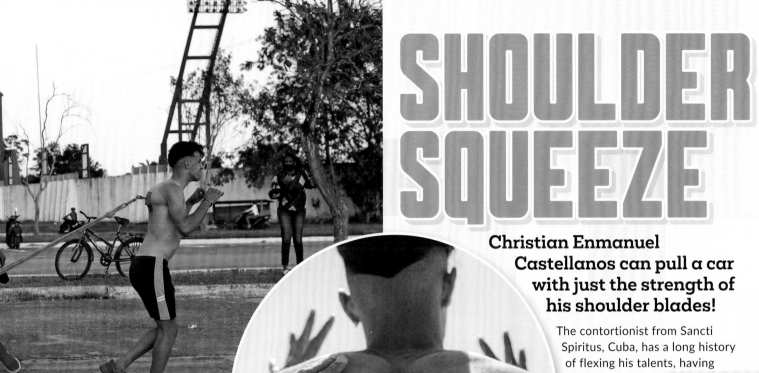

SHOULDER SQUEEZE

Christian Enmanuel Castellanos can pull a car with just the strength of his shoulder blades!

The contortionist from Sancti Spiritus, Cuba, has a long history of flexing his talents, having previously crushed 82 drink cans between his blades in just one minute! After that, Christian set his sights on something a bit heftier—a 2,425-pound (1,100-kg) car! Using only a rope and a block held between his shoulder blades, he successfully towed it 82 feet (25 m) down the street! While natural flexibility comes in handy for these feats, Christian spends a lot of his time doing strength and elasticity training to ensure his body is able to shoulder the load.

Melon Madness

Every two years, Australia's Chinchilla Melon Festival invites attendees to stick their feet into a pair of watermelons and hit the slippery slopes for some summer skiing! Known as the "Melon Capital of Australia," the town of Chinchilla grows 25 percent of the country's watermelons, and you don't need to tell them twice that it's worth celebrating! The event includes many melon-themed obstacles like melon bungee, a melon chariot race, and melon ironman. Still, none is more popular than watermelon skiing, which requires competitors to dunk their toes into juicy watermelons and hold on for dear life as volunteers pull them across the plastic tarp!

GIANT TOWN

On the Italian island of Sicily, there is a small town shaped like a giant person!

Home to only 5,000 inhabitants, the village of Centuripe has an odd shape that is best observed from high above. With a bird's-eye view you can easily make out the head, torso, and limbs of the "body" (although some say it looks more like a sea star). Despite bearing a resemblance to Leonardo da Vinci's *Vitruvian Man*, the town's design was not created out of artistic desire, but rather to suit the area's natural terrain.

Centuripe has plenty to see at ground level as well. People have been coming and going through the area since prehistory, and modern visitors can visit numerous archeological sites ranging from ancient Greek and Roman structures to ruins from the Bronze and Iron Ages.

PRISON EXPERIENCE

More than 800 people volunteered to spend up to three days and nights behind bars to test the facilities at a new prison in Zurich, Switzerland, before it opened to real inmates. During their stay, the volunteers ate prison food and enjoyed a one-hour walk in the yard.

GOLF HAZARD

Golfers at the Carbrook Club in Brisbane, Australia, face an unusual hazard: a 46-foot-deep (14-m) inland lake containing a dozen aggressive bull sharks. It is thought the sharks were washed there by floods in the late 1990s.

MULTILINGUAL SINGER

On August 19, 2021, 16-year-old student Suchetha Satish performed a concert in Dubai, United Arab Emirates, where she sang in 120 different languages over a period of 7 hours 20 minutes.

GOAL TRIBUTE

To celebrate the life of Chilean soccer player Jaime Escandar, who died in 2021, his Aparicion de Paine teammates placed his coffin in front of the goal and deliberately kicked the ball against it so that he could score one last goal, watched by hundreds of fans.

ANAGRAM FAMILY

Belgian couple Gwenny Blanckaert and Marino Vaneeno named all 12 of their children using different variations of the same four letters—A, E, L and X. They started with Alex, then followed with Axel, Xela, Lexa, Xael, Xeal, Exla, Leax, Xale, Elax, Alxe, and Laex.

DIFFERENT YEARS

Twins Alfredo and Aylin Trujillo were born only 15 minutes apart at the Natividad Medical Center in Salinas, California—but they were born in different years. Alfredo was born at 11:45 p.m. on December 31, 2021, and his sister followed at the stroke of midnight on January 1, 2022.

DONUT LOGO

In July 2022, the Bashas' grocery store in Chandler, Arizona, created a mosaic of the store's ninetieth-anniversary logo using 14,400 iced donuts. The donut logo covered an area of 903 square feet (84 sq m).

CULTURAL DIVERSITY

More than 300 different languages are spoken on Roosevelt Avenue, New York City.

COW AIRLIFT

Any Swiss cows that suffer injuries while living in their summer pastures high in the Alps are airlifted by helicopter further down the mountain to save them from having to walk to their lowland winter home like the rest of the herd.

BIZARRE *Stars*

Sea stars, a.k.a. starfish, are more than just SpongeBob's best friend! Along with their close relatives, the brittle stars, sea stars are some of the ocean's strangest residents. With otherworldly looks, brutal hunting methods, and other unusual characteristics, here are some of the most bizarre of the bunch!

BRANCHING OUT

If you didn't know any better, you might see a basket star and assume it's some sort of underwater plant from the way its arms branch out like tree limbs. When they aren't by waiting for food to swim into its outstretched arms, they keep their fractal-like limbs curled up and close to the body.

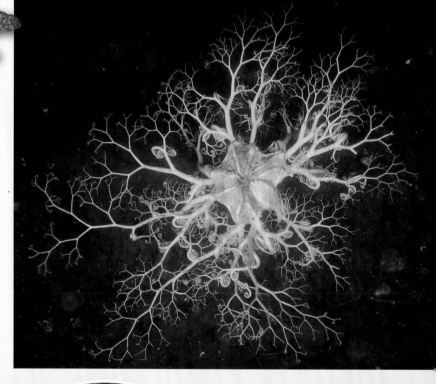

HEAVILY ARMED

The largest and fastest of all sea stars, the sunflower sea star can grow more than 3 feet (0.9 m) wide and have up to 24 arms! All those arms and the 15,000 tiny tube feet that cover their undersides help sunflower sea stars crawl across the ocean floor at speeds of up to 3.3 feet (1 m) per minute!

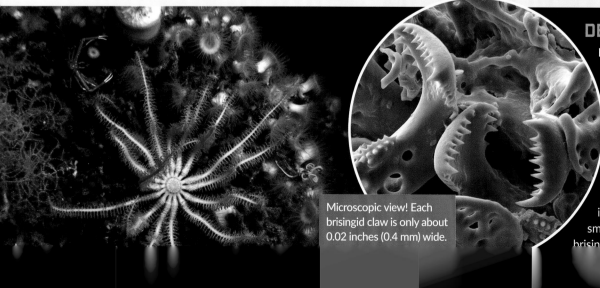

DEATH GRIP

Brisingids are a group of sea stars with a catchy way of capturing prey. Their long arms are covered with hundreds of spines, which in turn are covered in millions of miniscule claws known as "pedicellariae." These tiny pincers act like Velcro, resulting in an inescapable death grip for any small creatures that swim into a brisingid's arms.

Microscopic view! Each brisingid claw is only about 0.02 inches (0.4 mm) wide.

SLICK GETAWAY

Slime stars are so named thanks to the massive amounts of mucus they excrete when stressed. This unusual defense mechanism helps protect the animal's extremely soft body from predators. Slime stars kept in aquariums have been known to produce enough goo to block pipes and cause water to overflow!

ROUGH EXTERIOR

The crown-of-thorns starfish is about as mean as it looks! The hundreds of spines covering its colorful body contain venomous toxins. More painful than the starfish's sting, however, is its appetite for coral. When crown-of-thorns starfish populations grow too large and eat too much, it can be devastating for reefs that are already struggling to survive.

APPETIZING APPEARANCE

What you decide to call this creature may depend on whether you prefer pasta or pastries. Its scientific name is *Plinthaster dentatus*, but most people refer to it as a "cookie" or "ravioli" star. With its stubby arms, golden-brown coloring, crimped edges, and pillowy body, it's easy to see how it earned these tasty titles!

NOT FOR EATING!

LEVEL UP
SEE PAGE 7!

SCAN AND PLAY!

Canopy Cone

Peeking above the treetops of Gisselfeld Klosters forest in Denmark you'll find a strange structure that looks a bit like a giant ice cream cone! Known as Forest Tower, it's part of the Camp Adventure climbing park found about an hour south of Copenhagen. And while you won't find any soft serve ice cream swirled inside this cone, the view from the top of its 147-foot-tall (45-m) spiral walkway is a treat nonetheless!

VANISHING SOCKS

Scientists have calculated that the average person in the UK loses 15 socks a year while clothes are being washed, which works out to around 1,200 lost socks during a lifetime.

FALSE ALARM

After firefighters were called to Hope Ranch Beach, California, to rescue a woman reported to be hanging perilously from rocks 30 feet (9 m) down a cliff, they found on arrival that the victim was really a long-haired mannequin left behind after a recent movie shoot.

FAST FINGERS

The highest acceleration that the human body is capable of producing occurs when you snap your fingers. Humans snap their fingers more than 20 times faster than the blink of an eye.

PEPPA EFFECT

Some U.S. preschool children started to develop English accents as a result of watching a lot of *Peppa Pig* shows. The phenomenon was so widespread it became known as the Peppa Effect.

POSTHUMOUS VICTORY

Ramiro Rodriguez, Jr. was reelected mayor of Palmhurst, Texas, in May 2022 by more than 100 votes despite having died a month earlier.

WITCH BOTTLE

While searching a forest in Shropshire, England, in 2021, metal detectorist Chris Langston discovered an old bottle containing urine, hair, and a human tooth! It is thought to be a witch bottle, which was used in the nineteenth century to keep homes free of evil spells and curses.

TOILET TRAP

At the top of Mount Walker in Washington State, a woman was rescued by firefighters after she fell into a toilet while trying to retrieve her cell phone and was trapped there for 15 minutes.

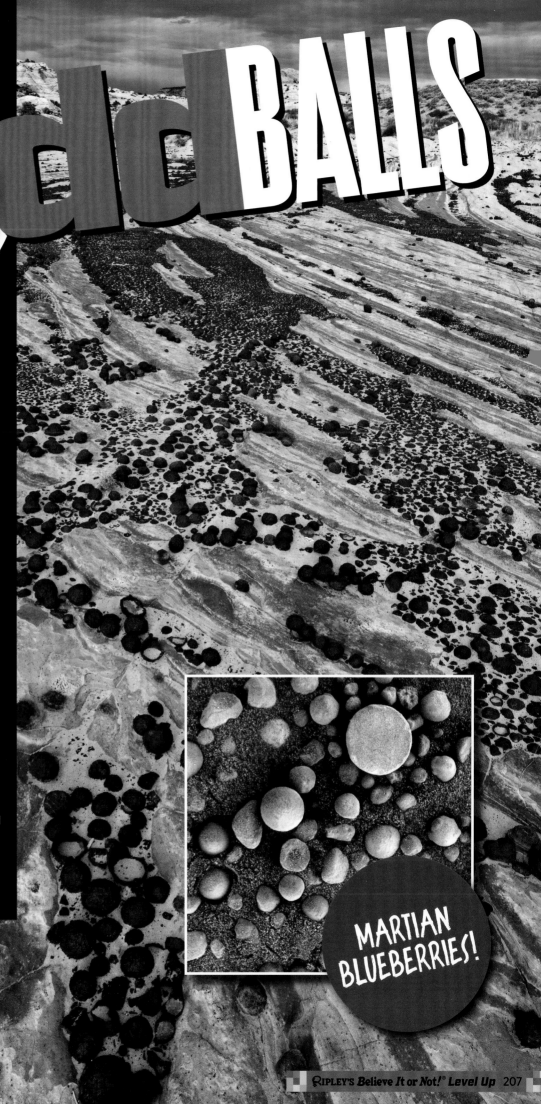

OddBALLS

Thousands of strange stone spheres can be found scattered across the American Southwest, but how they got there was a mystery until answers were found in an unexpected place: Mars!

They are called *moqui marbles*—small sandstone balls with hard shells of rust, ranging in shape from pea-sized spheres to frisbee-sized discs. The origin of these oddballs was a mystery until NASA's Mars Exploration Rover *Opportunity* discovered similar formations on the red planet in 2004. Dubbed "Martian blueberries," they reignited interest in the moqui marbles because they could be studied to find out how the ones on Mars were formed.

So, how are they made? Research revealed that moqui marbles are formed underground as erosion causes minerals to seep into the groundwater and then harden around wet sandstone clumps. Since the Martian blueberries likely formed in a similar manner, that led to some of the earliest evidence of water on Mars!

MARTIAN BLUEBERRIES!

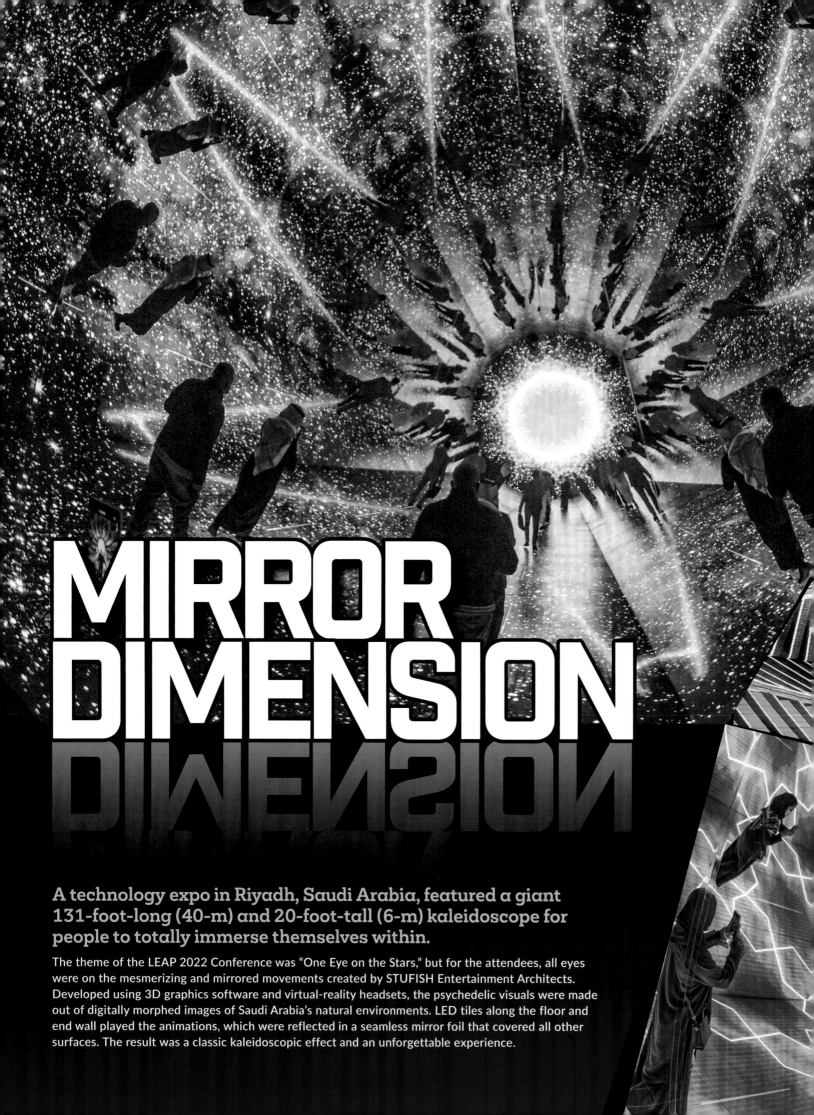

MIRROR DIMENSION

A technology expo in Riyadh, Saudi Arabia, featured a giant 131-foot-long (40-m) and 20-foot-tall (6-m) kaleidoscope for people to totally immerse themselves within.

The theme of the LEAP 2022 Conference was "One Eye on the Stars," but for the attendees, all eyes were on the mesmerizing and mirrored movements created by STUFISH Entertainment Architects. Developed using 3D graphics software and virtual-reality headsets, the psychedelic visuals were made out of digitally morphed images of Saudi Arabia's natural environments. LED tiles along the floor and end wall played the animations, which were reflected in a seamless mirror foil that covered all other surfaces. The result was a classic kaleidoscopic effect and an unforgettable experience.

FOR THE BIRDS

Situated between two trees in the middle of a Swedish forest and surrounded by 350 birdhouses, Treehotel's Biosphere room is a birdwatcher's dream!

The 366-square-foot (34-sq-m) hotel room is contained within a large cube, surrounded by a metal bird cage with different-sized birdhouses attached, creating a spherical shape. Guests can observe the birds through the floor-to-ceiling windows, which should remain clear of droppings, as birds prefer not to poop where they nest. A collaboration between Danish architecture studio BIG and Swedish ornithologist Ulf Öhman, the sustainability and ecotourism-focused hotel aims to aid in the conservation of local bird populations with its innovative design.

BRINY BOURBON

In May 2022, Tamworth Distilling released a sustainable bourbon made with a *sea*-cret ingredient—invasive crabs! Green crabs have been wreaking havoc on the New England coast since hitching a ride on British ships more than 200 years ago, constantly taking out shellfish populations, destroying seagrass beds, and generally messing up entire ecosystems. With the help of New Hampshire's NH Green Crab Project, Tamworth was able to remove some of the invasive species, giving them a good cleaning before tossing them in a pot and making a crab stock to incorporate into their specialty spirit: Crab Trapper.

CAUGHT ON CAMERA

Gioacchino Gammino, a Sicilian mafia fugitive who had been on the run for nearly 20 years, was finally caught after being spotted on Google Street View outside a fruit store in Galapagar, Spain.

MAILED SNOWMAN

Discovering that most of her kindergarten students had never seen snow, Robin Hughes, a teacher in Tampa, Florida, arranged for a snowman to be mailed to her class. Following a blizzard in January 2022, Hughes's sister, Amber Estes, built a snowman at her home in Danville, Kentucky, wrapped it in foil, carefully packed it with ice, and mailed the snowman overnight so that it arrived intact in Florida the next day.

TRUCK BURIAL

Don Adán Arana, from Puerto San Carlos, Mexico, was buried in his favorite truck. A crane lowered the truck into a brick-lined tomb, and his coffin was then placed in the bed of the truck.

TINY BOOK

A 1952 German prayer book measuring only 0.2 inches (5 mm) on each side sold at auction in Brussels, Belgium, in 2021 for $4,739. The text is so tiny it can only be read with a strong magnifying glass.

TOOTHBRUSH SCULPTURE

Using around 80,000 toothbrushes, pharmaceutical firm Dr. Reddy's Laboratories created a 40-foot-tall (12.1-m) sculpture of a giant tooth in Navi Mumbai, India.

SMALL DICE

A team of welders from the Mazda Motor Corporation in Japan made a metal dice with faces measuring just 0.04 inches (1 mm) across. The six faces of the dice were created in a T shape and then bent into a cube using tiny tweezers before finally being welded together. In order to keep their hands perfectly still, the welders had to hold their breath throughout the process. The finished dice is so small it is barely visible when placed on a fingertip.

ROBOT ESCAPE

A robot vacuum cleaner escaped through the open front door of a hotel in Cambridge, England. Realizing it was missing, staff searched for it for hours until it was eventually found the next day nestled under a hedge next to the parking lot.

FISH WITHIN A FISH

One fish, two fish. . . one fish? Paleontologist George F. Sternberg was shocked when, in June 1952, he uncovered an 80-million-year-old, 14-foot-long (4.3-m) fossil of an extinct fish containing the remains of its last meal—a smaller, but still quite large, 6-foot-long (1.8-m) fish! It is believed the larger fish, *Xiphactinus audax*, overestimated how much it could eat and died after gulping down the smaller *Gillicus arcuatus*. The duo then sank to the seafloor and were quickly covered in mud that preserved their remains for millennia. The Fish-Within-a-Fish can be seen today at the Sternberg Museum of Natural History in Hays, Kansas, not far from where it was originally discovered!

FAMOUS LAST MEAL!

GRADUATING TWINS

Thirty-five pairs of twins and one set of triplets graduated from the six high schools in Texas's Mansfield Independent School District in 2022.

SURGICAL TIPS

Studies show that surgeons who regularly play video games make 37 percent fewer mistakes in the operating room. And listening to Australian rock band AC/DC while operating is thought to make surgeons faster and more efficient.

SENIOR SAILOR

In 2022 at age 83, Japan's Kenichi Horie sailed solo nonstop across the Pacific Ocean, covering the 5,500 miles (8,850 km) from San Francisco, California, to Cape Hinomisaki, Japan, in 69 days. He has been sailing for more than 60 years, and back in 1962 he became the first person to sail solo nonstop across the Pacific from Japan to California.

EGG BALANCE

Ibrahim Sadeq from Iraq can balance 18 eggs simultaneously on the back of his hand.

PEE PALS

Bottlenose dolphins recognize their friends partly by the taste of their urine.

WASTED JOURNEY

Constance Kampfner traveled 537 miles (864 km) by car and ferry from London, England, to the remote Scottish island of Mull to take what is regarded as the UK's easiest driving test. Even though there is little traffic on the island, no traffic lights, nowhere to parallel park, and only one roundabout, she still failed.

Crowley Columns

The curious stone columns rising 20 feet (6 m) out of the beaches of Crowley Lake in California baffled scientists and visitors alike for decades. The pillars had actually gone unseen for thousands of years until waves from a new reservoir eroded the sand and exposed the columns for the world to see in the 1940s. It wasn't until 2015 that researchers determined how the strange structures were formed! It's believed the columns were created when cold water met hot ash after a massive volcanic eruption 760,000 years ago.

STANDING TALL

The Garuda Wisnu Kencana statue towers above the city of Bali as the tallest statue in Indonesia!

The copper and brass statue alone is 246 feet (75 m) tall and depicts the Hindu god Vishnu riding on the back of his flying mount Garuda. If you include the statue's base, its total height is a staggering 397 feet (121 m). Believe it or not, from conception to completion, it took almost 30 years to build! Indonesian sculptor Nyoman Nuarta came up with the design in 1990, and the construction process began in 1997. The statue was not finished until 2018 due to financial troubles and various setbacks. When all was said and done, it ended up costing nearly $100 million!

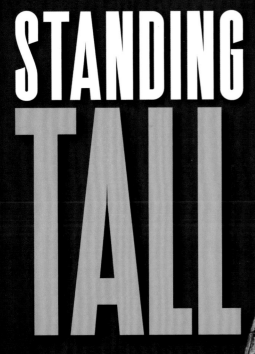

WINGING IT

Every autumn, spectators gather in St. Hilaire du Touvet, France, to watch as frogs, windmills, Chinese dragons, and more soar across the sky !

The Alpine farming village is the location of the Coupe Icare (Icarus Cup), a six-day paragliding and hang-gliding festival best known for its Masquerade Flight Contest in which competitors take to the skies dressed in outrageous costumes. Upward of 100 glider pilots commit to the challenge each year, donning all kinds of outfits, makeup, and masks as they launch themselves over the edge of a mountain in what has been called "the world's biggest international ultralight air sports event."

GRASS CUTTING

When predatory shrikes are flying overhead, Brandt's voles from Asia instinctively start trimming tall grasses in their territory because the birds associate short grass with poor hunting grounds. The grass cutting also gives the voles a better view of the skies and a clue as to where the shrike might strike.

TINY SNAIL

A newly discovered species of land snail, *Angustopila psammion*, found on a cave wall in northern Vietnam, is so tiny that one could fit inside a grain of sand. Its shell is only 0.18 inches (0.48 mm) high and 0.2 inches (0.6 mm) in diameter.

LOVE TRAIN

When the Australian echidna (or spiny anteater) prepares to mate, as many as 10 males line up nose-to-tail behind the female. This ritual can last for six weeks, and when she is finally ready, the rival males dig a trench around her and then attempt to push each other out of it. The last male in the trench earns the right to mate.

QUICK GAME

Brazilian software developer and video game enthusiast Matheus Furtado completed the 1990 Super Nintendo game *Super Mario World* in only 41 seconds. He used a glitch in the game to reach the end credits without finishing a single level.

FAKE POOP

To encourage transplanted burrowing owls to settle in their new surroundings in Southern California, biologists at the San Diego Zoo Wildlife Alliance played recordings of owl calls and scattered fake poop made from white paint. This made the birds feel at home because they were tricked into believing that other owls already lived there.

KILLER CAT

Africa's smallest feline, the nocturnal black-footed cat, kills an average of 12 rodents or small birds every night. It is three times more successful at hunting than a lion, but weighs around 200 times less than the big cat.

CAVE FREEZER

Tuktoyaktuk, a tiny village on the shores of the Arctic Ocean in Canada's Northwest Territories, has its own communal freezer, the Tuktoyaktuk Icehouse, a man-made cave that extends nearly 30 feet (9 m) underground and where local Inuvialuit people can store perishable food.

MARBLE VOTE

In the African country of Gambia, votes are cast in elections by dropping a glass marble into the container that bears the name of their preferred candidate.

MILLION STEAKS

Gayle Dudley has grilled more than one million steaks during the 20 years that she has worked at the LongHorn Steakhouse in Columbus, Georgia.

CHOPSTICK FURNITURE

Engineer Felix Böck has founded a company called ChopValue, which turns some of the 350,000 chopsticks that are thrown out every day after use by restaurants in Vancouver, British Columbia, Canada, into items of wooden furniture, including desks, cabinets, and tablet stands.

BEE-YONCÉ

Beyoncé is a keen beekeeper and has 80,000 bees at her home. She makes hundreds of jars of honey a year.

Yikes on Trikes!

Every spring, San Francisco's curviest street gets shut down while hundreds of thrill seekers race to the bottom on big-wheel bikes! Lombard Street may be the city's most photographed road, but the most crooked can actually be found in the Potrero Hill neighborhood. What Vermont Avenue lacks in curb appeal, it makes up for with way more curves, making it the perfect place for the Bring Your Own Big Wheel (BYOBW) race. This whimsical event sees hundreds of children and adults race toy bikes down the wonky road. Originally hosted on Lombard Street beginning in 2000, BYOBW later moved to Vermont Avenue to take full advantage of its roller coaster–like twists and turns.

TOUGH STUFF

Believe it or not, inventor Leo Krause was shot more than 4,000 times over the course of 27 years!

Though not the first person to develop bulletproof body armor, Leo and his business partner Bernard Spooner helped popularize it by traveling the U.S. demonstrating the groundbreaking technology. Photos of people withstanding gunshots thanks to the vests garnered much public interest, and the duo capitalized on the intrigue as a genius way to market and generate more sales! The vests were adopted by the New York City Police Department for officers who faced consistent danger. Even criminal figures such as Chicago's Al Capone approached Leo and Bernard about purchasing the unbelievable technology in an effort to keep himself protected while navigating a life of crime!

BULLET BLOCKERS

Scientists are experimenting with **liquid armor!** Non-Newtonian fluids quickly change from liquid to solid when hit with force and can possibly be used **to stop bullets!**

Larry McElroy of Lee County, Georgia, **accidentally shot his mother-in-law,** Carol Johnson, **after his bullet bounced off an armadillo!**

Toronto tailor Garrison Bespoke designed a **bulletproof three-piece suit** using **state-of-the-art carbon nanotechnology.**

Spider silk is stronger than **steel and tougher than Kevlar,** absorbing up to **three times as much energy** before breaking!

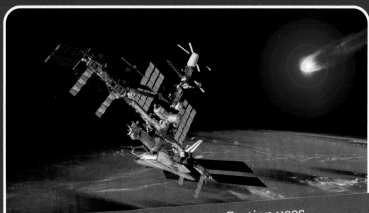

The International Space Station uses **Whipple Shields**—layers of Kevlar, Nextel, and aluminum—**to protect it from space debris** that can travel up to 17,500 mph (28,164 kmph)!

The U.S. president's official limousine, **"The Beast,"** is fully armored with 5-inch-thick (12.7-cm) **bulletproof windows,** and **Kevlar reinforcement on its tires!**

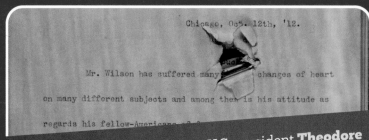

On **October 14, 1912,** former U.S. president **Theodore Roosevelt** gave a 90-minute speech despite having **just been shot!** Although it **still reached his chest,** the would-be assassin's bullet was slowed by items in Roosevelt's coat pocket, including **pages of his speech!**

Cat. No. 17139

THREE-HORNED SHEEP

This unusual sheep lived a normal life despite the extra horn growing from the side of its head, making it a polycerate—an animal with more than two horns. Believe it or not, horns are made of keratin, the same protein that makes up your hair and fingernails!

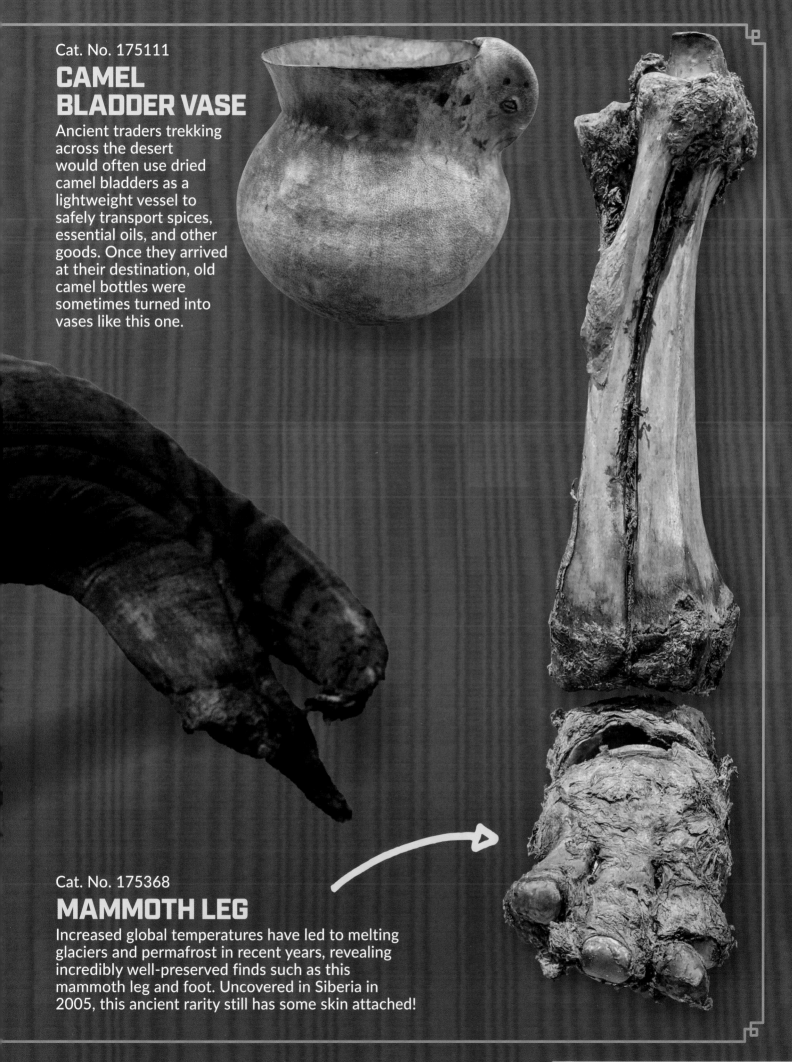

CAMEL BLADDER VASE

Cat. No. 175111

Ancient traders trekking across the desert would often use dried camel bladders as a lightweight vessel to safely transport spices, essential oils, and other goods. Once they arrived at their destination, old camel bottles were sometimes turned into vases like this one.

Cat. No. 175368

MAMMOTH LEG

Increased global temperatures have led to melting glaciers and permafrost in recent years, revealing incredibly well-preserved finds such as this mammoth leg and foot. Uncovered in Siberia in 2005, this ancient rarity still has some skin attached!

GRAVEYARD Goodies

RIPLEY'S EXCLUSIVE

> "Food is this beautiful memory tool that connects us better than just a name and date."

SPRITZ COOKIES

1 cup of butter or margarine
3/4 cup sugar
1 teaspoon vanilla

1 egg
2 1/4 cups of flour
1/2 teaspoon baking powder
1/8 teaspoon salt

Some recipes are so good, they get taken to the grave. Aspiring archivist Rosie Grant has been uncovering those family favorites and baking them back to life on TikTok!

Like many, Rosie picked up baking during the COVID-19 lockdown, but unlike others, she also began studying cemeteries. Taking daily walks through her local graveyard, she began reading the headstones as she passed. Realizing people include way more than names and dates, she decided to merge her newfound hobbies into one. Since then, Rosie has documented herself traveling across the U.S. on a hunt for new recipes from the departed, gaining millions of views along the way. Ripley's caught up with Rosie to learn more about her curious cooking.

Q: What was the first gravestone recipe you made?

A: The first grave I learned about was that of Naomi Miller-Dawson in Brooklyn, New York. It's carved to be a beautiful open book with the ingredients for a spritz cookie recipe. There aren't instructions on it, so I made it like a sugar cookie, mixing everything together and baking it in small circular shapes.

After I posted on TikTok, a lot of people commented on how their own families made spritz cookies, and I learned I needed a cookie press to properly make them. I began using a press and was surprised how well the recipe worked, so I brought a plate of them to Naomi's grave with my mom. We had a cookie in her honor, and that started the journey of visiting these graves in person.

KAY'S FUDGE
2 SQ. CHOCOLATE
2 TBS. BUTTER
MELT ON LOW HEAT
STIR IN
1 CUP MILK
BRING TO BOIL
3 CUPS SUGAR
1 TSP. VANILLA
PINCH OF SALT
COOK TO SOFTBALL STAGE
POUR ON MARBLE SLAB
COOL & BEAT & EAT

WHEREVER SHE GOES,
THERE'S LAUGHTER

Mom's Christmas Cookies
Cream: 1 cup sugar
       1/2 cup oleo
Add: 2 beaten eggs
       1 tsp. vanilla
Add: 3 cups flour
       3 tsp. baking powder
       1 tsp. salt
Add alternately with 1 cup cream.
Chill and roll out with flour.
Bake 350 degrees oven, and frost.

Q: What type of food are most gravestone recipes?

A: Until recently, all the grave recipes I knew about were desserts and mostly on the graves of women. But I just learned about the grave of Debra Ann Nelson, who has a savory cheese dip recipe on her gravestone!

Something more complicated like lasagna might take up a lot of real estate and putting text onto stones is not cheap or easy. I also think desserts send the message, "We're all going to die someday, why not eat a cookie?!"

Q: What do you like about cemeteries?

A: I think cemeteries are peaceful, though I only started visiting them regularly because I interned at Congressional Cemetery in Washington, DC. After the internship, I started seeing cemeteries as lively places, like outdoor museums, that rely on their local communities to be continuously cared for and preserved.

Q: Why do you think people put recipes on their gravestones?

A: Food is this beautiful memory tool that connects us better than just a name and date. When I think of my own grandmothers, I also think about their cooking and the meals we had together. I can still taste the yellow cake with chocolate icing my Grandma Kay used to make for my family's birthdays.

We all have that one family recipe that connects us to these memories, and so I think sharing a recipe on a gravestone is a way to continue to connect over food.

Q: What recipe would you put on your gravestone?

A: There are so many I love! I know I'd want a savory recipe, and I think it's a tie between a simple mac 'n' cheese or a clam pasta that I love to make for dinner parties.

GAME SNOW

Swedish skier Jesper Tjäder went from the slopes to the screen in a series of Japanese game show–inspired stunts that put his talents to the test!

Japanese game shows are famous for their wacky challenges, and the feats attempted by Jesper were no exception! To make his TV dreams a reality, Jesper teamed up with Red Bull to create a film set inside an icy tunnel filled with ramps, rails, and. . . walls? As a tribute to one of the most iconic and viral Japanese game show challenges, Jesper attempted to ski through a series of oddly shaped holes without hitting the surrounding wall, with varying degrees of success. Other stunts included performing a backflip off a miniature ramp, jumping through a ring of fire, and spinning atop a giant can of Red Bull.

LEVEL UP
SEE PAGE 7!

SCAN AND PLAY!

SWORDFISH STRUGGLE

Peter Schultz, from Annapolis, Maryland, caught a 301-pound (137-kg) swordfish after an eight-hour struggle. He was competing in the Big Fish Classic Tournament in Ocean City when he hooked the monster fish about 50 miles (80 km) offshore.

BOARD GAMERS

Lea Poole, Dale Poole, Adam Bircher, and Luke de Witt Vine played the board game Dune—based on American author Frank Herbert's 1965 science fiction novel of the same name—for more than 85 hours straight in Herefordshire, England. In total they played 79 rounds of the game.

INSPIRATIONAL DISH

The title of Paul Simon's song "Mother and Child Reunion" was inspired by a dish of fried chicken and boiled eggs at a Chinese restaurant in New York.

NEW ALBUM

Pianist Ruth Slenczynska, from Sacramento, California, released a new album in 2022—at age 97. A former child prodigy who gave her first recital when she was only four, she is the last surviving pupil of famous Russian composer Sergei Rachmaninoff.

BACK HOME

When Catherine Graham, from Boston, Massachusetts, flew out to Los Angeles to appear on TV game show *The Price Is Right* and won a five-day dream vacation, she hoped for a retreat to somewhere exotic like Tahiti. Instead, it was a trip back to New Hampshire, just across the state border from her home!

INVISIBLE ART

Twentieth-century French artist Yves Klein sold numerous pieces of invisible art in exchange for gold. To prove the buyers' ownership of the non-existent artworks he would issue receipts, and in 2022 one such framed receipt sold at auction for $1.2 million.

ONLINE BARGAIN

A painting of *The Last Supper* purchased by Welsh farmer Huw Lewis as the sole bidder on eBay for $70 turned out to be a long-lost work by eighteenth-century American artist Benjamin West worth $70,000.

DANCE INJURY

After Nicole Kidman fractured two ribs and injured her knee while rehearsing a dance routine, she had to shoot the final scenes of *Moulin Rouge* in a wheelchair with her leg up. To conceal the accident, she was only filmed from the chest up.

PAPER PEACOCKS

In 16 days, math teacher Ravi Kumar Toleti, from Hyderabad, India, folded 1,776 origami peacocks—India's national bird.

PLAYING WITH FIRE

World champion rope skipper Timothy Ho Chu-ting heats up his act by setting both himself and his rope on fire! The Hong Kong native has been jumping into competitions for more than 20 years, including making and breaking his own world record for number of skips in three minutes. In 2012 he became the first person to ever skip more than 500 times in the short timeframe before breaking his record with 522.5 skips in 2014. Timothy continues to challenge himself, and after being inspired by a fire dancing video, he turned himself into a "Fire Dragon" in May 2022 by setting both his rope and body suit on fire!

CRICKET KID

While most kids his age were busy learning to walk and talk, three-year-old Korey Adams of Gloucestershire, England, was busy training to become a world-class cricket player! Korey began playing the game at only 12 months old, mastering bowling and batting before he could even walk. Despite being too young for preschool, Korey has already played with kids nearly three times his age in an under-11s game and dreams of one day joining the England cricket team.

Bin Traveling

Welsh travel bloggers Craig Holmes and Aimee Bannister, a.k.a. Kinging-It, traveled 200 miles (322 km) across Wales taking turns pushing one another in a trash can! The couple used the creative idea and their social media following to bring about awareness for mental health support after losing a friend to suicide. The whole trip took 17 days and included extreme heat, mountain terrain, and utter physical fatigue. But with encouragement and support, Craig and Aimee persevered and raised more than £62,000 (around $75,000 USD) for charity!

the wheelie bin challenge raising money for mental health

bigmoose

#SPEAKUPFORLEE

RARE TRIPLETS

On July 8, 2021, parents Gabriela Mosquera and Mark Bodrog, of Gloucester Township, New Jersey, welcomed a set of rare identical triplet daughters, Anastasia, Olivia, and Nadia, beating odds of up to one in 200 million. By comparison, winning a lottery jackpot is about a one in 14 million chance.

HOLE IN HEAD

In 1863 during the U.S. Civil War, Union soldier Jacob C. Miller was shot in the forehead when a musket ball pierced him between the eyes at the Battle of Chickamauga. He miraculously survived, and the wound healed as a large hole that remained in the center of his forehead right up until he died in 1917 at age 88.

DOLL MYSTERY

Since January 2021, more than 30 creepy dolls—some just severed heads—have mysteriously washed ashore along a 40-mile (64-km) stretch of Texas coast. Others are missing arms and legs or have algae or barnacles growing inside their eyes and mouth.

STOMACH GURGLE

The scientific name for the gurgling noise your stomach and intestines sometimes make is "borborygmi."

FAN FEED

ROYAL TRIBUTE

Origami artist Kev Kendall of Suffolk, England, shared with us this portrait of Queen Elizabeth II he made by folding 6,400 individual pieces of paper! Kev began the project soon after the monarch's passing in September 2022 and completed it in just six days! Kev told us he always includes folded currency in his works, and in this case, banknotes double as the Queen's earring!

Spirit Sculptures

Established in what's considered one of the most haunted cities in the world, the York Ghost Merchants sell one-of-a-kind sculptures, each of which is said to have "a spirit all its own."

York, England, has a long, dark history of death stemming from incidents like Viking invasions, the Norman Conquest, and the Black Death (just to name a few), leading to its nickname: The City of One Thousand Ghosts. In fact, around 600 ghosts can be found in one storefront alone at any given time—a 1780s-era building on York's famed Shambles Steet that has been home to York Ghost Merchants since 2019. Living up to the city's reputation, the shop sells handmade "York Ghosts," whose spirits have been captured in the mold of classic bedsheet-style ghosts. The sculptures have become quite the collector's items for those hoping to take home a spooky souvenir.

THREADLIGHTLY

Lucy Simpson hand-stitches artworks so realistic, they'll have you doing a double take!

Lucy mastered knitting, sewing, and drawing at a young age, before earning a degree in Contemporary Crafts, working with wood, metal, ceramics, and textile techniques. She fell in love with stitching after receiving a cross-stitch kit from her sister and quickly left the restrictions of the kit behind, stitching thread-by-thread to create detailed pieces that look incredibly real. Her works resemble glass, scissors, bubble wrap, and even foil balloons!

SEE IT TO BELIEVE IT!

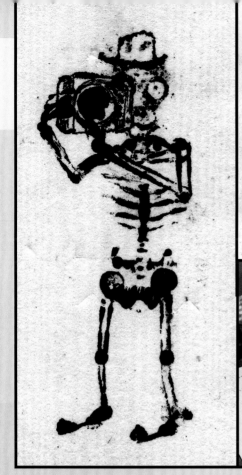

TRASHY ART

For Colby Simons, one person's trash is another's art! Using discarded items like wires, nails, gears, snail shells, coins, and everything in between, he creates haunting images of skeletons and detailed landscapes full of texture! Colby's upcycling doesn't stop there. He will often use something from an environment he is recreating to better showcase its characteristics, like using real leaves to paint a forest.

SHARP VISION

A golden eagle has such incredible eyesight that while high in the sky it can spot a rabbit on the ground 3 miles (4.8 km) away.

DIET CROC

An 8-foot-long (2.4-m) alligator broke into the garage of Laryn and Jamie Dobson's home in Naples, Florida, tore open a box of Diet Cokes, and guzzled down several cans of the soda.

EGG HAT

Gregory Da Silva, from Benin, West Africa, balanced 735 eggs on his hat. He spent three days carefully attaching them to the top of his hat, eventually creating an egg tower that was over 10 feet (3 m) tall.

PROFESSIONAL SCREAMER

In the same way that stunt people stand in for actors in dangerous scenes, New York-born Ashley Peldon works as a professional scream artist. She is hired to scream loudly into microphones for movies and TV shows to save the actors on screen from damaging their voice. Ashley discovered her talent for screaming at a young age, and it helped her win a number of roles as a child actor.

NUT FRENZY

A gray squirrel buries as many as 10,000 nuts each fall—but only ends up eating about 4,000.

WRONG FLAG

Rock band KISS mistakenly displayed the Australian national flag at the end of a June 2022 concert in Austria. As the show finished, a screen behind the stage read "KISS LOVES YOU VIENNA" but the KISS logo featured the flag of Australia instead of Austria.

MULTICOLORED IGLOO

To entertain their children, Ashley and Ryan Thorson built a 6-foot-tall (1.8-m), multicolored igloo in the front yard of their home in Owatonna, Minnesota. They used aluminum trays to freeze around 250 blocks of colored water and spent four days stacking them into an igloo, using snow to hold the blocks together.

NOT IN VEIN

Belmont and Hawthorne Lowe create works of art with a special draw—human blood! The Portland, Oregon-based brothers reached out to share how they transform blood supplied by their clients into custom pieces, including dice sets, jewelry, and more. Having lost their brother, Belmont and Hawthorne are passionate about creating art out of life, helping connect people with themselves, loved ones, or pets with their work. Don't try this at home, though! Samples must be drawn by a professional for the sake of both the artist and client's safety.

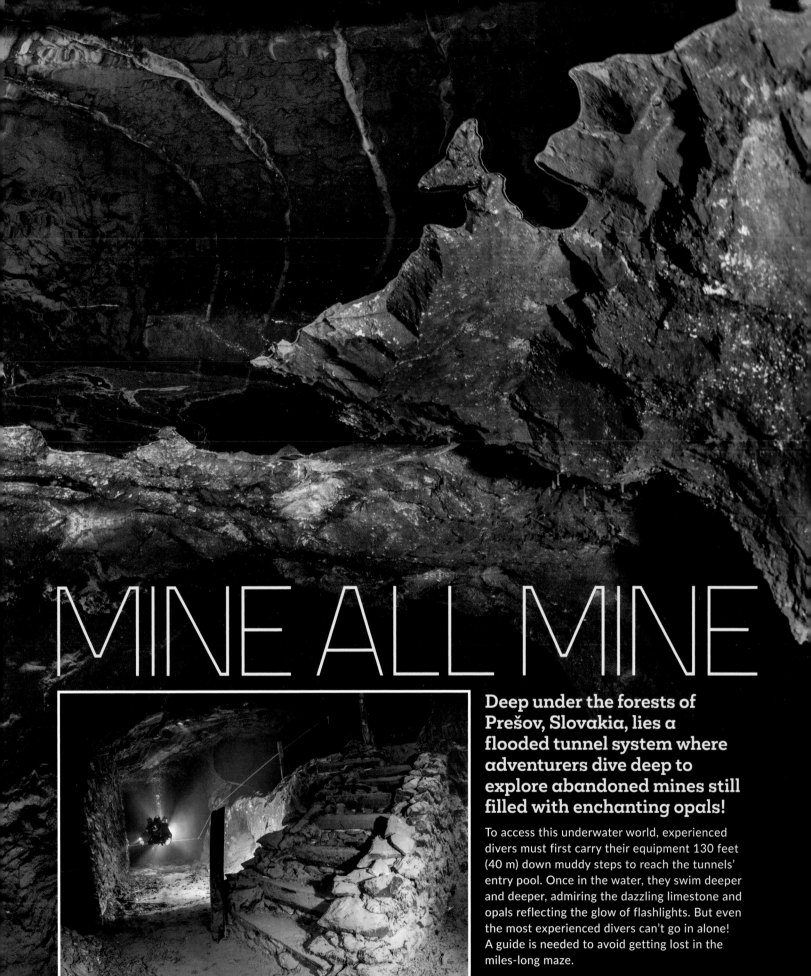

MINE ALL MINE

Deep under the forests of Prešov, Slovakia, lies a flooded tunnel system where adventurers dive deep to explore abandoned mines still filled with enchanting opals!

To access this underwater world, experienced divers must first carry their equipment 130 feet (40 m) down muddy steps to reach the tunnels' entry pool. Once in the water, they swim deeper and deeper, admiring the dazzling limestone and opals reflecting the glow of flashlights. But even the most experienced divers can't go in alone! A guide is needed to avoid getting lost in the miles-long maze.

The area is protected today, but for decades up until 1922 the now-waterlogged tunnels were part of the largest opal-mining operation in the world. Workers chipping away at the walls collected 25 thousand carats of the precious gem every year!

WOAH, DEER!

Muntjacs are an unusual group of deer. To begin, they have bizarre glands on their foreheads and near their eyes that they inflate to spread their scent! While at rest, these glands just look like wrinkles, but once the muntjac becomes excited, territorial, or has to go to the bathroom, they'll begin to flare up. While that in itself is truly a sight to behold, it's not the only weird thing about these quirky deer. Weighing about 30 pounds (13.6 kg), muntjacs find creative ways to protect themselves from predators, such as barking, headbutting, or chomping down with their fangs! One more strange fact: The most common muntjac species, the Indian muntjac, has the fewest chromosomes of any mammal—even fewer than a fruit fly!

DEER WITH FANGS!

FEISTY OCTOPUSES

Female octopuses throw objects at male octopuses who are harassing them. The females use their tentacles to propel sand, shells, and algae at the males, usually accompanied by a jet of water, to deter them from attempting to mate.

CRIMEBUSTING GOAT

When a suspect fled a property in Fieldale, Virginia, Gracie the goat chased him into nearby woods. Operating on opposite sides of the woods, a sheriff's deputy and the goat soon flushed the suspect out and he was arrested.

EVEREST PARTY

Overcoming sudden heavy snowfall brought on by a huge storm, endurance athlete Andrew Hughes, from Seattle, Washington, hosted a tea party at 21,312 feet (6,496 m) above sea level on Mount Everest. To reach that altitude they had to carry supplies through the treacherous Khumbu Icefall, where 44 climbers died between 1953 and 2016.

BEAR SCARE

Spotting a black bear lurking outside St. John's Academy in Shawnigan Lake, British Columbia, Canada, the school's music teacher, Tristan Clausen, scared the animal away by playing the trombone.

LEVEL UP SEE PAGE 7!

SCAN AND PLAY!

NONSTOP FLIGHT

In September 2020, a male bar-tailed godwit flew 7,580 miles (12,200 km) from Alaska to New Zealand in 11 days without rest.

SCARY SOUP

Restaurants in Guangdong Province, China, serve snake and whole scorpion soup. The chef extracts the venom from the scorpion before stewing it for three hours. According to traditional Chinese medicine, the soup can treat rheumatism and skin diseases.

PLANET PLUNGE

It would take 38 minutes for a person to fall through the center of the Earth from one side of the planet to the other—a distance of approximately 7,920 miles (12,680 km).

RADIOACTIVE BEACH

Areia Prata beach in Guarapari, Brazil, has black sand containing monazite, a phosphate mineral rich in uranium and thorium, making it radioactive. The sand there has radiation levels nearly 400 times greater than normal background radiation recorded in the U.S.

VIRGIN BIRTH

Female California condors sometimes give birth to young without mating—a very rare instance of parthenogenesis, or virgin birth.

REFLECT INSECT

The jewel scarabs of the *Chrysina* genus look like they are made from shiny metal, with some even having the appearance of chrome- or gold-plated jewelry! Some of these metallic bugs are so shiny that you can see your reflection in them, all thanks to a complex multilayer chitin coating. While you might think this polished look makes the beetles an easy target for predators, it's actually thought it may help them blend into their rainforest habitats by mimicking reflective beads of water.

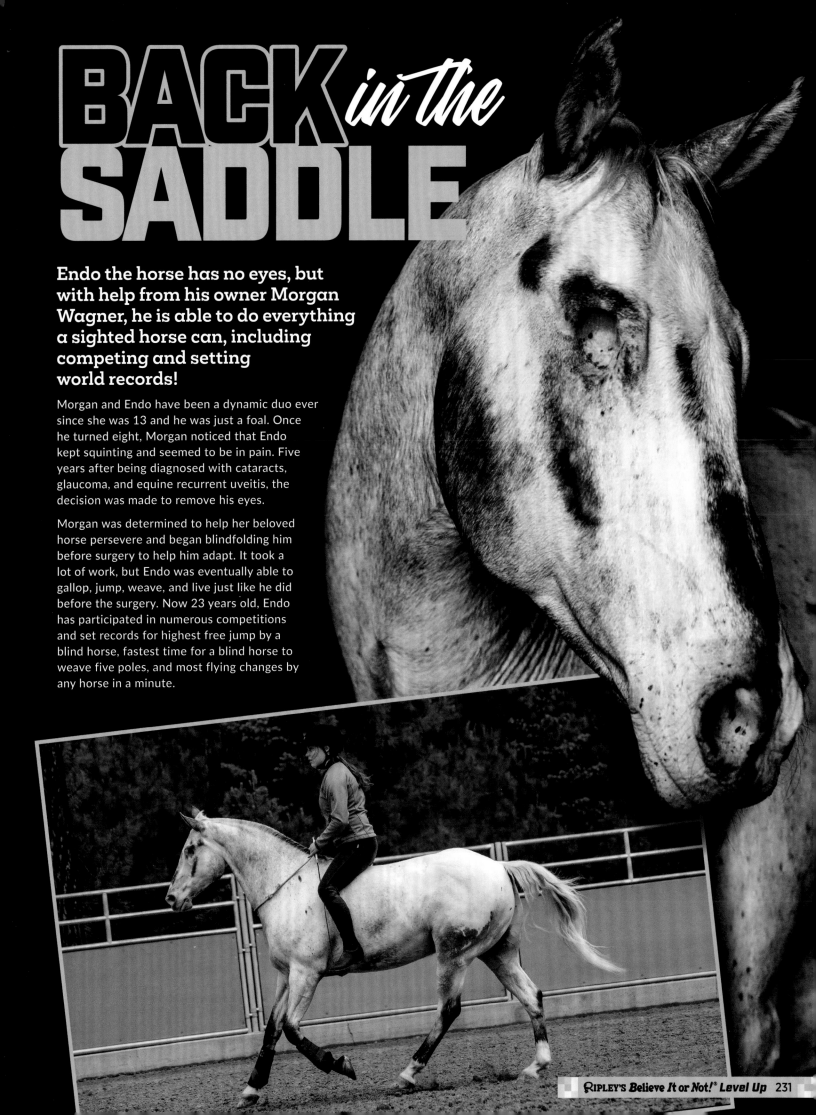

BACK *in the* SADDLE

Endo the horse has no eyes, but with help from his owner Morgan Wagner, he is able to do everything a sighted horse can, including competing and setting world records!

Morgan and Endo have been a dynamic duo ever since she was 13 and he was just a foal. Once he turned eight, Morgan noticed that Endo kept squinting and seemed to be in pain. Five years after being diagnosed with cataracts, glaucoma, and equine recurrent uveitis, the decision was made to remove his eyes.

Morgan was determined to help her beloved horse persevere and began blindfolding him before surgery to help him adapt. It took a lot of work, but Endo was eventually able to gallop, jump, weave, and live just like he did before the surgery. Now 23 years old, Endo has participated in numerous competitions and set records for highest free jump by a blind horse, fastest time for a blind horse to weave five poles, and most flying changes by any horse in a minute.

All NATURAL

The European Land Art Festival encourages participants to embrace their surroundings and create outdoor artwork using only natural materials.

Founded by James Craig Page in 2016, the annual festival encourages people of all ages to improve their mental and physical health by logging off their devices to enjoy nature and solitude. The event essentially turns the town of Dunbar, Scotland, into a giant art exhibit, with activities ranging from creating sandcastles and mosaics to surfing and, the most popular of all, stone stacking. During the Stone Stacking Championship, competitors spread out across the town's rivers, beaches, and parks to be at one with nature as they balance rocks one on top of another to construct intricate, mind-blowing sculptures that defy gravity.

Tight Squeeze

Travelers looking to *really* get away from it all can head to Just Room Enough Island, a speck of land so small there's no space for anything more than a single house! Located in New York's Thousand Islands, the tiny landmass (technically named Hub Island) was purchased by the Sizeland family in the 1950s as they searched for the perfect place to build a vacation home. With walls that almost go right to the island's coastline, visitors can theoretically jump straight from the house into the St. Lawrence River!

VOLCANO CLIMB

U.S. adventurer Victor Vescovo and marine scientist Dr. Cliff Kapono climbed the entire height of Hawaii's dormant volcano Mauna Kea, even though more than half of it is submerged beneath the Pacific Ocean. The mountain is 33,500 feet (10,213 m) high, making it much taller than Mount Everest, but only 13,802 feet (4,207 m) is above sea level. So, to make a complete ascent, the pair first had to descend thousands of feet below the waves in a submersible vehicle. After returning to the surface, they paddled 27 miles (43 km) to shore in a canoe and then cycled and hiked their way to the top of the mountain. It took them three days to climb from its seabed base to its snow-capped summit.

FISHING FAMILY

On July 3, 2021, 13-year-old Robert Audrain IV of St. Louis, Missouri, caught a 5-ounce (0.14-kg) longear sunfish at a private pond in Franklin County, breaking a state record that was set by his father while fishing in the same pond exactly one year earlier.

LITTER PICKER

Gonzalo Chiang's border collie Sam is so proficient at collecting discarded garbage from the main park in Santiago, Chile, that park officials used a cartoon image of Sam dressed in a superhero cape to promote their anti-litter campaign.

HISSING NOISE

Xi Yan called an animal welfare group to her Singapore home because she believed a snake was hissing in a cupboard near her bed. She sent a recording of the noise and the experts concluded that it was probably a black spitting cobra. But when they arrived, wearing protective eyewear and carrying snake grabbers, they discovered that the sound was being made by a malfunctioning electric toothbrush.

DOGGY DRIVER

Lexie, a Jack Russell terrier, not only rounds up sheep on Ian Zschech's farm near Hamilton, Victoria, Australia, she also sometimes "drives" the family's utility vehicle. Lexie stands on the driver's seat and uses her front paws to operate the steering wheel. Ian's son Cam puts the vehicle in first gear and allows it to move at a steady walking pace so that he can grab the wheel or the handbrake if Lexie loses interest.

SOCCER SNAKE

A top-league soccer match in Guatemala between Nueva Concepcion and Municipal was stopped for eight minutes while a long snake was removed from the pitch.

LIFE SAVER

Yorkshire terrier Chewie saved the life of his owner, Ray Whiteley, by performing CPR when he stopped breathing and went into cardiac arrest. Chewie licked Ray's face, jumped on his chest, and barked loudly to alert Ray's wife, Loretta, at their home in Lancashire, England. While waiting for the ambulance crew, Chewie never left his master's side. The Whiteleys adopted Chewie as a puppy and had taught him to perform CPR as a party trick.

THICK SKIN

The skin of a sperm whale is up to 14 inches (35 cm) thick, making it 200 times thicker than human skin.

Water Over the Bridge

The Veluwemeer Aqueduct in Harderwijk, the Netherlands, flips the script when it comes to bridges. Its design allows for a constant flow of automobile traffic while simultaneously letting boats pass overhead. The architects opted for this eye-catching reversal in order to avoid major traffic delays that a typical drawbridge would have caused on the busy N302 highway. Believe it or not, the road sits above the water level except for the 55.7 feet (17 m) that passes below the aqueduct, where it briefly dips lower than the lake's surface!

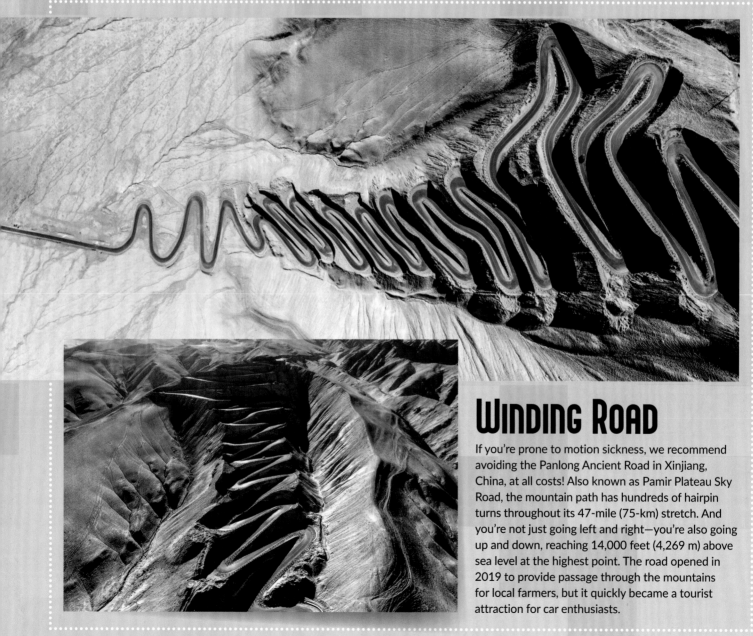

Winding Road

If you're prone to motion sickness, we recommend avoiding the Panlong Ancient Road in Xinjiang, China, at all costs! Also known as Pamir Plateau Sky Road, the mountain path has hundreds of hairpin turns throughout its 47-mile (75-km) stretch. And you're not just going left and right—you're also going up and down, reaching 14,000 feet (4,269 m) above sea level at the highest point. The road opened in 2019 to provide passage through the mountains for local farmers, but it quickly became a tourist attraction for car enthusiasts.

2.5 MILES (4 KM) ABOVE GROUND!

RIDING HIGH

AFMTÉLÉTHON

Ballon Offert par:

F-HTLT

The sky is the limit for French daredevil Rémi Ouvrard, who stood on top of a hot-air balloon flying more than 13,000 feet (3,962 m) in the air!

In a white pressure suit and helmet, Rémi started his journey by climbing to the top of the balloon while it was still grounded. The aircraft was piloted by his father, Jean-Daniel Ouvrard, who was able to speak to Rémi via walkie-talkie as they made their way higher and higher into the atmosphere. Despite the low temperatures and high altitude, Rémi stated that the heat coming off the balloon made him feel boiling hot! The feat was accomplished on November 10, 2021, as part of a telethon to raise money to fund research projects for genetic neuromuscular diseases.

SeaSONAL BLOOMS

Japanese artist Azuma Makoto's floral arrangements bring blossoming bouquets to unexpected places, including the ocean floor!

Rather than placing his botanical masterpieces in gardens or museums, Azuma prefers locations that defy nature, such as futuristic machines, frozen landscapes, and even space! In August 2022, he and a team of divers took his art to new depths—literally—with *Botanical Sculpture x In Bloom project Sea #2*, a delicate flower display installed on the ocean floor off the coast of Ishigaki Island, Okinawa, Japan.

COOL AWARD

Timothy Hutton, who won a Best Supporting Actor Academy Award for the 1980 movie *Ordinary People*, keeps his Oscar statuette in the fridge to amuse visitors.

SECRET TAPE

On June 13, 1980, Betty Eppes, a reporter for the *Baton Rouge Advocate* newspaper, secretly recorded a 27-minute conversation with reclusive U.S. author J. D. Salinger, who had last given an interview in 1953. It is the only known recording of his voice. Feeling guilty about the manner in which she obtained it, she never sold the tape but instead keeps it in a safety deposit box and says the recording will be cremated with her body when she dies.

WIZARD FAN

Tracey Nicol-Lewis, of Glamorgan, Wales, has more than 6,300 items of Harry Potter memorabilia that she has collected since 2002. Her collection, which includes 47 wands and more than 120 action figures, takes up three rooms of her house. Even her wedding in 2020 was Harry Potter–themed.

SEA SWORD

While diving off the coast of Israel, Shlomi Katzin discovered a 900-year-old sword on the seabed. The barnacle-encrusted weapon is believed to have once belonged to a knight during the twelfth-century Crusades.

TALL TEEN

At the age of only 12, Olivier Rioux, from Montreal, Quebec, Canada, already stood 6.9 feet (2.1 m) tall and towered over the other players in an under-12 basketball tournament. At 16, he is over 7.45 feet (2.26 m) tall and wears size 20 shoes. Height runs in the family, as both his parents are over 6 feet (1.8 m) tall.

SNOWBOARD RUNS

Snowboarder Myles Silverman made 56 runs on Sugarloaf Mountain's Narrow Gauge trail in Maine, traversing 95,088 vertical feet (28,990 m) in 12 hours.

MISSISSIPPI ROW

A team of four rowers—Bobby Johnson from Clearwater, Florida; Rod Price from Orlando, Florida; and father-daughter duo KJ and Casey Millhone from Wayzata, Minnesota—rowed the entire 2,350-mile (3,760-km) length of the Mississippi River in 17 days 19 hours 46 minutes. They set off from Lake Itasca, Minnesota, on April 22, 2021, and reached the Gulf of Mexico on May 10.

EYE OF THE EARTH

Located just north of Split in the foothills of the Dinara mountain range is Croatia's famous Cetina River Spring, a karst spring that looks like a giant blue eye! Also known as the "Eye of the Earth," the Cetina spring drops to depths of more than 492 feet (150 m), although no diver has been able to reach the bottom. The spring is the source of the 63-mile-long (101-km) Cetina River, with its clear cold water flowing all the way to Omis, leaving river rapids and spectacular waterfalls along its path.

Doodle Dwelling

British artist Sam Cox, a.k.a. Mr. Doodle, covered the entire inside and outside of his mansion in his signature squiggles!

Drawing on walls may be a big no-no in most homes, but for the Kent County–based artist, being surrounded by doodles is a dream come true. Sam's scribbles first gained attention in 2017 when a video of him freehanding thick black doodles went viral online, quickly earning him a massive social media following. By 2020, he had used the money earned from selling doodles to purchase a six-bedroom mansion in the English countryside, which he spent the following two years decking out with drawings of squiggles, smileys, animals, and other shapes. The final mansion mural took 238 gallons (900 l) of white paint, 401 cans of black spray paint, 286 bottles of black drawing paint, and 2,296 pen nibs to complete!

NOTHING LEFT UNDOODLED!

EVEN THE OUTSIDE!

Cat. No. 168335

A MATTER OF TIME

Palm Coast, Florida, artist Paul Baliker carved this out of cedar driftwood. Titled *A Matter of Time*, the 10-foot-tall (3.2-m) artwork addresses the dangers of extinction caused by ocean pollution and features more than 20 sea creatures tangled within the wild mane of Father Time.

Cat. No. 11021
HEX SIGN

Barn stars, a.k.a. hex signs, are a traditional decoration found on Pennsylvania Dutch farms established by German immigrants during the seventeenth and eighteenth centuries. There are numerous meanings and interpretations behind the designs, but many are inspired by the night sky, religion, or flowers.

Cat. No. 168335
TRUNK BARREL

Believe it or not, a tree trunk grew around the barrel of a U.S. Civil War weapon. Recovered near Union City, Tennessee, this Pattern 1861 Enfield musketoon was once used by a soldier of the Confederacy before the tree claimed it as its own!

Curious CUISINE

Europe is a foodie favorite and for good reason—Italian pasta, French pastries, and German sausages are just a few of the continent's iconic cuisines. But if you're looking to eat like the locals do, there are plenty of options for those with a more adventurous palate. While these meals may seem bizarre, many are rooted in generations of tradition and are still enjoyed by thousands today.

URUMIIT

While caviar, fois gras, and truffles may come to mind when thinking of delicacies, in some areas of Greenland, the finest food you can feast on is feces! In winter when resources are limited, gatherers collect *urumiit*, the dried-up droppings of the ptarmigan bird—or "snow chickens." The poop is then combined with seal meat and rancid seal oil to create a dish that provides some much-needed nutrition—and happens to smell like gorgonzola cheese!

BLACK PUDDING

Enjoyed in the UK and Ireland for hundreds of years, this English breakfast staple isn't a pudding at all, but rather a sausage made using animal blood! Though traditionally prepared using pig or cow blood mixed with fat, onions, herbs, spices, and a grain, any animal blood will do in a pinch. In fifteenth-century Britain, nobles even chowed down on pudding made of porpoise!

STARGAZY PIE

Every year on December 23, people in Cornwall, England, enjoy a pie made of eggs, potatoes, and. . . fish heads? Created in the village of Mousehole, stargazy pie first came to be when a fisherman named Tom Bawcock set sail into the stormy sea hoping to help feed starving villagers. He returned bearing seven types of fish, which were made into a pie that effectively saved the village from famine!

SMÖRGÅSTÅRTA

Ever find yourself eating a sandwich and wishing it was cake? Then smörgåstårta is the mash-up meal for you! This Swedish dish represents the best of both worlds with layers of bread, crème fraîche, and salmon, shrimp, or ham. The savory cake is then frosted and decorated, ready to be served at any and all celebrations!

ANGULAS

This may look like plain noodles, but it's actually baby eels! Called angulas, these Basque delicacies don't come cheap, with a pound costing around $500! Atlantic eels begin their lives off the coast of Bermuda before drifting into Spanish estuaries three years later, where they are snatched up by eager fishermen. The costly snake-like snack is said to have a flavor so delicate they must be eaten with wooden utensils.

PIE BARM

The English town of Wigan is known for its affinity for pies, a treat they love so much they even slap one between a bun and call it a pie barm. Also known as a Wigan kebab or a Wigan slappy, the pie barm is a carb lover's dream: meat and potatoes wrapped in pastry then sandwiched on a butter roll made with beer foam for a convenient meal that requires no clean up.

PIHTIJE

Serbian winters can get mighty cold, prompting families to make the most out of scarce resources by preparing pihtije, a jellied pork appetizer that utilizes the whole pig. Cooks strain the liquid from boiled ham hocks, head meat, and other spare parts mixed with seasonings before leaving it outside to cool and slicing it into cubes. The result is served cold with pickled vegetables and chased with a Balkan fruit brandy for warmth.

GATEWAY TO HELL

One of the most alien places on the planet, Ethiopia's Danakil Depression is made up of hot springs, salt flats, and acidic pools where aquatic life somehow thrives!

Also known as the "Gateway to Hell" or "Land of Death," the area has an average temperature of about 94°F (34.4°C) and can get as hot as 122°F (50°C), making it one of the hottest places on Earth. It is also one of the lowest, sitting 410 feet (125 m) below sea level at the spot where three tectonic plates are pulling away from each other. Despite its strong sulfuric smells, dangerously acidic waters, and slightly terrifying hissing sounds rising from its depths, the Danakil Depression attracts scientists, salt miners, and travelers from across the globe, making it one of Ethiopia's top destinations.

LEVEL UP
SEE PAGE 7!

SCAN AND PLAY!

For centuries, locals have led caravans of thousands of camels to and from the Danakil Depression to mine its salt.

INDEX

LEVEL UP
YOUR ADVENTURE

With more than 100 attractions around the world—from Odditoriums and Aquariums to Waxworks and Moving Theaters—the world of Ripley's embraces the spirit of discovery and curiosity. Here, you'll find that truth is always stranger than fiction, as the unbelievable comes alive right before your very eyes!

FIND A RIPLEY'S NEAR YOU!

SCAN TO PLAN!

COME SEE THE SHOW

SEA MORE AT RIPLEY'S

Get face-to-fin with hundreds of animals at Ripley's Aquariums!

Our world-class attractions foster conservation and provide exceptional animal care while bringing the wonders of the world's waters to life in a fun, family-friendly environment filled with awe-inspiring sights, hands-on experiences, and magical moments.